CHINESE (IDEOGRAMS & PĪNYĪN), ENGLISH & FRENCH LEVEL 1 & 2 WORDS IN USE

1800 Everyday Sentences to Master for It

HUA ZHANG

authorHOUSE®

AuthorHouse™ UK
1663 Liberty Drive
Bloomington, IN 47403 USA
www.authorhouse.co.uk
Phone: 0800.197.4150

Published by AuthorHouse 08/14/2017

ISBN: 978-1-5462-8094-1 (sc)
ISBN: 978-1-5462-8093-4 (e)

前言 Foreword *Avant-propos*

亲爱的语言学习者:

本书为您提供了掌握中文(640 词)、英文(1100 词)和法文(1050 词)的 1 级、2 级语言水平的必要词汇,并提供了使用这些词汇的一千八百多实用例句,以帮助您不但能掌握那些词汇,同时又学到日常生活、工作及社会交际的表达能力。

掌握单个词汇的正确使用不难,但在短期内掌握大量的必要词汇,并能使用其词汇组成的一千八百多日常生活、工作及社会交际常用句并不容易。如果这是您的目标 ---- 短期内大量的掌握 1 级 2 级词汇使用,我建议您只攻打每个词的一、两个例句,如框起来的前一、两例句 ---- 一般比较简单,容易记住。做到口头能熟练表达,并能熟练地认、读、写其单词或汉字。这样能使进展大大加快。例如:

例一 (第 12 页):

> 二 èr H1, S1 **two, *deux*** ~~得四。~~ dé sì. Twice two is four. *Deux fois deux est quatre.* 一公里等于~里。yì gōnglǐ děngyú ~ lǐ. A kilometre is equal to two li. *Un kilomètre est égal à deux li.*

他有~心。tā yǒu~ xīn. He's disloyal. *Il est déloyal.* 老通是个说一不~的人,你可以放心。Lǎo tōng shì gè shuōyī bú~ de rén, nǐ kěyǐ fàngxīn. Lao Tong is a man of his word, you can trust him. *Lao Tong est un homme de parole, tu peux lui faire confiance.* ~者必居其一。~zhě bì jū qí yī. It's either one or the other. *C'est tout l'un ou tout l'autre.*

例二 (第 32 页):

> 明白 míngbai G, H3, S1 **understand, clear, be franc, *comprendre, être clair, dire la vérité*** ~不~ / 明不~? ~ bù ~ / míng bù ~? Do you understand? *Est-ce que tu comprends?*

这句话的意思很~。zhè jù huà de yìsi hěn ~. The meaning of the sentence was clear. *Le sens de la phrase était clair.* 我看你跟我讲得不~。wǒ kàn nǐ gēn wǒ jǐng dé bù ~. I don't think you're being frank with me. *Je ne crois pas que tu me dises la vérité.*

请看第二个例子: [明白 míngbai G, H3, S1 **understand, clear, be franc, *comprendre, être clair, dire la vérité***]: 为快速进展,只学《明白不明白?》或《明不明白?》这个问句,并能熟练地读、写单词《明白》。过了一段时间学了其他新词以后,回头复习时,再学另外两句----《这句话的意思很明白》和《我看你跟我讲得不明白》。这样即能加快学习速度,又加深了掌握的程度。加油!

*   *   *

Dear language learner,

This book supplies you with the necessary 1 and 2 level vocabularies for you to grasp in your learning of Chinese (640 words and expressions) English (1100) and French (1050) languages. For this goal, it gives you more than 1800 everyday sentences to help you to master them, sentences of your everyday life and work as well as of your social communication activities.

Knowing a proper use of a single word is not difficult, but it is not easy at all to master a right use of a great deal of vocabulary by speaking more than 1800 sentences with those words for a short time. If this is your aim –

master the 1 or 2 level vocabularies for a short time, I propose you to study only one or two examples of each word, for instance the framed ones—less difficult and easier to remember. And try to skilfully use them and also read and write the concerned expression or ideogram(s) fast and well. And that will let you accelerate your language learning enormously.

Please look at the above 2nd example in the Chinese foreword: [明白 míngbai G, H3, S1 **understand, be clear, be franc,** *comprendre, être clair, dire la vérité*] In order to accelerate, just learn the framed example – a question "Do you <u>understand</u>?" Then you'll go on learning next new words with the same method. After grasping a number of easy sentences of the following new words, you'll come back, revise the first sentence and study the other two ones: "The meaning of the sentence <u>was clear</u>." and "I don't think you<u>'re being frank </u>with me." This will not only accelerate your advance greatly, but also get a deeper mastering. Come on!

*   *   *

Cher apprenant de langues, Chère apprenante de langues,

Ce manuel vous fournit un vocabulaire nécessaire des niveaux A1 et A2 à maîtriser dans l'apprentissage de langues chinoise (640 mots et expressions), anglaise (1100) et française (1050). Et pour atteindre cet objectif, il vous donne plus de 1800 phrases usuelles concernant la vie et le travail quotidiens ainsi que les activités de communication sociale pour vous aider à maîtriser l'emploi de ces mots et expressions.

Maîtriser l'emploi correct d'un seul mot n'est pas difficile, mais il n'est pas du tout facile de bien maîtriser un grand nombre de vocabulaire avec lesquels on compose plus de 1800 phrases en peu de temps. Si c'est votre objectif – maitriser ceux des niveaux A1 et A2 pendant une courte période, je vous propose d'étudier seulement un ou deux exemples pour chaque entrée, par exemple des exemples encadrés, qui sont souvent plus simples, et faciles à retenir. Et cela vous permettra d'arriver rapidement à bien dire la phrase, et à reconnaître, à lire et à écrire l'expression ou l'(les)idéogramme(s) concerné(s). Ce qui pourrait accélérer considérablement votre avance.

Prenons le 2ème exemple dans l'avant-propos chinois [明白 míngbai G, H3, S1 understand, be clear, be franc, comprendre, être clair, dire la vérité] Pour accélérer, apprenez seulement l'exemple encadré – la question « Est-ce que tu <u>comprends</u>? » Puis vous continuez à apprendre un certain nombre de nouveaux mots suivants de la même façon. Après les avoir appris avec des phrases toujours plus simples, vous reviendrez réviser la 1ère phrase et étudier les deux phrases suivantes : « Le sens de la phrase <u>était clair</u>. » et « Je ne crois pas que tu me <u>dises la vérité</u>. » Cela vous permettra d'accélérer votre avance, consolider et approfondir vos acquis. Allez-y!

目 录 Contents *Sommaire*

本书语言一、二级词汇包括 – The language levels 1 & 2 words and expressions of this book have – *Les niveaux A1 & A2 de langue des mots et des expressions dans ce livre contiennent :*

> ➢ **D**: 100 个最常用单音词 – most used monosyllabic words – *mots monosyllabiques les plus utilisés* [1] [D]
> ➢ **T**: 100 个在 10 个方面使用最多的汉字 – most used Chinese characters in 10 domains – *caractères chinois les plus utilisés dans l0 domaines* [2] [T]
> ➢ **N**: 100 个新闻界最常用双音词 (不包括人名) – most used disyllabic words in the press (not including people's names) – *mots dissyllabiques les plus utilisés dans la presse (non compris les noms de gens)* [3] [N]
> ➢ **G**: 100 个日常使用最常用双音词 - most used disyllabic words in general use – *mots dissyllabiques les plus utilisés dans l'emploi général* [4] [G]
> ➢ **H1 & H2**: 300 个汉语水平考试 1 级、2 级词汇 – vocabulary of the 1 and 2 levels of vocabulary of HSK – *vocabulaires des niveaux 1 et 2 de l'HSK* [5] [H1, H2]
> ➢ **S1 & H3 & H4**: 100 个其他必要词汇, 100 other necessary words, *100 autres mots nécessaires* : (1) 语言文字规范初级(一级)词汇 -- words of basic level of the language and writing standards – *mots de niveau élémentaire des standards de langue et de l'écriture* [6] [S1]; (2) 汉语水平考试 3 级、4 级词汇 vocabulary of the 3 and 4 levels of vocabulary of HSK – *vocabulaires des niveaux 3 et 4 de l'HSK* [7] [H3, H4] (见下页, see the next page, *voir la page suivante*)

书中使用的略语 -- abbreviations used in the text -- *abréviations utilisées dans le texte*

f: 法语阴性名词 French feminine noun, *nom féminin français*
m: 法语阳性名词 French masculine noun, *nom masculin français*
pl: 英语、法语复数名词, English and French plural noun, *nom pluriel anglais et français*
代: 代词 dàicí pronoun, *pronom*
动: 动词 dòngcí verb, *verbe*
方: 方言 fāngyán dialect, *dialecte*
副: 副词 fùcí adverb, *adverbe*
介: 介词 jiècí preposition, *préposition*
口: 口语词 kǒuyǔ cí oral, *oral*
量: 量词 liàngcí classifier, *spécificatif, classificateur*
名: 名词 míngcí noun, *nom*
数: 数词 shùcí numeral, *numéral*
形: 形容词 xíngróngcí adjective, *adjectif*
助: 助动词 zhùdòngcí auxiliary verb, *verbe auxiliaire*

---

[1] 现代汉语单字频率列表 Modern Chinese Character Frequency List, Jun Da, http://lingua.mlsu.edu
[2] 现代汉语通用字表 国家语言文字工作委员会汉字处编 语文出版社 1989 年 9 月第 1 版 pp.99-103
[3] Bigram frequency list for the news sub-corpus, Jun Da http://lingua.mlsu.edu
[4] Bigram frequency list for the general fiction sub-corpus Jun Da http://lingua.mlsu.edu
[5] www.chinesetest.cn
[6] 语言文字规范, 汉语国际教育用 音节、汉字、词汇等级划分 2010-02-01 实施 Beijing Language and Culture University Press, pp.25-50
[7] www.chinesetest.cn

I. S1 & H3 & H4: 其他 100 个关于旅行、教育、语言学习和东、西方文化等必要词汇, 100 other necessary words about travel, education, language learning, the east & west cultures, etc. *100 autres mots nécessaires sur le voyage, l'éducation, l'apprentissage de langues, les cultures orientales & occidentales, etc.*
II. "*" 编者所加 6 个词汇, 6 words added by the editor, *6 mots ajoutés par l'éditeur*

大学 (大學) dàxué 8
大学生 (大學生) dàxuéshēng 8
地 de 9
饿 (餓) è 12
*发音 (發音) fāyīn 13
*法国 (法國) fǎhuó 13
*法语 (法語) fǎyǔ 13
翻译 (翻譯) fānyì 13
工夫 gōngfu 16
汉字 (漢字) hànzì 19
护照 (護照) hùzhào 20
华人 (華人) huárén 20
华语 (華語) huáyǔ 20
话 (話) huà 21
火车 (火車) huǒchē 22
几 (幾) jǐ 22
交通 jiāotōng 23
交易 jiāoyì 23
京剧 (京劇) jīngjù 25
京戏 (京戲) īngxì 25
看病 kànbìng 26
没有 (沒有) méiyǒu 31
南方 nánfāng 34
*欧元 (歐元) ōuyuán euro 35
普通话 (普通話) pǔtōnghuà 36
汽车 (汽車) qìchē 37
签证 (簽證) qiānzhèng 37
人民币 (人民幣) rénmínbì 39
上学 (上學) shàngxué 41
生病 shēngbìng 42
实习 (實習) shíxí 42
是不是 shìbúshì 43
手续 (手續) shǒuxù 43
她们 (她們) tāmen 46
它(们) [它(們)] tā(men) 46
谈判 (談判) tánpàn 46
听力 (聽力) tīnglì 47
听说 (聽說) tīngshuō 47
停车 (停車) tíngchē 48

停车场 (停車場) tíngchēchǎng 48
同意 tóngyì 48
外国 (外國) wàiguó 49
外国人 (外國人) wàiguórén 49
外文 wàiwén 49
外语 (外語) wàiyǔ 49
晚安 wǎn'ān 49
为了 (為了) wèile 50
文明 wénmíng 50
文学 (文學) wénxué 50
文字 wénzì 50
午饭 (午飯) wǔfàn 51
武术 (武術) wǔshù 51
西餐 xīcān 51
西方 xīfāng 51
西医 (西醫) xīyī 51
洗手间 (洗手間) xǐshǒujiān 52
下车 (下車) xiàchē 52
下课 (下課) xiàkè 52
下周 xiàzhōu 53
现金 (現金) xiànjīn 53
香 xiāng 53
小学 (小學) xiǎoxué 54
小学生 (小學生) xiǎoxuéshēng 54
写 (寫) xiě 55
新年 xīnnián 55
新闻 (新聞) xīnwén 55
信 xìn 55
信息 xìnxī 55
信用卡 xìnyòngkǎ 55
行李 xínyli 56
熊猫 (熊貓) xióngmāo 56
亚洲 (亞洲) yàzhōu 57
研究生 yánjiūshēng 57
*阳 (陽) yáng 57
邀请 (邀請) yāoqǐng 58
一路平安 yílù píng'ān 59
以来 (以來) yǐlái 59
亿 (億) yì 60

意义 (意義) yìyì 60
艺术 (藝術) yìshù 60
银行 (銀行) yínháng 61
银行卡 (銀行卡) yínhángkǎ 61
*英国 (英國) yīngguó 61
英文 yīngwén 61
英语 (英語) yīngyǔ 61
邮局 (郵局) yóujú 61
语法 (語法) yǔfǎ 63
语音 (語音) yǔyīn 63
早饭 (早飯) zǎofàn 66
站 zhàn 66
这种 (這種) zhè(i)zhǒng 67
证件 (證件) zhèngjiàn 69
制造 (製造) zhìzào 69
中餐 zhōngcān 69
中华民族 (中華民族) zhōnghuá mínzú 69
中文 zhōngwén 69
中学 (中學) zhōngxué 69
中学生 (中學生) zhōngxuéshēng 69
中医 (中醫) zhōngyī 70
主任 zhǔrèn 70
祝 zhù 71
专业 (專業) zhuānyè 71
总理 (總理) zǒnglǐ 72

暗 àn T, H4, S2 **be dart, do secretly,** *faire nuit, faire en cachette* 天~下来了。tiān ~ xiàlai le. It's getting dart. *Il commence à faire nuit.*

冬季天~得很早。dōngjì tiān ~de hěnzǎo. It gets dark early in winter. *Il fait nuit de bonne heure en hiver.* 他把东西~中给了我。tā bǎ dōngxi ~zhōng gěile wǒ. He gave it to me secretly. *Il me l'a donné en cachette.*

案 àn T **case, law case,** *affaire f* 这是个 偷税 ~ / 凶杀 ~。 zhè shì gè tōushuì ~ / xiōngshā ~. It's a fraud / murder case. *C'est une affaire de fraude / meurtre.*

警察破~了吗? jǐngchá pò~ le ma? Did the police clear up that criminal case? *Est-ce que la police la cause judiciaire?*

爱(愛) ài T, H1, S1 **love, be mad about sb, be fond of, like,** *aimer, être amoureux* 我~你! wǒ ~ nǐ! I'm in love with you! *Je t'aime (d'amour)!* 她特别~音乐。tā tèbié ~ yīnyuè. She's very fond of music. *Elle aime beaucoup la musique.*

他~你~得发狂。tā ~ nǐ ~ de fākuáng. He's mad about you. *Il est follement amoureux de toi.* 我不~穿这件夹克。wǒ bú ~ chuān zhèjiàng jiákè. I don't like myself in this jacket. *Je ne m'aime pas dans cette veste.*

碍 ài T **hinder, be in the way of, be harmful to,** *gêner, être nuisible à* 这~着人过路。zhè àizhe rén guòlù. That is in the way. *Cela gène le passage.*

你们在这儿而呆着吧，~不着我。nǐmen zài zhèr dāizhe ba, ài bùzháo wǒ. Stay where you are. You're not in my way. *Restez où vous êtes. Vous ne me gênez pas.* 你作的事有~团结。nǐ zuòde shì yǒu~ tuánjié. What you're doing will be harmful to unity. *Ce que tu es en train de faire sera nuisible à l'unité.*

安全 ānquán N, H4, S1 **safety, be safe,** *sécurité f., être sûr* 要注意交通~! yào zhùyì jiāotōng ~. Be careful to traffic safety! *Attention à la sécurité routière!*

我负责他的~. wǒ fùzé tāde ~. I'm making sure he's safe. *Je veille à sa sécurité.* 她把我们带领到了一个~的地方。tā bǎ wǒmen dàidàole yígè ānquán de dìfang. She led us to a place of safety. *Elle nous a conduits à un lieu sûr.*

八 bā T, H1, S1 **eight,** *huit* 我孩子~岁了。wǒ háizi ~ suì le. My child is at the age of 8 (years old). *Mon enfant a 8 ans.* ~点了。~ diǎn le. It is eight (o'clock). *Il est huit heures.*

这是半斤~两。zhè shì bànjīn ~liǎng. It's six of one and half a dozen of the other. *C'est bonnet blanc et blanc bonnet.* ~月有三十一天。~yuè yǒu sānshíyī tiān. There are 31 days in August. *Il y a 31 jours au mois d'août.* (阴历) 8 月 15 是中秋节。(yīnlì) ~yuè shíwǔ shì zhōngqiūjié. 15th day of the 8th (lunar) month is the Mid-autumn Festival / the Moon Festival. *Le 15ème du 8ème mois (lunaire) est la fête de la mi-automne / de la lune.*

巴 bā T **look foward to, be close / next to, *attendre impatiemment, à proximité de, tout près de*** 我~不得再见到她。wǒ ~budé zài jiàndào tā. I'm looking forward to seeing her again. *J'attends impatiemment de la revoir.*

我们前不~村，后不着店。wǒmen qián bù ~ cūn hòubù zháodiàn. We are with no village ahead and no inn behind. *Il n'y a aucun village devant nous, pas d'auberges derrière.*

把 bǎ (介) T, H3, S1 **bǎ + object + transitive verb, *bǎ + objet + verbe transitif*** 他~东西都吃了。tā ~ dōngxi dōu chī le. He's eaten everything (up). *Il a tout mangé.* 我~衣服洗了(洗)。wǒ ~ yīfu xǐle(xǐ). I washed the clothes. *J'ai lavé des vêtements.*

把 bǎ (量) T, H3, S1 **[a classifier], *[un classificateur]*** 我需要一~尺子。wǒ xūyào yì~ chǐzi. I need a rule. *J'ai besoin d'une règle.* 还缺少三~叉子。hái quēshǎo sān~ chāzi. There are still three forks missing. *Il manque encore trois fourchettes.*

爸爸 | 爸 bàba | bà T, H1, S1 **papa, dad, father, *papa, m*** 嗨, ~! 妈妈在哪儿? hèi, bàba! māma zài nǎr? Hello, Papa! Where's Mum? *Hé, papa! Où est maman?* ~生气了。bàba shēngqì le. Dad got angry. *Papa s'est mis en colère.*

~的书架上有很多书。bàba de shūjià shang yǒu hěnduō shū. Dad has a bookcase with a lot of books. *Papa a une bibliothèque avec beaucoup de livres.*

吧 ba T, H2, S1 **[a particle expressing a suggestion, a request, order...], *[un particule qui exprime une suggestion, une demande, un ordre...]*** 咱们走~! zánmen zǒu ba! Let's go! *Allons-y!* 这您就放心~。zhè nín jiù fàngxīn ba. Set your mind at rest on that point. *Rassurez-vous là-dessus.*

明天有工夫再来~。míngtiān yǒu gōngfu zài lái ba. Come again tomorrow if you have time. *Reviens demain si tu as le temps.*

白 bái (形) (1) T, H2, S1 **white, clear, *blanc, clair*** 她皮肤~。tā pífū ~. She has a fair complexion. *Elle a le teint clair.* 我们~天去。wǒmen ~tiān qù. Let's go in the daytime. *On y va pendant la journée.*

你喜欢~巧克力吗? nǐ xǐhuan ~ qiǎokèlì ma? Do you like white chocolate? *Est-ce que tu aimes le chocolat blanc?* 他头发一夜之间变~了。tā tóufà yíyè zhījiān biàn~ le. He went white overnight. *Ses cheveux sont devenus blancs en l'espace d'une nuit.*

白 bái (副) (2) T, H2, S1 **in vain, for nothing, *en vain, pour rien*** 我~忙了半天。wǒ ~ mángle bàntiān. I went for a lot of trouble for nothing. *Je me suis dérangé beaucoup pour rien.* 他们~费了力气。tāmen ~ fèi le lìqi. They made fruitless efforts. *Ils ont fait des efforts sans résultat*

百 bǎi H2, S1 **hundred, numerous, all kinds of, *cent, un grand nombre de, toutes sortes de*** 我有一~个。wǒ yǒu yì~ gè. I've got a hundred. *J'en ai cent.* 每人大约要一~克。měirén dàyuē yào yì~ kè. You need about a hundred grams per person. *Il faut à peu près cent grammes par personne.*

您~分之~的正确。nín ~fēn-zhī~ de zhèngquè. You're absolutely right. *Vous avez cent fois raison.* 我重复了上~遍叫你不要做。wǒ chóngfù le shàng~ biàn jiào nǐ búyào zuò. I've told you a hundred times not to do it. *Je t'ai répété cent fois de ne pas le faire.*

板 bǎn T, S1 **board, shutter, stiff, *planche f, volet m, être difficile*** 妈妈新买了个切菜~。māma mǎile yígè xīn cài~. Mum just bought a chopping board. *Maman vient d'acheter une planche à découper.*

窗户上~了吗? chuānghu shàng ~ le ma? Have you closed the shutters? *Est-ce que tu as fermé les volets?* 他很~，很难接触。tā hěn bǎn, hě nán jiēchù. He is very stiff and you can't easily be in touch with. *Il est d'un abord difficile et tu ne peux pas facilement être en contact avec.*

办 (辦) bàn T, S1 **do, faire** 我去~。wǒ qù ~. I'll do it. *Je vais le faire.* ~叫你~的事。~ jiào nǐ bànde shì. Do as you're told. *Fais ce qu'on te dit.*

我不知道怎么~。wǒ bù zhīdào zěnme bàn. I don't know what is to be done. *Je ne sais quoi faire.* 这个~不得。zhège ~ bùdé. It isn't done. *Cela ne se fait pas.* 一般都这么~。yìbān dōu zhème ~. It is quite commonly done. *C'est de pratique courante.* ~完了 / ~好了! ~wán le / ~hǎo le! It is as good as done / That's done it! *C'est une affaire faite / Ça y est!*

帮（幫）bāng T, S1 **help, side of a boat, a group of,** *aide f, le côté du bateau, un groupe de* 她需要(人)~一下。tā xūyào (rén) ~ yíxià. She needs help. *Elle a besoin d'aide.*

巨大的海浪撞击船~。jùdà de hǎilàng zhuàngjī chuán~. Big waves crashed against the side of the boat. *De grandes vagues se sont écrasées contre le côté du bateau.* 电影院前面有一~年轻人。diànyǐngyuàn qiánmiàn yǒu yì~ niánqīngrén. There was a group of youngsters in front of the cinema. *Il y avait un groupe de jeunes devant le cinéma.*

帮助（幫助）bāngzhù H2, A1 **help, assist,** *aider, assister* 能~我一把吗(能~一把我做作业吗)? néng bāng wǒ yìbǎ ma (néng bāng yìbǎ wǒ zuò zuòyè ma)? Can you help me (with my homework)? *Peux-tu m'aider (pour faire le devoir)?*

他~了我学外文 / 他~我学了外文。tā ~le wǒ xué wàiwén / tā ~ wǒ xuéle wàiwén. He helped me learn a foreign language. *Il m'a aidé à apprendre une langue étrangère.* (我)感谢您~了我 / 对您的~我表示感谢。(wǒ) gǎnxiè nín ~ le wǒ / duì nínde bāngzhù wǒ biǎoshì gǎnxiè. Thank you for helping me. *Je vous remercie de m'avoir aidé.*

包 bāo T, H3, S1 **leave it all to sb, make, wrap,** *faire tout seul, faire, emballage* 这事由我~了吧。zhè shì yóu wǒ ~ le ba. Just leave it all to me. *Laissez-moi le faire tout seul.*

咱们~饺子(吃)吧。zánmen ~ jiǎozi chī ba. Let us make dumplings ourselves. *Allons faire des raviolis nous-mêmes.* 您想用礼物纸~起来吗? nín xiǎng yòng lǐwù-zhǐ bāo qǐlái ma? Would you like it gift-wrapped? *Voudriez-vous le mettre sous emballage-cadeau?*

饱（飽）bǎo T, H3, S2 **have eaten one's fill, be full,** *avoir mangé à sa faim, être rassasié* 我吃~了。wǒ chī~ le. I'm full. *Je suis rassasié.* 他们吃得很~。tāmen chīde hěn ~. They have eaten their fill. *Ils ont mangé tout leur content.*

宝（寶）bǎo T, S2 **precious, treasure,** *sacré, joyau m, trésor m* 这是我的~(贝)。zhè shì wǒde ~ (bei). That's my treasure. *C'est mon trésor.* 这是你那本~书! zhè shì nǐ nàběn ~ shū. Here's your precious book! *Le voilà ton sacré livre!*

博物馆有很多文艺复兴的艺术之~。bówùguǎn yǒu hěnduō wényì-fùxīng de yìshù zhī ~. The museum has many treasures of Renaissance art. *Le musée contient de nombreux joyaux de la Renaissance.*

保 bǎo T, S1 **preserve, protect, defend,** *conserver, garder* 田地要~水~肥。tiándì yào ~ shuǐ ~ féi. You have to preserve moisture and fertility in the soil. *Il faut conserver l'humidité et la fertilité de la terre cultivée.*

晚饭你能给我~一下暖吗? wǎnfàn nǐ néng gěi wǒ ~ yíxià nuǎn ma? Will you keep dinner warm for me? *Peux-tu me garder le dîner chaud?*

报导（報導）bàodǎo
报道（報道）bàodào N, H4, S1 **cover, story,** *(faire) le reportage, histoire f* 他~了会议情况。tā ~ le huìyì qíngkuàng. He covered the conference. *Il a fait le reportage de la conférence.*

各家日报星期一大量~了此事。gèjiā rìbào xīngqī-yī dàliàng ~ le cǐshì. Monday's dailies were full of the story. *Les quotidiens de lundi ont été pleins de cette histoire.*

报纸（報紙）bàozhǐ H2, S1 **newspaper,** *journal m* 他每天都看~。tā měitiān dōu kàn ~. He reads newspapers every day. *Il lit des journaux tous les jours.*

她去给奶奶取了~。tā qù gěi nǎinai qǔle ~. She fetched a newspaper for her grandma. *Elle est allée chercher un journal pour sa grand-mère.* 您希望我们把~送到家里吗? nín xīwàng wǒmen bǎ ~ sòngdào jiālǐ ma? Do you want your newspaper (to be) delivered? *Est-ce que vous voulez qu'on vous livre votre journal?*

杯子 bēizi H1, S1 **cup, glass,** *verre m, tasse f* 我没有~。wǒ méitǒu ~. I don't have any glasses. *Je n'ai pas de verres.*

我不需要玻璃~, 给我一个塑料~就行了。wǒ bù xūyào bōli ~, gěi wǒ yígè sùliào ~ jiù xíngle. I don't need a glass. Just give me a plastic cup. *Je n'ai pas besoin d'un verre. Donne-moi juste une tasse en plastique.* 桌子上有五个酒杯(子)。zhuōzi shàng yǒu wǔgè jiǔ-bēi(zi). There're five wine glasses on the table. *Il y a cinq verres à vin sur la table.*

北京 běijīng N, H1, S1 **Beijing, Peking,** *Beijing, Pékin* 我是从~来的。wǒ shì cóng ~ lái de. I come from Beijing. *Je viens de Beijing / Je* *suis originaire de Beijing.* ~是中国的首都。 ~ shì zhōngguó de shǒudū. Beijing is the capital of China. *Beijing est la capitale de la Chine.*

~是直辖市。 ~ shì zhíxiáshì. Beijing is a municipality directly under the Central Government. *Beijing est une municipalité relevant directement du gouvernement central.* ~有 3000 年的历史了。 ~ yǒu sānqiān nián de lìshǐ le. Beijing has had a history of 3000 years. *Beijing a eu une histoire de 3000 ans.*

本 běn (量) H1 S1 **[a classifier],** *[un classificateur]* 我想买这~书和这两~杂志。 wǒ xiǎng mǎi zhè~ shū hé zhè liǎng~ zázhì. I'd like to buy this book and these two magazines. *Je voudrais acheter ce livre et ces deux magazines.* 我去买一~中文词典。 wǒ qù mǎi yì~ zhōngwén cídiǎn. I'll go and buy a Chinese dictionary. *Je vais acheter un dictionnaire chinois.*

这~书是面向大众的。 zhè~ shū shì miànxiàng dàzhòng de. This is a book aimed at a wide public. *C'est un livre qui s'adresse à un large public.*

本 běn (代、副) H1, S2 **this, according to, by,** *ce, comme, selon* ~周没有课。 ~zhōu méiyǒu kè. There aren't any classes this week. *Il n'y a pas de cours cette semaine.*

她~月的健康状况有了好转。 tā ~yuè de jiànkāng zhuàngkuàng yǒule hǎozhuǎn. Her health has been improving this month. *Son état (de santé) s'est amélioré ce mois.* 一切都是~着计划进行的。 yíqiè dōu shì ~zhe jìhuà jìnxíng de. Everything went according to the plan. *Tout s'est passé comme prévu.* 我们是~着规则行事的。 wǒmen shì ~zhe guīzé xíngshì de. We acted by the rules. *Nous avons agi selon les règles.*

本报 běnbào N **our newspaper,** *notre journal* ~报道了会议情况。 ~ bàodào le huìyì qíngkuàng. Our newspaper has covered the conference. *Notre journal a fait le reportage de la conférence.*

比 bǐ H2, S1 **compare, more...than, comparable, plus...que** 俄国~中国大。 éguó ~ zhōngguó dà. Russia is bigger than China. *La Russie est plus grande que la Chine.* 他~不上您。 tā ~ búshàng nín. He can't compare with you. *Il ne vous est pas comparable.*

他开车~我小心。 tā kāichē ~ wǒ xiǎoxīn. He drives more carefully than I do. *Il conduit plus prudemment que moi.*

别 （別）bié (1) H2, S1 **don't, ne (fais) pas, ne (fais) plus** ~忙! ~ máng! Don't hurry! *Ne vous pressez pas!* ~当老好人! ~ dāng lǎohǎorén! That's the expense of principles! *Il ne faut pas sacrifier les principes!*

~三心二意了, 一块儿跟我们走吧! ~ sānxīn èryì le, yíkuàir gēn wǒmen zǒu ba. Don't shilly-shally, let's go together! *Plus d'hésitation, partons ensemble!*

别 （別）bié (动) (2) H2; S1 **fasten, pin to, wear,** *attacher, épingler* 不要忘了把安全带~好。 búyào wàngle bǎ ānquándài ~ hǎo. Don't forget to fasten your seatbelt. *N'oublie pas d'attacher ta ceinture de sécurité.*

她上衣~着一个饰针。 tā shàngyī ~zhe yígè shìzhēn. There was a brooch pinned to her jacket. *Elle portait une broche épinglée à sa veste.* 他衣服纽扣上~着一朵花儿。 tā yīfú niǔkòu shang biézhe yì duǒ huār. He's wearing a flower in his button hole. *Il a une fleur à la boutonnière.*

并不 bìngbù G **actually not,** *vraiment pas* 您~能去。 nǐ ~ néng qù. You really mustn't go to it. *Il ne faut absolument pas que vous y alliez.*

这与那些事实~矛盾。 zhè yǔ nàxiē shìshí ~ máodùn. That isn't really at variance with the facts. *Cela n'est vraiment pas en contradiction avec les faits.* 他们被削弱了, 但是 ~ / 并没(有) 泄气。 tāmen bèi xuēruò le, dànshì ~ / bìng méi(yǒu) xièqì. They were weakened, but not discouraged. *Ils étaient affaiblis, mais non pas découragés.*

薄 bó T **ungenerous, trivial, set,** *peu généreux, frivole, décliner* 这一提供并不~。 zhè yì tígōng bìng bù ~. The offer was not ungenerous. *L'offre n'est pas peu généreuse.*

他的那些话太轻~。 tāde nàxiē huà tài qīng~. He had trivial remarks. *Il a eu des propos frivoles.* 日~西山了。 rì ~ xīshān le. The sun is setting behind the western hills. *Le soleil décline dernière les collines de l'ouest.*

不客气 （不客氣）bú kèqi H1 **blunt; you're welcome, don't mention it,** *sans détour; pas de quoi, de rien* 多谢! 多谢! --- ~! (~!) duō xiè! duō xiè! --- ~! (~!) Thank you very much indeed! – You're welcome. *Merci infiniment! – Pas de quoi.*

他的回答 / 他回答得 很~。 tāde huídá / tā huídá dé hěn ~. He answered bluntly / In answer he

4

didn't mince his words. *Il a répondu sans ménagement / sans mâcher ses mots.* 自己拿, 别客气! zìjǐ ná, bié ~. Help yourself! *Sers-toi!*

不 bù bú D, H1, S1 [expressing the negation, *exprimer la négation*] 我~ 说 / 来 / 走。 wǒ ~ shuō / lái / zǒu. I won't speak / come / go. *Je ne parle pas / viens pas / pars pas.*

这个并~便宜, 你怎么说便宜? zhègè bìng ~ piányi, nǐ zěnme shuō piányi? It isn't cheap really, and why do you say it is? *Ce n'est vraiment pas bon marché, alors pourquoi tu dis le contraire?* 他~会表示自己要说的意思。 tā ~ huì biǎoshì zìjǐ yào shuō de yìsi. He has difficulty in expressing himself. *Il a du mal à s'exprimer.*

不能 bùnéng G cannot, not be able to, *ne pas pouvoir, ne pas capable de* 我们绝~ 做。 wǒmen jué ~ zuò. We cannot possibly do it. *Nous ne pouvons absolument pas le faire.* 她再也 ~唱歌了。 tā zàiyě ~ chànggē le. She'll never be able to sing again. *Jamais plus elle ne sera capable de chanter.*

不知 bùzhī G not know, *ne pas savoir* 那个人~好歹。 nàgè rén ~ hǎodǎi. That person doesn't know what's good for him / her. *Cette personne ne comprend pas où se trouve son intérêt.*

~不觉已过了 两个星期 / 两周。 ~ bùjué yǐ guòle liǎnggè xīngqī / liǎngzhōu. Two weeks had passed before we knew it. *Deux semaines ont passé sans qu'on s'en aperçoive.*

菜 cài H1, S1 Vegetable, cooking, course, *légume m, cuisine f, plat m* 我种~。 wǒ zhòng ~. I grow vegetables. *Je cultive des légumes.* 她在做(中国) ~ / 饭。 tā zài zuò (zhōngguó) cài / fàn. She's doing the (Chinese) cooking. *Elle est en train de faire la cuisine (chinoise).*

我们吃了三道~, 最后(一道 ~)是甜食。 wǒmen chīle sān dào ~, zuìhòu (yídào ~) shì tiánshí. We had three courses and a sweet. *Nous avons eu trois plats et le dessert.*

茶 chá H1, S1 tea, *thé m* 喝~吗? hē ~ ma? Would you like tea? *Vous voulez boire du thé?*

我喜欢喝淡一点儿的~。 wǒ xǐhuan hē dàn yìdiǎr de ~. I prefer the weak tea. *Je préfère le thé léger.* 我烧水泡~。 wǒ shāoshuǐ pào~. I'll put the kettle on for tea. *Je mets l'eau à chauffer pour le thé.*

长 (長) cháng H2, S1 long, length, be good at, strong point, *longueur f, long, être doué pour, qualité f* ~江很~。 ~jiāng hěn ~. The Yangtze River is very long. *Le Yangzi Jiang est très long.* 这张桌子有多~? zhè zhāng zhuōzi yǒu duō~? How long is the table? *Quelle est la longueur de la table?*

我们会有~时间的好天气。 wǒmen huì yǒu ~ shíjiān de hǎo tiānqì. We'll have a long spell of fine weather. *Nous aurons une longue période de beau temps.* 这是条(有)两百公里~的河。 zhèshì tiáo (yǒu) liǎngbǎi gōnglǐ ~ de hé. It's a river 200 kilometres in length. *C'est un fleuve long de 200 kilomètres.* 她~于绘画。 tā ~ yú huìhuà. She is good at painting. *Elle est douée pour la peinture.*

一个人要取人之~, 补己之短。yígè rén yào qǔ rén zhī~, bǔ jǐ zhī duǎn. One should overcome one's shortcomings by learning from others' strong points. *On devrait corriger ses propres défauts en prenant exemple sur les qualités d'autrui.*

唱歌 chàng gē H2, S1 **sing (a song),** *chanter (une chanson)* 她(~儿)唱得很好。tā (~r) chàng de hěnhǎo. She sings well. *Elle chante bien.* 我不会~。wǒ bú huì ~. I can't sing. *Je ne sais pas chanter.*

她除了很会~, 还能拉小提琴。tā chúle hěn huì ~, hái néng lāi xiǎotíqíng. Besides being a good singer, she also plays the violin. *C'est une bonne chanteuse, et de plus elle joue du violon.*

成 chéng D, S1 **become, develop into,** *devenir, se développer en* 他~了将军。tā ~le jiāngjūn. He became a general. *Il devint général.* 他们不久就~了朋友。tāmen bùjiǔ jiù ~ le péngyou. They were soon making friends. *Ils se sont bien vite fait des amis.*

事件会很快发展~丑闻。shìjiàn huì hěnkuài fāzhǎn~ chǒuwén. The affair will soon develop into a scandal. *L'affaire ne va pas tarder à se développer en scandale.*

成为 (成為) chéng wéi D, H4, S1 **become, develop into,** *devenir, se développer en* 青蛙~王子了。qīngwā ~ wángzǐ le. The frog changed into a prince. *La grenouille s'est transformée en prince.*

他~了一个电脑专家。tā ~le yígè diànnǎo zhuānjiā. He's become a computer expert. *Il est devenu un expert en informatique.*

吃 chī H1, S1 **eat, take,** *manger, prendre* 他在~苹果。tā zài ~ píngguǒ. He's eating an apple. *Il est en train de manger une pomme.*

只有方便面~, 行不行? zhǐyǒu fāngbiànmiàn ~, xíngbùxíng? There are only instant noodles, is that all right? *Il y a seulement des nouilles à cuisson instantanée, ça va?* 咱们午饭包饺子~吧! zánmen wǔfàn bāo jiǎozi ~ ba! Let's make dumplings ourselves at lunch. *Allons faire des raviolis nous-mêmes pour le déjeuner.* 什么~的都没有。shénme chīde dōu méiyǒu. There's nothing to eat. *Il n'y a rien à manger.*

出 chū D, H2, S1 **go out, [a classifier], [a result of an action],** *sortir, [un classificateur], [le résultat d'une action]* 她~去了。tā ~qù le. She went out. *Elle est sortie.* 他~了什么事儿了? tā ~le shénme shìr le. What

has happened to him? *Qu'est-ce qui lui est arrivé?*

他是这~话剧的导演。tā shì zhè~ huàjù de dǎoyǎn. He's the director of the modern drama. *Il est metteur en scène du théâtre parlé.* 我们需要一个专家对此作~评价。wǒmen xūyào yígè zhuānjiā duì cǐ zuò~ píngjià. We need to have it valued by an expert. *Nous devons le faire évaluer par un expert.*

出来 chūlai G, S1 **go out, [a result of an action],** *sortir, [le résultat d'une action]* 她从屋里~了。tā cóng wūlǐ ~ le. She came out of the room. *Elle est sortir de la pièce.*

他从一个门进去, 又从另一个门~了。tā cóng yígè mén jìnqù, yòu cóng lìng yígè mén chūlái le. He went in at one door and out at the other. *Il est entré par une porte et sorti par l'autre.* 树上(生)长不出钱来。shùshàng (shēng)zhǎng bù chū qián lái. The money doesn't grow on trees. *L'argent ne pousse pas sur les arbres.*

出租车 (出租車) chūzūchē H1, S1 **taxicab, taxi, cab,** *taxi m* 我打电话叫辆~。wǒ dǎ diànhuà jiào liàng ~. I'll phone for a taxi. *J'appellerai un taxi.* 我坐~去。wǒ zuò ~ qù. I'll go by taxi. *J'y vais en taxi.*

穿 chuān H2, S1 **dress, cross,** *habiller, traverser* 他~得很暖和。tā ~de hěn nuǎnhuo. He's warmly dressed. *Il est habillé chaudement.*

这双鞋我~上正合适。zhè shuāng xié wǒ ~shàng zhèng héshì. These shoes are just my size. *Cette paire de chaussures est tout à fait à ma pointure.* 我们在等那些奶牛~过公路去。wǒmen zài děng nàxiē nǎiniú ~guò gōnglù qù. We're waiting for the cows to cross the road. *Nous attendons que ces vaches traversent la route.*

船 chuán H2, S1 **boat,** *bateau m* 上~吧! shàng ~ ba! Let's go on board. *Montons à bord.*

我们乘~去美洲。wǒmen chéng ~ qù měizhōu. We're going to America by boat. *Nous allons en Amérique en bateau.* ~在暴风雨中沉了。~ zài bàofēngyǔ zhōng chéng le. The boat sank in the storm. *Le bateau a coulé dans la tempête.*

次 cì (量) (1) H2, S1 **time,** *fois f* 我去过好几~他家。wǒ qùguo hǎo cǐ ~ tājiā. I went to his place several times. *Je suis allé chez lui plusieurs fois.*

那个电子邮件我给他发过两~。nàge diànzǐ-yóujiàn wǒ gěi tā fāguò liǎng~. I sent him the same e-mail twice. *Je lui ai envoyé le même courrier électronique deux fois.*

次 cì (形) (2) H2, S1 **no good, terrible, inferior,** *nul, médiocre, moins bon* 这个真~。zhègè zhēn ~. That's really no good. *Ceci est vraiment médiocre.*

我(的)数学太~了。wǒ(de) shùxué tài ~ le. I'm terrible at maths. *Je suis nul en math.* 她的第二本小说~多了。tāde dì èr běn xiǎoshuō ~duō le. Her second novel is a much inferior work. *Son deuxième roman est bien moins bon.*

存 cún T, H5, S1 **keep,** *conserver* 大热天西红柿~不住。dà rètiān xīhóngshì ~búzhù. Tomatoes won't keep in hot weather. *Les tomates ne se conservent pas quand il fait trop chaud.*

这是保险单，要~好。zhèshì bǎoxiǎn-dān, yào ~ hǎo. It's the guarantee form. You must keep it. *C'est le bon de garantie. Il faut le conserver.*

寸 cùn T, S2 **cun, a unit of length (= 1/3 decimetre),** *cun m, une unité de longueur (= 1/3 de décimètre)* 一分米等于三~。yì fēnmǐ děngyú sān~. A decimetre (dm.) is equal to 3 cun (a unit of Chinese length). *Un décimètre (dm) est égal à 3 cun (une unité de longueur chinoise).*

我们~土必争。wǒmen ~tǔ bìzhēng. We're fighting for every inch of land. *Nous nous battons pour chaque pouce de terrain.*

错 (錯) cuò H2, S1 **wrong, mistake, fault,** *mauvais, erreur f, faute f* 我对，你~了。wǒ duì, nǐ ~ le. I'm right, and you're wrong. *J'ai raison, et tu as tord.* 他回答~了。tā huídá ~ le. He gave the wrong answer. *Il a donné une mauvaise réponse.*

这个~儿你忘改了。zhègè cuòr nǐ wàng gǎi le. You forgot to correct this mistake. *Tu as oublié de corriger cette erreur.* 他虽然有~儿，我仍然爱着他。tā suīrán yǒu ~r wǒ rēngrán àizhe tā. In spite of his faults, I still love him. *Malgré ses fautes, je l'aime toujours.*

打电话 (打電話) dǎ diànhuà H1, S1 **phone, be on the phone,** *téléphoner, être au téléphone* 请等一下，我在~。qǐng děng yíxià, wǒ zài ~. Just a minute, I'm on the phone. *Un instant, je suis au téléphone.* 好几个人给我们打了电话。hǎo jǐgè rén gěi wǒmen dǎle diànhuà. Several people have phoned in. *Plusieurs personnes nous ont téléphoné / nous ont appelés au téléphone.*

他~请了病假。tā ~ qǐngle bìngjià. He phoned in sick. *Il a appelé pour dire qu'il était malade.* 我的会开到 11 点，开完会后再给我~。wǒde huì kāidào shíyī diǎn, kāiwán huì hòu zài gěi wǒ ~. I'll be in a meeting until eleven o'clock, but phone me afterwards. *Je serai en réunion jusqu'à onze heures, mais téléphone-moi après.*

打篮球 (打籃球) dǎ lánqiú H2 **play basketball,** *jouer au basketball* 咱们去~吧。zánmen qù ~ ba. Let us go and play basketball. *Allons jouer au basket.*

大 dà D, H1, S1 **big, loud,** *grand, fort* 中国很~, 俄国更~。zhōngguó hěn ~, éguó gèng ~. China is big, and Russia is bigger. *La Chine est grande, et la Russie est plus grande.* 这是个~问题。zhèshì gè dà ~. That's a big problem. *C'est un grand problème.*

收音机声音太~。shōuyīnjī shēngyīn tài ~. The radio is too loud. *La radio joue trop fort.* 她变化多~呀! tā biànhuà duō dà ya! How she has changed! *Ce qu'elle a changé!*

大家 dàjiā G, H2, S1 **everybody, all of us...; great master, authority on,** *tout le monde, tous; grand maître, spécialiste en* ~好! ~ hǎo! Hello / Hi everyone! *Bonjour à tous / à tout le monde!* ~都知道此事。~ dōu zhīdào cǐ shì. Everybody knows that. *Tout le monde sait cela.*

他为~做好事。tā wèi ~ zuò hǎoshì. He does all of us good turns. *Il rend service à nous tous.* 他是个书法~。tā shì gè shūfǎ ~. He's a great master of calligraphy. *C'est un grand maître de la calligraphie.* 他是个经济学~。tā shì gè jīngjìxué ~. He's an authority on economics. *C'est un grand spécialiste en sciences économiques.*

大陆（大陸）dàlù N, S2 **continent, mainland,** *continent m* 亚洲、非洲是两个最大的~。yàzhōu, fēizhou shì liǎnggè zuìdà de ~. Asia and Africa are the two biggest continents. *L'Asie et l'Afrique sont les deux plus grands continents.* 她划船返回了~。tā huáchuán fǎnhuí le ~. She sailed back to the continent. *Elle a regagné le continent en bateau.*

大学（大學）dàxué S1 **university,** *université f* 我上~。wǒ shàng ~. I go to university. *Je vais à l'université.* 他受过~教育。tā shòuguò ~ jiàoyù. He's had a university education. *Il a fait des études supérieures.* 褚小姐~(本科)毕业了。chǔ xiǎojiě ~ (běnkē) bìyè le. Miss Chu has graduated (from university). *Mlle Chu a obtenu sa licence.*

大学生（大學生）dàxuéshēng S1 **a university student,** *un(e) étudiant(e) universitaire* 他们是~。tāmen shì ~. They are university students. *Ils sont étudiants à l'université.* 她是生物学(专业)~。tā shì shēngwùxué (zhuānyè) ~. She's a biology student. *Elle est étudiante en biologie.* 他是一年级~ / 二年级~。tā shì yī niánjí ~ / èr niánjí ~. He's a first- / second-year student. // a freshman / sophomore. *C'est un étudiant de première / seconde année.*

代 dài (动) (1) T, S1 **take the place of, on behalf of,** *remplacer, au nom de* 请~向你父母致意。qǐng ~ xiàng nǐ mùmǔ zhìyì. Please give your parents my regards. *Fais mes amitiés à tes parents.*

我~(表)这里所有的人, 向您表示感谢。wǒ ~(biǎo) zhèlǐ suǒyǒu de rén, xiàng nín biǎoshì gǎnxiè. On behalf of everyone here, I thank you. *Au nom de tous ceux qui sont ici présents, je vous remercie.*

代 dài (名) (2) S1 **generation,** *génération f* 他们不是同一~人。tāmen búshì tóng yí~ rén. They are not of the same generation. *Ils ne sont pas de la même génération.*

现在这一~人对未来很担忧。xiànzài zhè yí~ rén duì wèilái hěn dānyōu. The present generation is / are anxious about the future. *La génération actuelle est inquiète face à l'avenir.* 这是世世~~留下来的传统。zhè shì shìshì ~~ liú xiàlái de chuántǒng. These are traditions that have been practiced for generations. *Ce sont des traditions en vigueur depuis des générations.*

代表 dàibiǎo N, H4, S1 **representative, delegate,** *représentant(e), délégué(e)* 我是公司~。wǒ shì gōngsī ~. I'm the representative of the company. *Je suis le représentant / la représentante de la société.*

各地~都到了。gèdì ~ dōu dàole. The delegates of all parts of the country have arrived. *Les délégués des différents endroits du pays sont tous arrivés.* 她声称自己~人民的声音。tā shēngchēng zìjǐ ~ rénmín de shēngyīn. She claims to be the voice of the people. *Elle se fait passer pour la voix du peuple.*

但 dàn D, S1 **but,** *mais* 他个子矮，~很结实。tā gèzi ǎi, ~ hěn jiēshi. He's small but strong. *Il est petit mais fort.*

~您对文件不是很了解的吗？~ nǐ duì wénjiàn búshì hěn liǎojiě de ma? But you are familiar with the case, aren't you? *Mais vous connaissez le dossier?* 他可以是老板，~你毕竟有你的权力。tā kěyǐ shì lǎobǎn, ~ nǐ bìjìng yǒu nǐde quánlì. He may be the boss but you've still got your rights. *Il est peut-être le patron mais tu as quand même tes droits.*

但是 dànshì G, H2, S1 **but,** *mais* 他不太聪明，~很能苦干。tā bú tài cōngming, ~ hěn néng kǔgàn. He's not very intelligent but he's a hard worker. *Il n'est pas très intelligent mais il est très travailleur.*

~我告诉你我是亲眼看见的。~ wǒ gàosù nǐ wǒ shì qīnyǎn kànjiàn de. But I tell you I saw it. *Mais puisque je t'ai dit que je l'ai vu.*

当然（當然）dāngrán G, H3, S1 **of course, naturally,** *bien sûr, naturellement* 真的吗？--- ~(是真的)。zhēnde ma? --- ~ (shì zhēnde). Is it true? – Of course it is. *C'est vrai? – Bien sûr que oui.*

您生气了吗? --- ~! nín shēngqì le ma? --- ~. You resented it? – Naturally! *Vous vous en êtes fâché? – Naturellement!* 她~ 一点儿 / 什么 也没懂。tā ~ yìdiǎr / shénme yě méi dǒng. Of course she hadn't understood a thing. *Bien sûr qu'elle n'avait rien compris.*

到 dào D, H2, S1 **arrive, it's time..., gain, arriver, il est temps que..., gagner** 我们快~了。wǒmen kuài ~ le. We're almost there. *Nous sommes presque arrivés.*

我出发的时间~了。wǒ chūfā de shíjiān ~ le. It's time I went. *Il est temps que je parte.* 你什么成果都得不~。nǐ shénme chéngguǒ dōu débú ~. You will gain nothing. *Tu n'y gagneras rien.*

道 dào D, S1 **road, detour, river, priest, voie f, circuit m, rivière f, prêtre m** 咱们抄近~儿去。wǒmen chāo jìn~r qù. Let's go by the shortest road. *Prenons par le plus court.*

我们去那儿绕了~(儿)。wǒmen qù nàr ràole ~(r). We made a long detour to get there. *Nous avons fait un long circuit pour y arriver.* 这条河~开通了。zhè tiáo hé~ kāitōng le. This river has opened / dredged. *Cette rivière a été ouverte / draguée.* 我向一位老~鞠了躬。tā xiàng yíwèi lǎo~ jūle gōng. I made / paid obeisance to an old Taoist priest. *J'ai rendu hommage à un vieux prêtre Taoïste.*

得 dé D, S1 **get, winner, look, all right, obtenir, médaillé, ça va** 七减四~三。qī jiǎn sì ~ sān. Seven minus four is three. *Sept moins quatre égale trois.* 他~金牌了! tā ~ jīnpái le! He is a gold medal winner! *Il est médaillé d'or!*

~了, 又搞错了! ~ le, yòu gǎocuò le! Look, I've got it wrong again! *Zut, je me suis trompé encore une fois!* ~了, 就这么办! ~ le, jiù zhème bàn! All right, just go ahead! *Ça va, allons-y!* (> 得 de, děi)

地 de H3, S1 **[an adjective / a phrase+地 =an adverb / adverbial modifier], [un adjective / une expression+地=un adverbe / complément circonstanciel]** 你要很快~回答。nǐ yào hěn kuài ~ huídá. You must reply quickly. *Il faut que tu répondes rapidement.* 他慢慢~走下了小山(来)。tā mànmàn ~ zǒu xià le xiǎoshān (lái). He slowly came down the hill. *Il a descendu la côte lentement.* 你应该实事求是~处理这个问题。nǐ yīnggāi shíshì qiúshì ~ chǔlǐ zhègè wèntí. You should handle that problem in a practical and realistic way. *Tu devrais traiter le problème de façon pratique et réaliste.* (> 地 dì)

的 de D, H1, S1 **of, [noun +的: demonstrative], de [nom+的: démonstratif]** 这是我~母亲。zhèshì wǒ~ mǔqin. She's my mother. *C'est ma mère.*

我喜欢有一个自己~房子。wǒ xǐhuān yǒu yígè zìjǐ~ fángzi. I'd like a home of my own. *J'aimerais avoir mon chez-moi.* 她是部门~负责人。tā shì bùmén ~ fùzérén. She's a head of department. *Elle est chef de service.*

得 de, dé H2, S1 **[verb+得+complement: appreciation], [verbe+得+complément: appréciation]** 他走~很 快 / 慢。tā zǒu ~ hěn kuài / màn. He is walking fast / slowly. *Il marche vite / lentement.*

她长~漂(亮)不漂亮? tā zhǎng ~ piào(liang) bú piàoliang? --- (长~)很漂亮 / 漂亮~很。(zhǎng ~) hěn piàoliang / piàoliang ~ hěn. Does she look pretty? – Yes, she does. *Est-elle belle? – Oui, très belle.* 我看他钢琴弹~不好。wǒ kàn tā gāngqín tán ~ bùhǎo. In my opinion, he doesn't play the piano well. *D'après moi, il ne joue pas bien de piano.* (> 得 dé, děi)

等 děng (动) H2, S1 **wait, attendre** 你~谁 / 什么 呢? nǐ ~ shéi / shénme ne? Who / What are you waiting for? *Qui attends-tu / Qu'attends-tu?*

那, 我们就~着吧! nà, wǒmen jiù děngzhe ba! In that case, it's best to wait! *En ce cas, il vaut mieux attendre!* 别~我们! bié ~ wǒmen. Don't wait for us! *Ne nous attends pas!*

地 dì D, S1 **land, terre f, terrain m** 这块~很肥。zhè kuài dì hěn ~. This is a good farming land. *C'est de la bonne terre.*

他下~种田(谋生)。tā xià ~ zhòng tián (móushēng). He works on the land. *Il travaille la terre.* "这块~出售" zhè kuài ~ chūshòu. "Land for sale", *"Terrain à vendre".* (> 地 de)

地方 dìfāng (1) D, H3, S1 **local, local** 他是~政府雇员。tā shì ~ zhèngfǔ gùyuán. He is an employee in the local government. *Il est fonctionnaire dans l'administration locale.*

你今天听~新闻了吗? nǐ jīntiān tīng ~ xīnwén le ma? Have you heard the local news today? *As-tu écouté les informations locales aujourd'hui?*

地方 dìfang (2) D, H3, S1 **place, local, endroit m** 你放在什么~了? nǐ fàngzài shénme ~ le? Whereabouts did you put it? *A quel endroit tu l'as mis?*

他们在我前面很远的~。tāmen zài wǒmen qiánmiàn hěn yuǎn de ~. They're a long way ahead us. *Ils sont loin devant nous.* 这个~的人很好客。zhègè ~ de rén hěn hàokè. The local people are very friendly. *Les gens de l'endroit sont très accueillants.*

地区 (地區) dìqū N, H5, S1 **area, region, *région f*** 我对这个~不了解。wǒ duì zhègè ~ bù liǎojiě. I don't know the area. *Je ne connais pas la région.*

我想买一张~交通图。wǒ xiǎng mǎi yì zhāng ~ jiāotōngtú. I'd like to buy a road map of the region. *Je voudrais acheter une carte routière de la région.* 这个~需要绿化。zhègè ~ xūyào lǜhuà. This region need reforestation. *Cette région a besoin d'être reboisée.*

弟弟|弟 dìdi | dì H2, S1 **younger brother, little brother, *frère cadet, petit frère*** 我~是中学生。wǒ ~ shì zhōngxuéshēng. My younger brother is a secondary school pupil / a high school student. *Mon petit frère est lycéen.*

那里有几个人，其中包括你~。nàlǐ yǒu jǐgè rén, qízhōng bāokuò nǐ ~. There were a few people there, including your little brother. *Quelques-uns étaient là, dont ton frère cadet.*

第一 dìyī G, N, H2 **first, front, *premier(ère)*** 他(是)~。tā (shì) ~. He's in first place. *Il est en tête.*

她中国文学(的分数)~。tā zhōngguó wénxué (de fēnshù) ~. She was first in Chinese Literature. *Elle était première en littérature chinoise.* 我们的座位在~行。wǒmen de zuòwèi zài ~ háng. We have seats in the front row. *Nous avons des places au premier rang.*

点 (點) diǎn H1, S1 **o'clock, it, a bit, *heure f, un peu*** 下午五~了。xiàwǔ wǔ ~ le. It's five (o'clock) p.m. *Il est cinq heures dans l'après-midi.*

这一~我不否认。zhèyì ~ wǒ bù fǒurèn. I'm not denying it. *Je ne le nie pas.* 我们看事情客观~儿吧。wǒmen kàn shìqíng kèguān ~r ba. Let's be a bit objective. *Voyons les choses un peu objectivement.*

电话 (電話) diànhuà G, S1 **telephone, phone, call, *téléphone m, appel m*** 您的~号码是多少? nín de ~ hàomǎ shì duōshǎo? What's your telephone number? *Quel est votre numéro de téléphone?*

下午有三个找你的~。xiàwǔ yǒu sāngè zhǎo nǐ de ~. There were three calls for you this afternoon. *Il y a eu trois appels pour toi cet après-midi.* 我往她家里打了~。wǒ wǎng tā jiāli dǎle ~. I called her house. *J'ai téléphoné chez elle.*

电脑 (電腦) diànnǎo H1, S1 **computer, *ordinateur m*** 她是搞~的。tā shì gǎo ~ de. She's in computers / She's a computer scientist. *Elle est dans l'informatique / Elle est informaticienne.*

~网络现在不通。~ wǎngluò xiànzài bù tōng. The network of computers is not going now. *Le réseau des ordinateurs ne marche pas maintenant.* 他整天都玩儿~游戏。tā zhěngtiān dōu wár ~ yóuxì. He spends his days playing computer games. *Il passe ses journées à jouer à des jeux électroniques.*

电视 (電視) diànshì H1, S1 **television, TV, telly, *télévision f, TV f, télé f*** 你~看个没完了! nǐ ~ kàn gè méiwán le! You watch television too much! *Tu regardes trop la télévision!*

您上~了吧? nín shàng ~ le na? You have been on television, haven't you? *Vous êtes passé à la télévision, n'est-ce pas?* 今晚~没什么好看的。jīnwǎn ~ méi shénme hǎokàn de. There's nothing on TV / telly tonight. *Il n'y a rien ce soir à la télé.*

电影 (電影) diànyǐng H1, S1 **film, motion, moving picture, *cinéma m, film m*** 那部~你看了吗? nà bù ~ nǐ kànle ma? Have you seen that film? *As-tu regardé ce film?*

她孩子长大要当~演员。tā háizi zhǎngdà yào dāng ~ yǎnyuán. Her child wants to be a film actor when he grows up. *Son enfant veut devenir un acteur de film quand il grandira.* 他是个~明星。tā shì gè ~ míngxīng. He's a film star. *C'est une star de cinéma.* 我把昨天晚上的~录了下来给你看。wǒ bǎ zuótiān wǎnshàng de ~ lùle xiàlái gěi nǐ kàn. I recorded last night's film for you. *J'ai enregistré le film d'hier soir pour toi.*

定 dìng D, S1 **fix, make up, *fixer, prendre la décision*** 结婚的日期~下来了吗? jiéhūn de rìqī ~ xiàlái le ma? Has the date of the marriage been fixed? *La date de mariage a-t-elle été fixée?*

他看来还没有拿~主意。tā kànlái hái méiyǒu ná~ zhǔyì. Evidently he has not made up his mind yet. *Il semble qu'il n'a pas encore pris la décision.*

东西 (東西) dōngxī (1) G, H1 **east and west, from east to west, *l'est et l'ouest, d'est en ouest*** 这个地方~两公里，南北四公里。This district is two kilometres across from east to west and four from north to south. *Cet arrondissement s'étend sur 2 kilomètres d'est en ouest et sur 4 du nord au sud.*

这是本关于~方文化交流的书。zhè shì běn guānyú ~ fāng wénhuà jiāoliú de shū. It's a book about the East-West cultural exchanges. *C'est un livre au sujet des échanges culturels entre l'Est et l'Ouest.*

东西 (東西) dōngxi (2) G, H1 **thing, creature, *choses f, sujet m*** 我去买~。wǒ qù mǎi ~. I'm going shopping. *Je vais faire des courses.* 他把~都吃了。tā bǎ ~ dōu chīle. He's eaten everything (up). *Il a tout mangé.*

我把~寄给你。wǒ bǎ ~ jì gěi nǐ. I'll post it to you. *Je te l'enverrai par la poste.* 真不是~! zhēn bú shì ~! What a despicable creature! *Quel mauvais sujet!*

动 (動) dòng D, S1 **move, fidget, *remuer, bouger, agiter*** 他闪了腰，~不了了。tā shǎnle yāo, ~ bùliǎo le. He has sprained his back and can't move. *Il s'est fait mal au rein et ne peut plus remuer.*

别~, (不然)我开枪了! bié ~, (bùrán) wǒ kāiqiāng le! Don't move, or I fire! *Ne bougez pas ou je tire!* 小曲, 别~个没完没了的! xiǎo qǔ, bié ~ gè méiwán méiliǎo de! Xiao Qu, stop fidgeting! *Xiao Qu, arrête de t'agiter!* 这个句子里缺~词。zhè gè jùzi lǐ quē ~cí. The verb is missing from this sentence. *Il manque le verbe dans cette phrase.*

都 dōu D, H1, S1 **everybody, everyone, even, already, *tout, chacun, même, déjà*** 大家~到了吗? dàjiā ~ dàole ma? Is everybody here? *Tout le monde est là?*

每个人~有自己的短处。měigè rén ~ yǒu zìjǐ de duǎnchù. Everyone has his faults. *Chacun a ses défauts.* 连老师~笑了。lián lǎoshī ~ xiàole. Even the teacher laughed. *Même le professeur a ri.* 他~八十了，身体还那么好。tā ~ bāshí le, shēntǐ hái nàme hǎo. Already eighty, he is still on top form. *Déjà quatre-vingts ans il est toujours en pleine forme.*

读 (讀) dú H1, S1 **read, read aloud, *lire, lire à haute voix*** 他能~会写。tā néng ~ huì xiě. He can read and write. *Il sait lire et écrire.*

我喜欢~经典作品。wǒ xǐhuan ~ jīngdiǎn zuòpǐn. I enjoy reading classics. *J'aime lire des œuvres classiques.*

对 (對) duì (形) D, H2, S1 **be right, *avoir raison*** 你不~。nǐ bú ~. You're not right. *Tu n'as pas raison.*

她基本上回答~了。tā jīběn shàng huídá ~le. She gave basically the right answer. *Elle a donné la bonne réponse dans son ensemble.* 他~了吗? --- 不全~ / 没有全~。tā ~le ma? --- bù quán ~ / méiyǒu quán ~. Was he right? – Not entirely. *Avait-il raison? – Pas entièrement.*

对 (對) duì (介、动) D, H2, S1 **[introducing concerned person(s) / thing(s)], *[introduire qn / qch concerné]*** 我~这个地区不了解。wǒ ~ zhègè dìqū bù liǎojiě. I don't know the area. *Je ne connais pas la région.*

时间~对方有利。shíjiān ~ duìfāng yǒulì. Time's on the other side. *Le temps travaille pour nos adversaires.* 她俩公开~骂。tāliǎ gōngkāi ~ mà. They insulted each other in public. *Elles se sont insultées en public.*

对不起 (對不起) duìbuqǐ H1, S1 **I'm sorry, sorry, excuse me, pardon me, I beg your pardon, *excusez-moi, je m'excuse, pardon, je vous / te demande pardon*** ~, 我来晚了。~, wǒ láiwǎn le. Sorry, I'm late. *Excusez-moi, je suis en retard.* 跟 夫人 / 阿姨 说~。gēn fūren / āyí shuō ~. Say sorry to the lady. *Demande pardon à la dame.*

~, 您说(的是)什么? ~, nín shuō (de shì) shénmen? (I beg your) pardon? What did you say? *Pardon, qu'est-ce que vous avez dit?* 他的行为不能说~而(得到)宽恕。tā de xíngwéi bùnéng shuō ~ ér (dédào) kuānshù. There is no excuse for his behaviour. *Sa conduite est inexcusable.*

多 duō (形) (1) H1, S1 **much, many, *beaucoup, nombreux*** 时间不~。shíjiān bù ~. We don't have much time. *On n'a pas beaucoup de temps.* 音乐会有很~人。yīnyuèhuì yǒu hěn ~ rén. There were many people at the concert. *Il y avait beaucoup de monde au concert.*

她吃得不~。tā chī de bù ~. She doesn't eat much. *Elle ne mange pas beaucoup.* 他们人太~了。tāmen rén tài ~ le. There were too many of them. *Ils étaient trop nombreux.*

多 duō (副) (2) H1, S1 **more, well, how, *plus, bien, comme, particulièrement*** ~想

想。~ xiǎngxiang. Think a little more. *Réfléchis un peu plus.*

开瓶前要~~摇动。kāi píng qián yào ~~ yáodòng. Shake well before opening. *Bien agiter le flacon avant d'ouvrir.* 她~伤心呀! tā ~ shāngxīn ya! How sad she is! *Comme elle est triste!* ~蠢呀! ~ chǔn ya! How stupid was that! *C'était particulièrement stupide!*

多少 duōshao H1, S1 **how many, how much, combien** 这个~钱? zhègè ~ qián? How much is it? *Combien ça coûte?* 我不知道他们有~人。wǒ bù zhīdào tāmen yǒu ~ rén. I don't know how many of them there are. *Je ne sais pas combien de personnes il y a.*

~教员(参加)罢课了? ~ jiàoyuán (cānjiā) bàkè le? How many teachers are on strike? *Combien de profs sont en grève?*

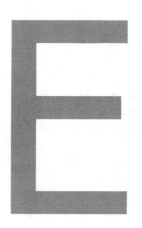

饿 (餓) è H3, S1 **hungry, starve, faim f, affamer** 她看起来又累又~。tā kànlái yòu lèi yòu ~. She looked tired and hungry. *Elle avait l'air fatiguée et affamée.* 我 ~极了 / ~死了! wǒ ~ jí le / ~ sǐ le! I'm very hungry / I could eat a horse. *J'ai très faim / J'ai une faim de loup.* 几个灾民没人援救~死了。jǐgè sāimín méi rén yuánjiù ~ sǐ le. Some disaster victims starved death without rescue. *Quelques personnes sinistrées sont mortes de faim sans être sauvées.*

而 ér D, H4, S2 **[linking two elements], but, [expressing a reason], [lier deux éléments], mais, [exprimer une raison]** 他出去~没有穿鞋袜。tā chūqù ~ méiyǒu chuān xiéwà. He went out without his shoes and socks on. *Il est sorti sans mettre ses chaussures et ses chaussettes.*

我想去，~他不想去。wǒ xiǎng qu, ~ tā bù xiǎng qù. I want to go but he doesn't. *Je veux aller, mais lui ne veut pas.* 我们为工作~去了维也那。wǒmen wèi gōngzuò ~ qùle wéiyěnà. We went to Vienna for work. *Nous sommes allés à Vienne pour le travail.*

而且 érqiě G, H3, S1 **[placing side by side or presenting another level], [mettre en parallèle ou présenter un autre niveau]** 我不想出去，~太冷了。wǒ bù xiǎng chūqù, ~ tài lěng le. I don't want to go out and besides, it's too cold. *Je n'ai pas envie de sortir, d'ailleurs il fait trop froid.*

他不但能看中文，~说得也不错。tā búdàn néng kàn zhōngwén, ~ shuō dé yě búcuò. He can not only read in Chinese, but also speak it quite well. *Non seulement il lit en chinois, mais aussi parle assez bien cette langue.*

儿子 (兒子) érzi G, H1, S1 **son, fils m** 这是我的~。zhèshì wǒde ~. He's my son. *C'est mon fils.* 您的~叫什么名字? nín de ~ jiào shénme míngzi? What's your son's name? *Comment s'appelle votre fils?*

这个当~的很象他父亲! tā zhēnshì tā fùqin de ~. He's just like his father! *Il est bien le fils de son père!* 这是个娇生惯养的~。zhè shì gè jiāoshēng guànyǎng de ~. He's a young man with an influantial father. *C'est le fils à papa.* 她的两个~长大成人了。tā de liǎng gè ~ zhǎngdà chéngrén le. She has two grown-up sons. *Elle a deux grands fils / deux fils adultes.*

二 èr H1, S1 **two, deux** ~~得四。~~ dé sì. Twice two is four. *Deux fois deux est quatre.* 一公里等于~里。yì gōnglǐ děngyú ~ lǐ. A kilometre is equal to two li. *Un kilomètre est égal à deux li.* 他有~心。tā yǒu~ xīn. He's disloyal. *Il est déloyal.* 老通是个说一不~的人，你可以放心。Lǎo tōng shì gè shuōyī bú~ de rén, nǐ kěyǐ fàngxīn. Lao Tong is a man of his word, you can trust him. *Lao Tong est un homme de parole, tu peux lui faire confiance.* ~者必居其一。~zhě bì jū qí yī. It's either one or the other. *C'est tout l'un ou tout l'autre.*

F

pronounced? *Comment est-ce que ça se prononce?* 这个字母不~。zhègè zìmǔ bù ~. This letter is not pronounced. *Cette lettre ne se prononce pas.*

发展（發展）fāzhǎn N, H4, A1 **develop, development, *(se) développer, développement m*** 有了新的~。yǒu le xīnde ~. A new development occured. *Un nouveau développement s'est produit.*

那个孩子~得很快 / 有很快的~。nàgè háizi ~ dé hěn kuài / yǒu hěn kuài de ~. The child is developing rapidly. *L'enfant se développe rapidement.* 这一地区~得不够快。zhèyí dìqū ~ dé búgòu kuài. The region isn't developing very quickly. *Ça ne se développe pas beaucoup dans la région.*

法 fǎ D, S2 **law, method, mode, *loi f, méthode f, manière f*** 我们要守~。wǒmen yào shǒu ~. We must observe the law. *On doit observer la loi.* 他违~了。tā wéi ~ le. He broke the law. *Il a violé la loi.*

她的教~遭到了批评。tāde jiāo~ zāodào le pīpíng. Her teaching method has come under fire. *Sa méthode d'enseignement a été critiquée.* 这个表达~不对。zhègè biáodá~ búduì. The mode of expression isn't correct. *Cette manière d'expression n'est pas correcte.*

法国（法國）fǎguó * **France, *France*** 1789 年发生了~大革命。yīqībājiǔ nián fāshēng le ~ dàgémìng. French Revolution took place in 1789. *La Révolution française se passa en 1789.* ~的奶酪很有名。~ de nǎilào hěn yǒumíng. France is famous for the cheeses. *La France est réputée pour ses fromages.*

法文 fǎwén * (= 法语 fǎyǔ *)

法语（法語）fǎyǔ * S2 **French (language), *français m, langue française*** 你不懂~吗？nǐ bùdǒng ~ ma? Don't you understand (plain) French? *Tu ne comprends pas le français?* 我觉得你~说得很好。wǒ juédé nǐ ~ shuō dé hěn hǎo. I think you speak very good French. *Je pense que tu parles très bien français.*

翻译（翻譯）fānyì H4, S2 **translate, interpret, translator, *interpreter, traduire, traducteur(trice), interprète nmf*** 李小姐是~。lǐ xiǎojiě shì ~. Miss Li is an interpreter. *Mlle Li est interprète.* 这是从俄语~(过来)的。zhèshì cóng éyǔ ~(guòlái) de. It is a translation from the Russian. *C'est traduit du russe.* 你能把这个~

发（發）fā D, H4, S1 **send, deliver, *envoyer, partir, délivrer*** 我昨天给他~了一个电子邮件。wǒ zuótiān gěi tā ~le yígè diànzǐ yóujiàn. I sent him an e-mail / email yesterday. *Je lui ai envoyé un courriel / un courrier électronique / un mél hier.*

信今天能~走吗? 什么时候可以到? xìn jīntiān néng ~ zǒu ma? shénme shíhou kěyǐ dào? Will the letter be sent today? When will it arrive? *La lettre partira-t-elle aujourd'hui? Quand arrivera-t-elle?* 我们已经~货了。wǒmen yǐjīng ~ huò le. We have already delivered goods. *Nous avons déjà livré / délivré des marchandises.*

发生（發生）fāshēng N, H4, S1 **happen, *arriver, se passer*** ~了意外。~ le yìwài. Something unexpected happened. *Un événement imprévu s'est passé.*

~的事儿没什么不平常的。~ de shìr méi shénme bù píngcháng de. Nothing out of the ordinary happened. *Il n'est rien arrivé d'inhabituel.* 警察已在~事故的地点。yǐngchá yǐ zài ~ shìgù de dìdiǎn. The police are at the scene of the accident. *La police est sur les lieux de l'accident.* 在进行化学实验时~了(一起)爆炸事故。zài jìnxíng huàxué shíyàn shí ~ le (yìqǐ) bàozhà shìgù. There was an explosion during the chemistry experiment. *Il y a eu une explosion pendant l'expérience de chimie.*

发音（發音）fā yīn * **pronounce, *prononcer*** 他法语~(不)很好。tā fǎyǔ ~ (bù) hěn hǎo. He has (not) a very good accent in French. *Il a / (Il n'a pas) un très bon accent en français.* 这个怎么~? zhègè zěnme ~? How's it

成平易的英语吗? nǐ néng bǎ zhège ~ chéng píngyì de yīngyǔ ma? Can you translate that into plain English, please? *Peux-tu traduire en anglais de tous les jours?*

饭馆（飯館）fànguǎn H1, S2

restaurant, *restaurant m* 在家吃饭还是下~去? zài jiā chīfàn háishì xià ~ qù? Shall we eat at home or shall we eat out? *On mange à la maison ou on va au restaurant?*

他们常 吃 / 去 / 下 ~。tāmen cháng chī / qù / xià ~. They often eat out. *Ils vont souvent au restaurant.* 他开~。tā kāi ~. He is a restaurant owner. *C'est un restaurateur.*

方 fāng (形) (1) D, H5, S2 **square,** *carré* 我

们刚买了张~桌子。wǒmen gāng mǎile yì zhāng ~zhuōzi. We just bought a square table. *Nous venons d'acheter une table carrée.* 我找一条~头巾。wǒ zhǎo yìtiáo ~tóujīn. I'm looking for a square scarf. *Je cherche un foulard carré.*

方 fāng (名) (2) G, H5, S2 **direction, side,**

direction f, côté m 他们去法国南~了。tāmen qù fǎguó nán ~ le. They've gone to the South of France. *Ils sont allés au Midi (de la France).*

您还没听我~的解释。nín hái méi tīng wǒ ~ de jiěshì. You haven't heard our side of the story yet. *Vous n'avez pas encore entendu notre version de l'histoire.*

方面 fāngmiàn N, H4, S1 **aspect, field,**

aspect m, domaine m 她是这个~的专家。tā shì zhège ~ de zhuānjiā. She's an expert in this field. *Elle est experte en la matière.*

从预防这个~来看，还有很多事要作。cóng yùfáng zhège ~ lái kàn, háiyǒu hěnduō shì yào zuò. As far as prevention action concerned, there's still a lot to do. *Dans le domaine de la prévention, il y a encore beaucoup à faire.*

房间（房間）fángjiān H2, S1 **room,**

chambre f, pièce f 他们进了那间~。tāmen jìnle nà jiān ~. They entered that room. *Ils sont entrés dans cette salle.*

你们能把行李放到我的房间里去吗? nǐmen néng bǎ xíngli fàngdào wǒde ~ lǐ qù ma? Could you take up my luggage to my room? *Pourrez-vous monter mes bagages à ma chambre?*

非常 fēicháng H2, S1 **extraordinary,**

awfully, perfectly, unusually, highly, *vraiment, parfaitement, extraordinaire, exceptionnel* 我~抱歉。wǒ ~ bàoqiàn. I'm

awfully sorry. *Je suis vraiment / sincèrement désolé.* 您~正确。nín ~ zhèngquè. You are perfectly right. *Vous avez parfaitement raison.*

这是一次~会议。zhèshì yícì ~ huìyì. It is an extraordinary session. *C'est une session extraordinaire.* 她~聪明。tā ~ cōngming. She's unusually intelligent. *Elle est d'une intelligence exceptionnelle.* 他~赞扬她的工作。tā ~ zànyáng tāde gōngzuò. He praised her work highly. *Il a chanté (haut) les louanges de son travail.* 晚会的气氛~好。wǎnhuì de qìfen ~ hǎo. There was a very good atmosphere at the party. *Il y avait une très bonne ambiance à la soirée.*

飞机（飛機）fēijī H1, S1 **plane,**

avion m ~起飞了。~ qǐfēi le. The plane has taken off. *L'avion a décollé.* 您坐~(去)还是坐火车去? nín zuò ~ (qù) háishì zuò huǒchē qù? Are you flying or going by train? *Irez-vous en avion ou en train?*

我坐~去纽约。wǒ zuò ~ qù niǔyuē. I'll take the plane to New York. *Je prendrai l'avion pour aller à New York.* 我不喜欢坐~。wǒ bù xǐhuan zuò ~. I hate flying. *Je déteste (prendre) l'avion.*

分 fēn (名、量) (1) D, H3, S1 **minute,**

centime, mark, grade, fraction, *minute f,* *centime m, note f, fraction f* 九点五~了。jiǔ diǎn wǔ ~ le. It's five past nine. *Il est neuf heures cinq.* 我得了个好~(儿)! wǒ déle gè hǎo ~(r). I've got a good mark / grade! *J'ai eu une bonne note!*

能借我两毛三~钱吗? néng jiè wǒ liǎng máo sān ~ qián ma? Can you lend me twenty three centimes? *Tu peux me prêter vingt-trois centimes?* 她看了三~之一了。tā kànle sān ~ zhī yī le. She's a third of way through (reading it). *Elle en a lu un tiers.*

分钟（分鐘）fēnzhōng H1, S1

minute, *minute f* 三点过十分(钟)了。sān diǎn guò zhí fēn(zhōng) le. It is ten minutes past three / after three. *Il est trois heures dix.*

他走了一、两~了。tā zǒu le yì、liǎng ~ le. He's been gone for a minute or two now. *Il est parti depuis une bonne minute.* 一~也不要浪费了。yì ~ yě bú yào làngfèi le. There's not a minute to lose. *Il n'y a pas une minute à perdre.*

服务（服務）fúwù N, S1 **service,**

serve, *service m, servir* "包括~费", bāokuò ~ fèi; "Service included", *"Service compris";*

对我们的~很周到, 谢谢! duì wǒmen de ~ hěn zhōudào, xièxie! We have a very good help, thanks a lot! *Nous sommes très bien servis, merci beaucoup!* 我们要为人民~。wǒmen yào wèi rénmín ~. We must serve the people. *Nous devons servir le peuple.*

服务员 (服務員) fúwùyuán H2 **waiter, waitress, attendant,** *serveur(se),* *monsieur, madame, mademoiselle* 喂, ~! wèi, ~! Waiter! *S'il vous plaît, monsieur / madame!*

酒巴的~不太和气。jiǔbā de ~ bútài héqi. The pub barman wasn't very nice. *Le serveur du pub n'était pas très amiable.*

改革 gǎigé N, H5, S2 **reform,** *réformer,* *réforme f* 我们将选择~的道路。wǒmen jiāng xuǎnzé ~ de dàolù. We shall opt for a policy of reform. *Nous choisirons la voie des réformes.*

他们引进了 / 进行了~。tāmen yǐnjìn le ~ / jìnxíng le ~. They've introduced / made reforms. *Ils ont introduit / fait des réformes.*

感到 gǎndào G, S1 **feel,** *sentir* 我~好多了。wǒ ~ hǎo duō le. I'm feeling a lot better. *Je me sens beaucoup mieux.*

她~增加了勇气。tā ~ zēngjiā le yǒngqì. She felt full of courage. *Elle se sentait du courage.* 你不~惭愧吗？nǐ bù ~ cánkuì ma? Aren't you ashamed of yourself? *N'as-tu pas honte?*

干部 (幹部) gànbù N **cadre,** *cadre m* 她是 (个 / 位 / 名) ~ / 女~。tā shì (gè / wèi / míng) ~ / nǚ ~. She's an executive / a female executive. *Elle est cadre / une femme cadre.*

他是 (个 / 位 / 名) 高级~ / 中级~。tā shì (gè / wèi / míng) gāojí ~ / zhōngjí ~. He's a senior executive / a middle manager. *C'est un cadre supérieur / un cadre moyen.*

高兴 (高興) gāoxìng H1, S1 **please, happy, like,** *content, aimer* 见到您很~! jiàndào nín hěn ~! I'm very pleased to see you. *Je suis très content de vous voir.*

我一点儿也不~。wǒ yìdiǎr yě bù ~. I'm not at all happy. *Je ne suis pas content du tout.* 他~也好不~也好，自己看着办! tā ~ yě hǎo, bù gāoxìng yě hǎo, zìjǐ kànzhe bàn! He can like it or lump it! *S'il n'aime pas, qu'il s'arrange.*

告诉 (告訴) gàosu H2, S1 **tell, let know,** *faire savoir, dire, annoncer* ~你一个消息。~ nǐ yígè xiāoxi. I've some news for you. *J'ai une nouvelle à t'annoncer.*

他来了就~我一声。tā láile jiù ~ wǒ yìshēng. Let me know when he arrives. *Fais-moi savoir lorsqu'il sera là.* ~我你愁什么呢。~ wǒ nǐ chóu shénme ne. Tell me what's worrying you. *Dis-moi ce qui te préoccupe.*

哥哥 | 哥 gēge | gē H2, S1 **elder brother,** *grand frère, frère aîné* 她有两个~、一个弟弟。tā yǒu liǎnggè ~、yígè dìdi. She has two elder brothers and a younger one. *Elle a deux frères aînés et un (frère) cadet.*

这是我~的银行卡。zhèshì wǒ ~ de yínhángkǎ. It's the credit card of my older brother. *C'est la carte bancaire de mon grand frère.*

个 (個) gè D, H1, S1 **[classifier], verb+个+complement,** *[classificateur m], verbe+个+complément* 房间里有两~人。fángjiān lǐ yǒu liǎng ~ rén. There're two people in the room. *Il y a deux personnes dans la pièce.* 有三~苹果。yǒu sǎn ~ píngguǒ. There're three apples. *Il y a trois pommes.*

我睡了~好觉。wǒ shuìle ~ hǎo jiào. I had a good sleep. *J'ai fait un bon somme.* 他活动~没完没了的。tā huódòng ~ méiwán wéiliǎo de. He moves around, never staying in one place. *Il se déplace sans arrêt.*

给 (給) gěi H2, S1 **give, to,** *donner, à* 我把那本书~他了。wǒ bǎ nàběn shū ~ tā le. I gave him the book. *Je lui ai donné le livre.* 他~我写了封信。tā ~ wǒ xiě le fēng xìn. He wrote a letter to me. *Il m'a écrit une lettre.*

这能~你带来什么好处? zhè néng ~ gěi nǐ dàilái shénme hǎochù? What good can that do you? *Qu'est-ce que ça peut t'apporter?*

更 gèng T, H5, S1 **more,** *plus, avantage*

您阔，可他~阔。nǐ kuò, kě tā ~ kuò. You're rich, but he's richer. *Vous êtes riche, mais il l'est davantage.*

那个建筑里地方~多。nà gè jiànzhù lǐ dìngfang ~ duō. There's much more room in the other building. *Il y a beaucoup plus de place dans l'autre bâtiment.*你应该~乐观些! nǐ yīnggāi ~ lèguān xiē. You could be a bit more optimistic! *Tu pourrais être un peu plus optimiste!*

公共汽车（公共汽車）

gōnggòng qìchē H2, S1 **bus,** *bus m, autobus m* 你坐~去吗? nǐ zuò ~ qù ma? Are you bus(s)ing it? *Tu y vas en autobus?*

我们走回家或坐~回家都可以。wǒmen zǒu huíjiā huò zuò ~ huíjiā dōu kěyǐ. We can walk or bus it home. *Nous pouvons rentrer à pied ou en autobus.* 一辆~刚刚过去。yíliàng ~ gānggāng kāi guòqu. A bus has just passed by. *Un bus vient de passer.*

公斤 gōngjīn H2, A1 **kilogram (kg.), kilo,** *kilogramme (kg.) m, kilo m* 一~有一千克。yì ~ yǒu yìqiān kè. There are 1000 grams in a kilogram. *Il y a 1000 grammes pour un kilogramme.*

这个包裹 20 ~重。zhègè bāoguǒ yǒu èrshí ~ zhòng. The package weighs 20 kilos. *Le paquet pèse 20 kilos.*

公司 gōngsī N, H2, S1 **company, firm, corporation,** *société f, compagnie f, firme f* 这位是~经理先生。zhè wèi shì ~ jīnglǐ xiānsheng. Here is Mr the Director of the company. *Voici M. le Directeur de la société.*

这家~是前年成立的。zhè jiā ~ shì qiánnián chénglì de. The company was set up the year before last. *La société a été établie il y a deux ans.* 这是国际上第一流的~。zhè shì guójì shàng dìyī liú de ~. It's a world prominent firm. *C'est une firme de premier plan mondial.*

工厂（工廠）gōngchǎng T, H5, S1 **factory, plant, works,** *usine f, fabrique f* 她男朋友在~工作。tā nán-péngyou zài ~ gōngzuò. Her boy-friend works in a factory. *Son petit ami travaille en usine.*

这是一家制鞋(工)厂 / 军~。zhè shì yìjiā zhì xié (gōng)chǎng / jūn ~. It's a factory that manufactures shoes / It's an arms factory. *C'est une usine qui fabrique des chaussures / C'est une fabrique d'armes.*

工夫 gōngfu H5, S1 **spare time, exercise, martial arts,** *temps libre, exercice m, arts martiaux* 他没什么闲~。He hasn't got much spare time. *Il n'a pas beaucoup de temps libre.* 我去练练~。I'll take some exercise. *Je vais prendre de l'exercice.* 你喜欢看~片(儿)吗? Do you like to see martial arts movies? *Aimes-tu voir des films des arts martiaux?*

工作 gōngzuò G, N, H4, S1 **work, job,** *travailler, travail m, emploi m* 他有~。tā yǒu ~. He has a job. *Il a un travail / un emploi.* 您在哪个单位~? nín zài nǎge dānwèi ~? Where do you work? *Où travaillez-vous?*

她~得太多了。tā ~ dé tài duō le. She works too much. *Elle travaille trop.*

共 gòng T, S2 **share, altogether,** *se partager, en tout* 我(一)~该他两百英镑。wǒ (yī)~ gāi tā liǎngbǎi yīngbàng. I owe him £200 altogether. *Je lui dois 200 livres en tout.*

他们应该~负事故的责任。tāmen yīnggāi ~ fù shìgù de zérèn. They must share the blame for the accident. *Ils doivent se partager la responsabilité de l'accident.*

狗 gǒu T, H1, S2 **dog,** *chien(ne)* 小王的~很友好。Xiao Wang's dog is very friendly. *Le chien de Xiao Wang est très gentil.* «小心有~守卫»; "xiǎoxīn yǒu ~ shǒuwèi"; "Beware of the dog"; «Attention, chien méchant»;

别把我当~看待! bié bǎ wǒ dàng ~ kàndài! Don't treat me like a dog! *Ne me traite pas comme un chien!* 闭上(你的~)嘴! bìshàng (nǐde ~) zuǐ! Shut your (ugly) mug! *Ferme ta (grande / sale) gueule!*

古 gǔ T, S1 **ancient,** *antique, ancien(ne)* 这是本讲~希腊的书。zhè shì běn jiǎng ~ xīlà de shū. It's a book about the ancient Greece. *C'est un livre sur la Grèce antique.*

我有一本~诗集。wǒ yǒu yìběn ~ shījí. I have a collection of ancient poems. *J'ai un recueil de poèmes anciens.* ~时候有个学者叫老子。~ shíhou yǒu gè xuézhě jiào lǎozǐ. In ancient times, there was a scholar called Lao Zi. *Dans les temps anciens, il y avait un savant qui s'appelait Lao Zi.*

怪 guài (形) (1) T, S2 **strange, queer, bizarre, drôle** 她的一些主意很~。tāde yìxiē

zhǔyi hěn ~. She has some strange ideas. *Elle a des idées bizarres.*

这真是个~人! zhè zhēn shì gè ~rén! He's a queer fish! *C'est un drôle d'individu!*

怪 guài (副) (2) T, S2 **quite, rather,** *assez*

今天~冷的。jīntiān ~ lěng de. It's quite cold today. *Il fait assez froid aujourd'hui.*

我当时~累的。wǒ dāngshí ~ lèi de. I was rather tired. *J'étais assez fatigué.*

怪 guài (动) (3) T, S2 **blame,** *blâmer* 这不能~他。zhè bù néng ~ tā. He can't be blamed for it. *On ne peut pas l'en blâmer.*

这个事故~谁呢? zhè gè shìgù ~ shéi ne? Who are we to blame for this accident? *A qui attribuer cet accident?*

关系 (關係) guānxì H3, S1 **relation,** *lien m, rapport m, relation f* 他和你 有 / 是 什么亲属~? tā hé nǐ yǒu / shì shénme qīnshǔ ~? What relation is he to you? *Quel est son lien de parenté avec toi?* 他们的~有些紧张。tāmen de ~ yǒuxiē jǐnzhāng. Their relations are somewhat strained. *Ils ont des rapports assez tendus.*

两国 1962 年建立了外交~。liǎngguó yī-jiǔ-liù-èr nián jiànlì le wàijiāo ~. The two countries established diplomatic relations in 1962. *Les deux pays ont établi les relations diplomatiques en 1962.* 这事儿只~(到)你和我，别把她也往里拉。zhè shìr zhǐ ~ (dào) nǐ hé wǒ, bié bǎ tā yě wǎnglǐ lā. Don't bring her into this, it's between you and me. *Ne la mêle pas à cette affaire, il s'agit de toi et de moi.*

官 guān T, H5, S2 **boss, bureaucratic,** *chef m, bureaucrate nmf* 这儿谁是当~儿的? zhèr shéi shì dāng ~r de? Who's the boss here? *Qui est le chef ici?*

他总打~腔。tā zǒng dǎ ~qiāng. He is always speaking in a bureaucratic tone. *Il parle toujours d'un ton de bureaucrate.*

观 (觀) guān T **look at, watch, observe,** *regarder, voir, observer* 这个数目很可~。zhè gè shùmù hěn kě~. This is a considerable figure. *C'est un chiffre considérable.*

他对前途很 乐~ / 悲~。tā duì qiántú hěn lè~ / bēi~. He is optimistic / pessimist about the future. *Il a / Il n'a pas confiance dans l'avenir.*

管理 guǎnlǐ N, H4, S1 **manage,** *être gérant(e), gérer* 她~一个鞋店。tā ~ yígè

xiédiàn. She manages a shoe shop. *Elle est gérante d'une boutique de chaussures.*

我~公司的日常业务。wǒ ~ gōngsī de rìcháng yèwù. I manage company's everyday affairs. *Je gère les affaires quotidiennes de la société.*

广 (廣) guǎng T, S2 **wide, extensive, vast, large, extensive,** *vaste* 他兴趣很~。tā xìngqù hěn ~. He has very wide interests. *Il a des centres d'intérêts très larges.*

老钱知识很~。lǎo qián zhī hěn ~. Lao Qian has extensive knowledge. *Lao Qian a de vastes connaissances.* 西伯利亚地~人稀。xībólìyà dì ~ rén xī. Siberia is a vast and thinly populated area. *La Sibérie est une vaste région peu peuplée.*

归 (歸) guī T, S2 **return, converge, put in sb's charge,** *retour m, vers, être chargé de* 我们把~期定下来了。wǒmen bǎ ~qī dìng xiàlái le. We've set the date of return. *Nous avons fixé la date du retour.*

那个人无家可~。nàgè rén wú jiā kě ~. That man is homeless. *Cet homme est un sans-abri.* 公众关系~她管。gōngzhòng guānxì ~ tā guǎn. She's in charge of public relations. *Elle s'occupe des relations publiques.*

鬼 guǐ T, S2 **ghost, lazybones, coward, bad conscience, wretched,** *fantôme m, diable m, fainéant(e), mauvaise conscience* 今天是~天气。jīntiān shì ~ tiānqì. It's wretched / dreadful weathe today. *C'est un diable de temps / un temps du diable aujourd'hui.*

你(的样子)好象刚看见了~! nǐ (de yàngzi) hǎoxiàng gāng kànjiàn le ~. You look as if you've just seen a ghost! *On dirait que tu viens de voir un fantôme.* 嘿，懒~，帮我收拾盘子! hèi, lǎn~, bāng wǒ shōushi pánzi! Hey lazybones, help me with the dishes! *Hé, fainéant, aide-moi à ramasser les assiettes!* 别当胆小~。bié dāng dǎnxiǎo~. Don't be such a coward. *Ne sois pas aussi lâche.* 他心里有~。tā xīnlǐ yǒu ~. He has a bad conscience. *Il a mauvaise conscience.*

贵 (貴) guì H2, S1 **expensive, too dear, venerable,** *cher, hors de prix, vénérable* 您 / 你 ~姓? nín / nǐ ~ xìng? What is your (venerable) family name? *Quel est votre / ton (vénérable) nom de famille?*

太~了! tài ~ le! It's too dear / very expensive! *C'est trop cher!* 这条连衣裙~得可怕! zhètiáo liányīqún ~ dé kěpài! This dress is outrageously expensive! *Cette robe est hors de prix!*

国 (國) guó D, S1 **country, power,** *pays m, puissance f* 这是一个新工业发展~。zhè shì yígè xīn gōngyè fāzhǎn ~. It's a newly industrialized country. *C'est un nouveau pays industrialisé.* 此~渴望和平吗? cǐ ~ kěwàng hépíng ma? Does that country want peace? *Ce pays désire-t-il la paix?*

大~十九世纪瓜分了世界 / 中国。dà~ shíjiǔ shìjì guāfēn le shìjiè / zhōngguó. The powers divided the world / China in the 19th Century. *Les puissances divisèrent le monde / la Chine au 19ème siècle.* 我学(画)~画儿。wǒ xué (huà) ~huàr. I'm learning traditional Chinese painting. *J'apprends la peinture traditionnelle chinoise.*

国际 (國際) guójì N, H4, S1 **international,** *international* 我们队参加~锦标赛。wǒmen duì cānjiā ~ jǐnbiāosài. Our team is taking part in the international championship. *Notre équipe participe au championnat international.*

~形势更好了 / 更遭了。~ xíngshì gèng hǎole / gèng zāole. Internationally, the situation is even better / worse. *Sur le plan international, la situation est encore meilleure / pire.*

国家 (國家) guójiā N, H3, S1 **country, state, nation,** *pays m, Etat, m, nation f* ~支持我。~ zhīchí wǒ. I have the support of the country. *Tout le pays me soutient.*

~工商业很发达。~ gōngshāng yè hěn fādá. Industry and commerce are flourishing in the country. *L'industrie et le commerce sont prospères dans le pays.*

果 guǒ T **fruit, result,** *fruit m, conséquence f* 我每天至少吃两个水~。wǒ měitiān zhìshǎo chī liǎnggè shuǐ~. I eat at least two pieces of fruit a day. *Je mange au moins deux fruits par jour.*

他们的行为造成了恶~。tāmen de xíngwéi zàochéng le è~. They did it with disastrous results. *Ils l'ont fait avec des conséquences désastreuses.*

过 (過) guò (动) D, G2, S1 **past, cross, go across, go off,** *passer, traverser, se passer, durer* 我看见他(走)~去了。wǒ kànjiàn tā (zǒu) ~qù le. I saw him go past. *Je l'ai vu passer.* 你是怎么~河的? nǐ shì zěnme ~ hé de? How did you cross / go across the river? *Comment as-tu traversé la rivière?*

节日~得很好。jiérì ~ dé hěn hǎo. The holiday went off well. *La fête s'est bien passée.* 我日子~得很苦。wǒ rìzi ~ dé hěn kǔ. Life is hard for me. *La vie est dure pour moi.*

过 (過) guò (助) D, G2, S1 **[verb+过: meaning an action or state of the past],** *[verbe+过: exprimer une action ou un état du passé]* 他上~大学。tā shàng ~ dàxué. He's been to university. *Il a fait des études supérieures.* 她有~两辆车。tā yǒu ~ liǎng liàng chē. She had two cars in the past. *Elle avait deux voitures dans le passé.*

我在学校学~西班牙文。wǒ zài xuéxiào xué~ xībānyá wén. I learnt Spanish at school. *J'ai appris l'espagnol au collège.* 我们去~三次长城。wǒmen qù~ sāncì chángchéng. We went to the Great Wall three times. *Nous sommes allés à la Grande Muraille trois fois.* 她多年来(从)没病~。tā duōnián lái (cóng)méi bìng~. She hasn't been ill for years. *Elle n'a pas été malade depuis des années.*

过去 (過去) guòqù G, H3, S1 **past, bygone,** *passé m, ne plus exister* 这是~的事儿了。zhèshì ~ de shìr le. It is a thing of the past. *Ça n'existe plus.*

~的事就让他们过去吧。~ de shì jiù ràng tā guòqù ba. Let bygones be bygones / Let's forget the past. *Oublions le passé.*

过去 (過去) guòqu G, H3, S1 **go over, pass by,** *passer, aller, traverser* 我看见他(走)~了。wǒ kànjiàn tā zǒu ~ le. I saw him go past. *Je l'ai vu passer.*

一架飞机飞~了。yíjià fēijī fēi ~ le. A plane was flying in the sky. *Un avion passait dans le ciel.* 把这一页翻~ / 翻过(去)这一页。bǎ zhè yí yè fān ~ / fān guò(qu) zhè yí yè. Turn over this page. *Tournez cette page.*

还（還） hái D, H2, S1 **still, yet, also,** *toujours, encore, aussi* ~在下雨吗? ~ zài xiàyǔ ma? It it still raining? *Est-ce qu'il pleut toujours?*

她~没有到。tā ~ méiyǒu dào. She isn't here yet. *Elle n'est pas encore là.* 他~说意大利语。tā ~ shuō yìdàlì yǔ. He also speaks Italian. *Il parle aussi l'italien.*

还是（還是） háishi G, H3, S1 **nevertheless, or, after all,** *quand-même, ou, c'est tout* 我~去。wǒ ~ qù. I shall go nevertheless. *J'irai quand-même.*

您说普通话~(说)广东话? nín shuō pǔtōnghuà ~ (shuō) guǎngdōng huà? Do you speak Mandarin Chinese or Cantonese? *Vous parlez le chinois mandarin ou le cantonais?* 她毕竟~很年轻。tā bìjìng ~ hěn niánqīng. She's only young, after all. *Elle est jeune, c'est tout.*

还有（還有） háiyǒu G, S1 **still have,** *avoir d'autres, encore avoir* 你们~别的(什么)吗? nǐmen ~ biéde (shénme) ma? Have you got any different ones? *En avez-vous d'autres?*

我们现在~时间。wǒmen xiànzài ~ shíjiān. We still have time now. *Nous avons encore le temps à présent.*

孩子 háizi G, H2, S1 **child,** *enfant nmf* 他们有三个~。tāmen yǒu sāngè ~. They have three children. *Ils ont trois enfants.* 这是个漂亮的女~。zhè shì gè piàoliang de nǔ~. She is a beautiful child. *C'est une belle enfant.*

别跟~一样! bié gēn ~ yíyàng! Don't be such a child! *Ne fais pas l'enfant!* 不要把我当~看待! bú yào bǎ wǒ dāng ~ kàndài! Stop treating me like a child! *Arrête de me traiter comme un enfant!*

汉语（漢語） hànyǔ H1, S1 **Chinese (language),** *chinois m, langue chinoise* 他说~吗? tā shuō ~ ma? Does he speak Chinese? *Est-ce qu'il parle (le) chinois?* 他~一句话也不会说。tā ~ yíjù huà yě bú huì shuō. He doesn't speak a word of Chinese. *Il ne parle pas un mot de chinois.*

"这里讲~", "zhèlǐ jiǎng ~", "Chinese spoken", *"Ici on parle chinois"*; 我学了一些基础~。wǒ xuéle yìxiē jīchǔ ~. I have learned some basic Chinese. *J'ai appris les bases du chinois.*

汉字（漢字） hànzì S1 **Chinese character, ideogram,** *caractère chinois, idéogramme m* 这个~怎么写? zhè(i)gè ~ zěnme xiě? How to write this character? *Comment écrire ce caractère?* 我认识不少~了。wǒ rènshi bùshǎo ~ le. I already know quite a lot of characters / ideograms. *Je connais déjà pas mal de caractères / d'idéogrammes.*

好 hǎo (形) (1) D, H1, S1 **good, nice, fine, easy,** *bon, sympa, beau, excellent, facile* 她人很~。tā rén hěn ~. She's very nice. *Elle est très sympa.* 我们(不过)是~朋友。wǒmen (búguò) shì ~ péngyou. We're (just) good friends. *Nous sommes bons amis(, c'est tout).*

我们度假时天气很~。wǒmen dùjià shí tiānqì hěn ~. We had a good weather during the holiday. *Il faisait beau pendant nos vacances.* 这真是~酒。zhè zhēn shì ~jiǔ. This is a very fine wine. *C'est un vin vraiment excellent.* ~说不~做。~ shuō bù hǎo zuò. Easier said than done. *C'est plus facile à dire qu'à faire.*

好 hǎo (副) (2) D, H1, S1 **several, so, how,** *plusieurs, si, comme* 他们~几个(人)。tāmen ~ jǐ gè (rén). There are several of them. *Ils sont plusieurs.*

风景~漂亮。fēngjǐng ~ piàoliang. It was so beautiful a sight. *C'était un si beau spectacle / une si belle vue.* 她~伤心呀! tā ~ shāngxīn ya! How sad she is! *Comme elle est triste!*

好吃 hǎochī H2, S1 **delicious, tasty,** *délicieux, savoureux* 她做的这个菜很~。tā zuò de cài hěn ~. This dish of hers is delicious / tasty. *Ce plat qu'elle a fait est délicieux / savoureux.*

号（號）hào H2, S1 **date, number, mark, trumpet,** *date f, nombre m, point m, trompette f* 今天几~? --- 十六~。jīntiān jǐ ~? -- shíliù ~. What is the date today? – It's the 16th. *Quelle est la date aujourd'hui? – Il est le 16.*

这儿应该用问~。zhèr yīnggāi yòng wèn~. You should use a question mark here. *Tu devrais utiliser un point d'interrogation ici.* 我们住八十~。wǒmen zhù bāshí ~. We live at number 80. *Nous habitons au (numéro) 80.* 他吹小~。tā chuī xiǎo~. He's a trumpet player. *Il joue de la trompette.*

合 hé D, S1 **close, suit,** *fermer, convenir à* 他一夜没~眼。tā yíyè méi ~ yǎn. He didn't close his eyes all night long. *Il n'a pas fermé l'œil de la nuit.*

你这条裤子很~身。nǐ zhè tiáo kùzi hěn ~. Those trousers really suit you. *Ce pantalon te va vraiment bien.*

合作 hézuò N, H5, S1 **collaborate, cooperate, collaboration,** *collaborer, coopérer, collaboration f* 这一计划她同我们~过。zhè yí jìhuà tā tóng wǒmen ~ guo. She collaborated with us on the project. *Elle a collaboré avec nous au projet.*

她同妹妹~写了那本书。tā tóng mèimei ~ xiě le nàběn shū. She wrote the book in collaboration with her younger sister. *Elle a écrit le livre en collaboration avec sa jeune sœur.* 两国政府为反毒正采取~。liǎngguó zhèngfǔ wèi fǎn dú zhèng cǎiqǔ ~. The two government are cooperating in the drug war. *Les deux gouvernements coopèrent dans la lutte contre la drogue.*

黑 hēi H2, S1 **dark, black,** *noir* 天~了。tiān ~ le. It's dark. *Il fait noir.* 她总穿~衣服。tā zǒng chuān ~ yīfu. She always wears black. *Elle porte toujours du noir.*

这个人手~。zhè(i) gè rén shǒu ~. His hands were black. *Ils avaient les mains toutes noires.*

很 hěn H1, S1 **very, quite, awfully,** *très, beaucoup, tout à fait, infiniment* 他~饿。tā ~ è. He is very hungry. *Il a très faim.* 人不~多。rén bù ~ duō. There weren't very many people. *Il n'y avait pas beaucoup de gens.*

她~对。tā ~ duì. She's quite right. *Elle a tout à fait raison.* 我~感谢。wǒ ~ gǎnxiè. Thanks awfully. *Merci infiniment.*

红（紅）hóng H2, S1 **red, roux, blush, lights,** *rougir, rouge, feux m* 颜色是~的。yánsè shì ~de. The paint is red. *La peinture est rouge.* 他(是)~头发。tā (shì) ~ tóufa. He has red hair. *Il a les cheveux roux.*

她满脸通~。tā mǎnliǎn tōng~. She blushed to the roots of her hair. *Elle a rougi jusqu'aux oreilles.* 他闯~灯出了车祸。tā chuǎng ~dēng chūle chēhuò. He jumped the lights and had an accident. *Il a brûlé les feux et a causé un accident.*

后（後）hòu D, S1 **behind, after,** *derrière, après* 房~有一个花园 / 房子有一个~花园。fáng~ yǒu yígè huāyuán / fángzi yǒu yígè ~ huāyuán. There is a garden behind the house. *Il y a un jardin derrière la maison.*

(进门:) 您先进，我~进。(jìnmén:) nín xiān jìn, wǒ ~ jìn. After you (going through door). *Après vous (par la porte).*

后面（後面）hòumiàn H2, S1 (= 后边 hòubian) **back, behind,** *au fond, derrière, plus tard* ~还有座位。~ hái yǒu zuòwèi. There are vacant seats at the back. *Il y a des places libres au fond.*

他在~藏着。tā zài ~ cángzhe. He hid behind it. *Il s'est caché derrière.* 这个问题我~还要谈到。zhè gè wèntí wǒ ~ hái yào tándào. I'll come back to this question later. *Je reviendrai à la question plus tard.*

护照（護照）hùzhào H3, S1 **passport,** *passeport m* 这里检查~。zhè lǐ jiǎnchá ~. Here is the passport control. *Ici est le contrôle de passeports.* 请拿出您的~来。qǐng náchū nínde ~ lái. Show your passport please. *Montrez votre passeport, s'il vous plait.*

华人（華人）huárén S1 **a person of Chinese origin,** *une personne d'origine chinoise* 他们是美籍~。tāmen shì měijí ~. They're Americans of Chinese by birth. *Ce sont des américains d'origine chinoise.* 在洛山矶、纽约、伦敦、巴黎等城市都有~街。zài luòshānjī、niǔyuē、lúndūn、bālí děng chéngshì dōu yǒu ~ jiē. There are Chinatown's streets in cities such as San Francisco, New York, London and Paris. *Il y a des rues de Chinatown dans des villes comme San Francisco, New York, Londres et Paris.*

华语（華語）huáyǔ S1 **Chinese (language),** *chinois m, langue chinoise* 我每天都听~广播。wǒ měitiān dōu tīng ~ guǎngbō. I listen to the radio in Chinese every day. *J'écoute la radio en chinois tous les jours.* 这个地区有~小学吗? zhè gè dìqū yǒu ~ xiǎoxué ma? Is there any primary school in Chinese in the region? *Y a-t-il une école primaire en chinois dans la région?*

话（話）huà S1 **word, talk, sentence, Mandarin,** *mot m, phrase f, mandarin m* 让

我把~说完。 ràng wǒ bǎ ~ shuōwán. Let me finish what I have to say. *Laisse-moi finir ma phrase.* 这句~缺动词。 zhè jù ~ quē dòngcí. The verb is missing from this sentence. *Il manque le verbe dans cette* phrase. 我说普通话。 wǒ shuō pǔtōng~. I speak Mandarin Chinese. *Je parle le chinois mandarin.*

欢迎（歡迎）huānyíng H2, S1

welcome, *être le bienvenu / la bienvenue / les bienvenu(e)s* ~! ~! You are welcome! *Vous êtes le bienvenu / la bienvenue / les bienvenu(e)s.* ~你们来我们的城市! ~ nǐmen lái wǒmen de chéngshì! Welcome to our city! *Soyez les bienvenus dans notre ville!*

这些戏老百姓很~。 zhèxiē xì lǎobǎixìng hěn ~. These operas are popular with the men in the street. *Ces pièces d'opéra sont très populaires parmi les gens de la rue.*

回 huí (动) (1) H1, S1 **return, come back, at home,** *rentrer, revenir, retourner, retour m* 她~来了。 tā ~ lái le. She has returned, *Elle est revenue / de retour.*

我们星期日~家(去)。 wǒmen xīngqīrì ~jiā (qù). We'll come back home on Sunday. *Nous rentrerons dimanche.* 我每天都~(家)去吃午饭。 wǒ měitiān dōu ~ (jiā) qù chī wǔfàn. I have lunch at home every day. *Je rentre chez moi pour déjeuner tous les jours.*

回 huí (量) (2) H1, S1 **[classifier], [classificateur m]** 这完全是另外一~事。 zhè wánquán shì lìngwài yì~ shì. That's (quite) another matter. *C'est (tout) autre chose.*

我跟她打了三~电话。 wǒ gēn tā dǎle sān~ diànhuà. I called her three times. *Je l'ai appelée trois fois.* 他头一~做嘛，已经不错了。 tā tóu yì~ zuò ma, yǐjīng búcuò le. It was the first time he'd done it, it's quite good. *C'était la première fois qu'il l'a fait, c'est déjà pas mal.*

回答 huídá H2, A1 **answer, reply,** *réponse f, répondre* 他~错了。 tā ~ cuò le. He gave the wrong answer. *Il a donné une mauvaise réponse.*

她基本上~对了。 tā jīběn shàng ~ le. She gave basically the right answer. *Elle a donné la bonne réponse dans son ensemble.* 我~得很坚决。 wǒ ~ dé hěn jiānjué. I replied in a firm voice. *J'ai répondu d'une voix ferme.*

回来（回來）huílái G, S1 **come back, come home, be back,** *revenir, rentrer, être de retour* 他跟我一块儿~了。 tā gēn wǒ yíhuàir ~ le. He came back with me. *Il est revenu avec moi.*

晚上他 ~ / 回家来 吃饭。 wǎnshang tā ~ / huí jiā lái chīfàn. He's coming home to dinner tonight. *Il rentrera dîner ce soir.* 我会及时赶~。 wǒ huì jíshí gǎn ~ de. I shall be back in time. *Je serai de retour à temps.*

会（會）huì (动) (1) D, H1, S1 **can,** *savoir* 你~开车吗? nǐ ~ kāichē ma? Can you drive? *Sais-tu conduire?*

很多人 不~读写 / 不~读也不~写。 hěnduō rén bú ~ dúxiě / bú ~ dú yě bú ~ xiě. Many people can't read or write. *Beaucoup de gens ne savent ni lire ni écrire.* 这个活儿一天不~做完。 zhèigè huór yìtiān bú~ zuòwán. The job can't be finished in one day. *Le travail ne peut pas se faire en un jour.*

会（會）huì (名) (2) D, H1, S1 **meeting,** *réunion f* 我们开个短~。 wǒmen kāi gè duǎn ~. We'll have a brief meeting. *Nous ferons une brève réunion.*

我昨天在~上发了言。 wǒ zuótiān zài ~ shàng fā le yán. I spoke at the meeting yesterday. *J'ai pris la parole dans la réunion hier.*

会议（會議）huìyì N, H3, S1 **meeting,** *réunion f* 他现在有个~。 tā xiànzài yǒu gè ~. He's in a meeting. *Il est en réunion.*

谁做~记录? shéi zuò ~ jìlù? Who will take the minutes of a meeting? *Qui fera le procès-verbal?*

活动（活動）huódòng N, H4, S1 **exercise, move,** *exercice m, faire travailler, se déplacer* 我每天都~~。 wo měitiān dōu ~~. I exercise every day. *Je fais de l'exercice tous les jours.*

他~个没完没了的。 tā ~ gè méiwán méiliǎo de. He moves around, never staying one place. *Il se déplace sans arrêt.* 这个问题你~一下脑筋来解决。 zhège wèntí nǐ ~ yíxià nǎojīn lái jiějué. If you were to exercise your brain on the problem. *Si tu faisais travailler tes méninges pour régler ce problème.*

火车 (火車) huǒchē S1 **train, *train m*** 我坐~去。wǒ zuò ~ qù. I'll go by train. *J'y irai en train.* 快点儿，还有十分钟~就要开了! kuàidiǎr, háiyǒu shí fēnzhōng ~ jiù yào kāi le! Hurry up, the train leaves in ten minutes! *Vite, le train part dans dix minutes!* 她不在~上。tā bú zài ~ shàng. She wasn't on the train. *Elle n'était pas dans le train.*

火车站 (火車站) huǒchēzhàn H1 **railway station, *gare f*** 你能把我送到~去吗? nǐ néng bǎ wǒ sòngdào ~ qù ma? Can you take me to the station? *Tu peux m'emmener à la gare?*

火车进站了! huǒchē jìn zhàn le! The train steams into the station / pulls in! *Le train entre en gare!*

J

机场 (機場) jīchǎng H2, S1 **airport, *aéroport m*** 我去戴高乐~。wǒ qù dàigāolè ~. I'll go to Roissy-Charles-de-Gaule airport. *Je vais à l'aéroport de Roissy-Charles-de-Gaulle.* 他坐出租去~了。tā zuò chūzū qù ~ le. He got a taxi to the airport. *Il a pris un taxi pour l'aéroport.*

我们(的飞机)快到~降落了。wǒmen (de fēijī) kuài dào ~ jiàngluò le. We are about to land at the airport. *Nous allons atterrir à l'aéroport.*

鸡蛋 (雞蛋) jīdàn H2, S1 **egg, *œuf m*** 每人一个煮~。měirén yígè zhǔ ~. Each and every one will have a hard-boiled egg. *Chacun d'entre nous a un œuf dur.*

不要把~都放在一个篮子里。búyào bā ~ dōu fàngzài yígè lánzi lǐ. Don't put all your eggs into one basket. *Il ne faut pas mettre tous ses œufs dans le même panier.*

几 (幾) jǐ H3, S1 **how many, a few, several, some, *combien, quelques*** ~点了? ~ diǎn le? What time is it? *Quelle heure est-il?* 他这~年住在北京。tā zhè ~ nián zhù zài běijīng. He's been living in Beijing for the past few years. *Cela fait quelques années qu'il habite à Beijing.* 候选人没~个符合条件。hòuxuǎnrén méi ~ fúhé tiáojiàn. There are very few suitable candidates for the post. *Très peu de candidats ont le profil requis.*

几个 jǐgè G **how many, a few, several, some, *combien, quelques*** 我想问您~问题。wǒ xiǎng wèn nín ~ wèntí. I'd like to ask you some questions. *Je voudrais vous poser quelques questions.*

里面有~人。lǐmiàn yǒu ~ rén. There are some people inside. *Il y a quelques personnes dedans.* 做这个工作需要好~星期。zuò zhègè gōngzuò xūyào hǎo ~ xīngqī. You'll need several weeks to do the job. *On aura besoin de plusieurs semaines pour ce travail.*

记者 (記者) jìzhě G4, S1 **journalist, reporter, correspondent, *journaliste nmf, correspondant(e), reporter m*** 他想当~。tā xiǎng dāng ~. He wants to be a journalist. *Il veut devenir journaliste.*

这个电话是一个~(打来的)，他要访问您。zhègè diànhuà shì yígè ~ (dǎlái de), tā yào fǎngwèn nín. There's a journalist on the phone – he wants to interview you. *Il y a un journaliste on ligne, il veut vous interviewer.*

计划 (計劃) jìhuà N, H4, S1 **plan, programme, *plan m, programme m, prévu*** 定好~了吗? dìnghǎo ~ le ma? Have you drawn up a plan? *As-tu dressé un plan?*

~有了些变化。~ yǒu le miànhuà. There's a change in the programme. *Il y a un changement de programme.* 一切都是按~进行的。yíqiè dōu shì àn ~ jìnxíng de. Everything went according to plan. *Tout s'est passé comme prévu.*

技术 (技術) jìshù N, H4, S1 **skill, technology, *compétence f, technologie f, technique f*** (搞这个)你不需要什么专门~。You don't need any special skill (for it). *Ça ne demande aucune compétence précise (pour cela).*

他们掌握着最先进的~。They have all the latest technology. *Ils disposent de la technique / la technologie la plus avancée.*

家 jiā (1) D, H1, S1 **family, home, [classifier]**, *famille f, maison f, [classificateur m]* 我回~。 wǒ huí ~. I'll go home. *Je vais rentrer à la maison.*

他们~还不想要孩子。 tāmen ~ hái bù xiǎng yào háizi. They don't want to start a family yet. *Ils ne veulent pas encore avoir un enfant.* 她怎么跟在自己~一样! tā zěnme gēn zài zìjǐ ~ yíyàng! How she's like family! *C'est vraiment comme si elle était de la famille!* ~丑不可外闻。 ~ chǒu bùkě wàiwén! We will keep it in the family. *Ça restera de la famille.* 这是一~广告公司。 zhèshì yī ~ guǎnggào gōngsī. It's an advertising agency. *C'est une agence de publicité.*

...家 ...jiā (2) D, H1, S1 **specialist in a certain field**, *spécialiste nmf dans un domaine* 他是诗人还是小说~? tā shì shīrén háishì xiǎoshuō~? Is he a poet or a novelist? *C'est un poète ou un romancier?*

她是个(女)政治~。 tā shì gè (nǚ) zhènzhì ~? She's a politician. *C'est une femme politique.* 爱因斯坦是一个大科学~。 àiyīnsītǎn shì yígè dà kēxué ~. Einstein was a famous scientist. *Einstein était un scientifique renommé.*

家里 (家裡) jiāli S1 **of the family, be home**, *de la famille, chez soi* 他是~的一个朋友。 tā shì ~ de yígè péngyou. He's a friend of the family. *C'est un ami de la famille.*

她怎么跟在自己~一样! tā zěnme gēn zài zìjǐ ~ yíyàng! How she's like family! *C'est vraiment comme si elle était de la famille!* 他把我带到了他自己~。 tā bǎ wǒ dàidào le tā zìjǐ ~. He took me along to his house. *Il m'a entraîné chez lui.*

加强 (加強) jiāqiáng N, S1 **join, reinforce, reinforcement**, *renfort m, renforcer* 他来~我们的研究队伍。 tā lái ~ wǒmen de yánjiū duìwǔ. He will join our team of researchers. *Il viendra renforcer notre équipe de chercheurs.* ~的力量到了。 ~ de lìliàng dào le. Reinforcements have arrived. *Des renforts sont arrivés.*

件 jiàn H2, S1 **[classifier], letter**, *[classificateur m], lettre f* 这~衬衫是我的。 zhè ~ chènshān shì wǒde. It's my shirt. *C'est ma chemise.*

我跟您打听一~事儿。 wǒ gēn nín dǎting yí ~ shì. I'd like to ask you about something. *Puis-je vous demander un renseignement?* 我们星期一收到了

您的来~。 wǒmen xīngqīyī shōudào le nínde lái~. We received your letter on Monday. *Nous avons reçu votre lettre lundi.*

建设 (建設) jiànshè N, H5, S1 **build up, construction, constructive**, *construire, construction f, constructif* 那个地区~了很多房子。 nà gè dìqū ~ le hěnduō fángzi. That area has become quite built-up. *Cette région s'est beaucoup construite.*

~行业情况良好。 ~ hángyè qíngkuàng liánghǎo. Things are going well in the construction business / building trade. *Cela va bien dans la construction.* 您有什么~性的意见吗? nín yǒu shénme ~ xìng de yìjiàn ma? Have you got anything constructive to say? *Est-ce que vous avez quelque chose de constructif à dire?*

交通 jiāotōng H4, S1 **traffic, road**, *routier, trafic m, transport m* 要注意~安全! yào zhùyì ~ ānquán! Be careful to traffic safety! *Attention à la sécurité routière!* 我要买一张市区~图。 wǒ yào mǎi yìzhāng shìqū ~ tú. I'd like to buy a road map of the urban zone. *Je voudrais acheter une carte routière de la zone urbaine.*

交易 jiāoyì H6, S1 **deal, trade**, *marché m, foire f* 我想跟您做笔~。 wǒ xiǎng gēn nín zuò bǐ ~. I'll make a deal with you. *Je vous propose un marché.* ~拍板了! ~ pāi bǎn le! It's a deal! *Marché conclu!* 我不同意这笔~! wǒ bù tóngyì zhèbǐ ~! No deal! *Je ne marche pas!* 你今年去商品~会了吗? nǐ jīnnián qù shāngpǐn ~huì le ma? Have you been to the trade fair this year? *Est-ce que tu es allé à la foire commerciale cette année?*

叫 jiào (动) (1) H1, S1 **shout, call, be called, put through**, *crier, s'appeler, appeler, passer à* 别~! bié ~! Don't shout! *Ne crie pas!* 你~什么名字? nǐ ~ shénme míngzi? What's your name? *Comment t'appelles-tu?*

外面有人~你。 wàimiàn yǒu rén ~ nǐ. Someone outside is calling you. *On t'appelle dehors.* 您跟他的的电话~通了。 nín gēn tā de diànhuà ~ tōng le. I've put you through to him. *Je vous le passe.*

叫 jiào (介) (2) H1, S1 **[introducing an actor in a passive sentence]**, *[introduire un acteur dans une phrase de voie passive]* 她们~人看见了。 tāmen ~ rén kànjiàng le. They were seen. *Elles ont été vues.*

我不用~人提醒。 wǒ búyòng ~ rén tíxǐng. I didn't need to be reminded of it. *Je n'avais pas besoin qu'on me le rappelât.* 噪音~人很难集中精力。

zàoyīn ~ rén hěn nán jízhōng jīnglì. The noise made it hard to concentrate. *Le bruit faisait qu'il était difficile de se concentrer.*

教室 jiàoshì H2, S1 **classroom,** *salle de classe* 他们进了 / 出了 ~。tāmen jìnle / chūle ~. They went into / out of the classroom. *Ils sont entrés dans / sortis de la salle de classe.*

~换了。~ huàn le. The classroom has been changed. *La salle de classe a été changée.*

接 jiē T, H3, S1 **catch, fetch,** *attraper, chercher* 小马，~球! xiǎo mǎ, ~ qiú! Xiao Ma, catch the ball! *Xiao Ma, attrape le ballon!*

我去车站~人。wǒ qù chēzhàn ~ rén. I'll go and fetch someone from the station. *Je vais chercher quelqu'un à la gare.*

结（結） jié T, S2 **knot, forge,** *nœud m, sceller* 这个~没有打紧。zhègè ~ méiyǒu dǎjǐn. The knot wasn't tight enough. *Le nœud n'était pas assez serré.*

我们~下了深厚的友谊。wǒmen ~xià le shēnhòu de yǒuyí. We've forged a profound friendship. *Nous avons scellé une profonde amitié.*

解决（解決） jiějué N, H3, S1 **solve, solution,** *résoudre, solution f* 这个问题还没有 ~。zhègè wèntí hái méiyǒu ~. This question has not yet been solved. *Cette question n'est toujours pas résolue / reste toujours en suspens.*

找到~办法是很紧急的。zhǎodào ~ bànfǎ shì hěn jǐnjí de. A solution must be found urgently. *Il devient urgent de trouver une solution.*

姐姐｜姐 jiějie | jiě H2, S1 **elder sister,** *sœur aînée, grande sœur* 他~叫卡米拉。tā ~ jiào kǎmǐlā. His older sister's name is Camilla. *Sa sœur aînée s'appelle Camilla.*

我有 一个姐姐、一个妹妹 / 一姐一妹。wǒ yǒu yígè ~、yígè mèimei / yì~ yímèi. I have a big sister and a little sister. *J'ai une grande sœur et une petite sœur.*

介绍（介紹） jièshào H2, S1 **introduce, present, draw a sketch of,** *présenter, donner un résumé de* 我来~一下，这位是我的老朋友。wǒ lái ~ yíxià, zhè wèi shì wǒde lǎo péngyou. I must introduce you to my old friend. *Il faut que je vous présente mon vieil ami.*

老瞿简要地~了形势。lǎo qú jiǎnyào de ~ le xíngshì. Lao Qu drew a brief sketch of the situation. *Lao Qu a donné un bref résumé de la situation.*

今年 jīnnián N, S1 **this year,** *cette année* 你~去商品交易会吗? nǐ ~ qù shāngpǐn jiāoyìhuì ma? Are you going to the trade fair this year? *Vas-tu à la foire commerciale cette année?*

~中文课程很难。~ zhōngwén kèchéng hěn nán. The Chinese syllabus is hard this year. *Le programme de chinois est dur cette année.*

今天 jīntiān G, N, H1, S1 **today,** *aujourd'hui* ~星期几? --- (~)星期四。~ xīngqījǐ? --- (~)xīngqī sì. What day is it today? – It's Thursday. *Quel jour est-on aujourd'hui ? – C'est jeudi.* ~ (几月)几号 ? -- ~(三月)十七号。~ (jǐyuè) jǐhào? --- ~ (sānyuè) shíqī hào. Today is (March) 17th. *Aujourd'hui, on est le 17 (mars).*

尽（盡） jǐn T **as... as possible,** *le plus... possible* 你要~早来。nǐ yào ~ zǎo lái. Come as early as possible. *Viens le plus tôt possible.*

~着两天把事儿搞完。Get the job done in two days at the outside. *Fais ce boulot en deux jours au maximum.*

进（進） jìn H2, S1 **enter, come in, go in,** *entrer, rentrer* 请~! qǐng ~! Come in, please! *Entrez, s'il vous plaît!* 您先~! nín xiān ~! After you! *Après vous!*

我们~不了多少钱。wǒmen ~ bùliǎo bùshǎo qián. We don't have much money coming in. *Il n'y a pas beaucoup d'argent qui rentre.*

进行（進行） jìnxíng N, H4, S1 **get on, be in charge of,** *mener, aller, être chargé de* 你们这里环保~得怎么样? nǐmen zhèlǐ huánbǎo ~ dé zěnmeyàng? How are you getting on here with your environmental protection? *Comment va votre protection de l'environnement ici?*

她在(对一个暗杀事件)~调查。tā zài (duì yígè ànshā shìjiàn) ~ diàochá. She's in charge of the investigation. (She's investigating a murder). *Elle est chargée de l'enquête. (Elle mène une enquête sur un meurtre.)*

近 jìn H2, S1 **near,** *proche, près* 办公室离这儿非常~。bàngōngshì lí zhèr fēicháng ~. The office is very near from here. *Le bureau est tout proche d'ici.* 她住得相当~。tā zhù dé xiāngdāng ~. She lives quite near. *Elle habite tout près.*

快去最~的药店。kuài qù zuì ~ de yàodiàn. Go to the nearest chemist's (shop). *Allez à la pharmacie la plus proche.*

经（經）jīng D, T **be engaged in, holy, via, stand,** *faire, sacré, via, supporter* 我们公司在非洲~商。wǒmen gōngsī zài fēizhōu ~shāng. Our company is engaged in trade in Africa. *Notre société fait du commence avec l'Afrique.*

这是本圣~。zhèshì běn shèng~. It's the Holy Bible. *C'est la Bible (sacrée).* 我~巴梨回家的。wǒ ~ bālí huíjiā de. I returned home via Paris. *Je suis rentré via Paris.* 这个论据~不起推敲。zhè gè lùnjù ~ bùqǐ tuīqiāo. That argument does not stand investigation. *Cet argument ne supporte pas l'examen.*

经济（經濟）jīngjì N, H4, S1
economic, economical, economics, *rentable, économique, économie f* 这不大~。zhè búdà ~. It isn't economic. *Ce n'est pas rentable.* 大批买更~些。dàpī mǎi gèng ~ xiē. It's more economical to buy in bulk. *C'est plus économique d'acheter par grandes quantités.*

浦先生是~学讲师。pǔ xiānsheng shì ~ xué jiǎngshī. Mr Pu is an economics lecturer. *M. Pu est professeur d'économie.* 政府为了解决目前的~危机控制了进口。zhèngfǔ wèile jiějué mùqián de ~ wēijī kòngzhì le jìnkǒu. The government has introduced import controls to solve the current economic crisis. *Le gouvernement a mis en place le contrôle des importations pour résoudre la crise économique actuelle.* 西方国家对该国采取了~制裁。xīfāng guójiā duì gāiguó cǎiqǔ le ~ zhìcái. The western nations imposed economic sanctions on the country. *Les pays occidentaux ont imposé des sanctions économiques au pays.*

京剧（京劇）jīngjù H4, S1 **Beijing opera,** *opéra de Beijing* 我母亲常常去看~。wǒ mǔqin chángcháng qù kàn ~. My mother is often to the Beijing opera. *Ma mère va souvent à l'opéra de Beijing.* ~是典型的中国文化艺术。~ shì diǎnxíng de zhōngguó wénhuà yìshù. Beijing opera is the quintessential Chinese culture and art. *L'opéra de Beijing est la culture et l'art chinois typique.*

京戏（京戲）jīngxì S1 **Beijing opera,** *opéra de Bejing* (= 京剧 jìngjù)

井 jǐng T, H6, S2 **well, in perfect order,** *puits m, en bon ordre* 这口~很深。zhè kǒu ~

hěn shēn. This well is very deep. *Ce puits est très profond.*

我们用的是~水。wǒmen yòngde shì ~ shuǐ. We get our water from a well. *Notre eau vient d'un puits.* 一切真是~~有条! yíqiè zhēn shì ~~ yǒutiáo. Everything's shipshape / All shipshape and Bristol fashion! *Tout est impeccable / Tout est à sa place!*

九 jiǔ H1, S1 **nine,** *neuf* 有~个。yǒu ~ gè. There are nine. *Il y en a neuf.*

他十之八~要迟到。tā shí zhī bā~ yào chídào. He's late nine times out of ten. *Il est en retard neuf fois sur dix.* 现在是三~天。xiànzài shì sān~ tiān. Now we're in the coldest days of winter. *Maintenant nous sommes au cœur de l'hiver.* 这就是~天~地的差别。zhè jiù shì ~ tiān ~ dì de chābié. That makes all the difference. *Voilà qui change complètement les choses.*

就 jiù D, H2, S1 **at once, right away, already, as soon as, right after,** *bientôt, tout de suite, déjà, dès, aussitôt* (你)有事~不要来了。(nǐ) yǒu shì ~ búyào lái le. Don't come if you're busy. *Ne viens pas si tu n'as pas de temps.*

我家~在邮局对面。wǒjiā ~ zài yóujú duìmiàn. My house is opposite the post office. *Ma maison est juste en face du bureau de poste.* 火车还有五分钟~要开了! huǒchē hái yǒu wǔ fēnzhōng ~ yào kāi le! The train leaves in five minutes! *Le train part dans cinq minutes!*

就是 jiùshì N, S1 就是 **(+le): expressing a certainty,** *exprimer la certitude* 放心，我保密~了。fàngxīn, wǒ bǎomì ~ le. Don't worry. I'm under a promise of secrecy. *Ne t'inquiète pas. J'ai promis de garder le secret.*

他说的~不错嘛。tā shuō de ~ búcuò ma. His speech was quite something. *Son discours était tout à fait remarquable.* 这~孩子也知道。zhè ~ háizi yě zhīdào. Even the children knew it. *Même les enfants le savaient.*

举行（舉行）jǔxíng H3, S1 **hold, be held, give,** *avoir lieu, se tenir, offrir* 会议(将在)晚上 8 点~。huìyì (jiāng zài) wǎnshang fā diǎn ~. The meeting will be held at 8 pm. *La réunion aura lieu à 8 heures du soir.*

双方~了会谈。shuāngfāng ~ le huìtán. The two sides held talks. *Des discussions se sont tenues entre les deux parties.* 他为我们~了宴会。tā wèi wǒmen ~ le yànhuì. He gave us a banquet. *Il nous a offert un banquet.*

觉得（覺得） juéde G, H2, S2 **feel, think, *(se) sentir, penser*** 我~不大舒服。wǒ ~ bùdà shūfu. I don't feel very well. *Je ne me sens pas très bien.*

他~很累。tā ~ hěn lèi. He feels tired. *Il se sent fatigué.* 你~新来的老师怎么样? nǐ ~ xīn lái de lǎoshī zěnmeyàng? What do you think of the new teacher? *Comment trouves-tu le nouveau professeur?*

咖啡 kāfēi H2, S2 **coffee, *café m*** 您想喝（一杯）~吗? nín xiǎng hē (yìbēi) ~ ma? Would you like a (cup of) coffee? *Voulez-vous un café (une tasse de café)?*

我们一边喝~一边聊天。wǒmen yìbiān hē ~ yìbiān liáotiān. We talked over coffee. *Nous avons bavardé en prenant un café.*

开（開） kāi D, H1, S1 **switch on, go to, flower, *ouvrir, aller, fleurir*** 我能~灯吗? wǒ ~ kāidēng ma? Can I switch on the light? *Puis-je ouvrir la lumière?*

这列火车朝重庆~。zhè liè huǒchē cháo chóngqìng ~. This train goes to Chongqing. *Ce train va en direction de Chongqing.* 玫瑰花还没有~。méiguìhuā hái méiyǒu ~. The roses haven't flowered yet. *Les roses n'ont pas encore fleuri.*

开始（開始） kāishǐ G, H2, S1 **begin, start, *commencer, débuter*** 你什么时候~做? nǐ shénme shíhou ~ zuò? When will you begin to do it? *Quand vas-tu commencer à / de le faire?* (天)~下雨了。(tiān) ~ xiàyǔ le. It's beginning to rain. *Il commence à pleuvoir.*

这仅仅是~。zhè jǐnjǐn shì ~. This is only the beginning. *Ce n'est que le début.*

看 kàn D, H3, S1 **look, watch, read, depend on, *regarder, lire, être d'avis que, dépendre de*** 我从窗户往外~。wǒ cóng chuānghu wǎng wài ~. I'm looking out of the window. *Je regarde par la fenêtre.* 你常常~电视吗? nǐ chángcháng ~ diànshì ma? Do you often watch television? *Est-ce que tu regardes souvent la télévision?*

您 ~得懂 / ~得了 意大利文吗? nǐ ~ dédǒng / ~ déliǎo yìdàlì-wén ma? Can you read Italian? *Savez-vous lire l'italien?* 我~不懂乐谱。wǒ ~ bùdǒng yuè pǔ. I can't read music. *Je ne sais pas lire la musique.* 我~咱们应该等等。wǒ ~ zánmen yīnggāi děngdeng. I am of the opinion that we should wait. *Je suis d'avis que l'on attende.* 咱们出去吗? --- 这得~天气。zánmen chūqù ma? -- zhè děi ~ tiānqì. Are we going out? -- It depends on the weather. *Est-ce qu'on sort? -- Ça dépend du temps.*

看病 kàn//bìng S1 **(of a doctor) see a patient, (of a patient) see / consult a doctor, *(d'un médecin) voir un(e) patient(e), (d'un patient) voir / consulter un médecin*** 你得去~。nǐ děi qù ~. You should see a doctor. *Il faut te faire soigner.* 这个大夫给我~。zhèi gè dàifu gěi wǒ ~. I'm under the care of this doctor. *C'est le docteur qui me soigne.*

看到 kàndào G, S1 **look, see, *voir*** 我~了。wǒ ~ le. I saw it. *Je l'ai vu.*

你在那里处处可以~贫困。nǐ zài nàlǐ chùchù kěyǐ ~ pínkùn. Everywhere you look there is poverty. *De quelque côté que l'on se tourne, on voit la pauvreté.* 这个大教堂(你)很远就看得到。zhègè dà jiàotáng (nǐ) hěn yuǎn jiù kàn dé dào. The cathedral can be seen from a long way off. *La cathédrale se voit de loin.*

看见（看見） kànjiàn G, H1, S1 **catch sight of, see, *voir, apercevoir*** 我是亲眼~的。wǒ shì qīnyǎn ~ de. I saw it with my own eyes. *Je l'ai vu de mes (propres) yeux.*

我什么也没~。wǒ shénme yě méi ~. I didn't see anything. *Je n'ai rien vu.* 我什么也看不见。wǒ shénme yě kànbújiàng. I can't see anything. *Je ne vois rien.*

考试（考試） kǎoshì H2, S1 **examination, test, *examen m, épreuve f*** 他 ~ 不 / 没有 及格。tā ~ bù / méiyǒu jígé. He failed in the examination. *Il a été recalé à l'examen.* 我~及格了。wǒ ~ jígé le. I passed the examination. *Je suis reçu à / J'ai réussi à l'examen.*

你~得了几分 / 多少分? nǐ ~ déle jǐfēn / duōsgǎo fēn? What did you get in the exam? *Tu as eu combien à l'examen?*

科技 kējì N, S1 **science and technology,** *science f et technologie f* 他在(一所)~大学上学。tā zài (yìsuǒ) ~ dàxué shàngxué. He's studying in a university of science and technology. *Il étudie dans une université de sciences et technologies.*

他们对~着迷了。tāmen duì ~ zháomí le. They have a passion for science and technology. *Ils ont une passion pour les sciences et technologies.*

科学 (科學) kēxué N, H4, S1

science, *science f* 我一直对~很感兴趣。wǒ yìzhí duì ~ hěn gǎn xìngqu. I've always been interested in science. *J'ai toujours été intéressé par les sciences.*

对他来说园艺确实是一门~。duì tā láishuō yuányì quèshí shì yìmén ~. Gardening for him is quite a science. *Pour lui le jardinage est une véritable science.* 我女儿是个~工作者。wǒ nǚ'ér shì gè ~ gōngzuòshě. My daughter is a scientist. *Ma fille est une scientifique.*

可 kě D, S2 **be worth, suit,** *valoir la peine,* *convenir à* ~试一试。~ shì yí shì. It's worth a try / trying. *Cela vaut la peine d'essayer.* 工作~不要分心。gōngzuò ~ bùyào fēnxīn. Keep your mind on the job. *Ne vous laissez pas distraire du travail.*

他们轻松的态度~了我的心。tāmen qīngsōng de tàidù ~ le wǒde xīn. Their relaxed approach suits me fine. *Leur attitude décontractée me convient tout à fait.* 他对我的计划不置~否。tā duì wǒde jìhuà búzhì ~fǒu. He was very noncommittal about my plans. *Il s'est montré très réservé à mes plans.*

可能 kěnéng G, N, H2, S1 **possible,** **probable, probably, maybe,** *possible,* *probable, probablement, peut-être* 她~不知道。tā ~ bù zhīdào. She probably doesn't know. *Elle ne le sait peut-être pas.*

有这种~。yǒu zhèzhǒng ~. It's a possibility. *C'est une possibilité.* 他不大~在那儿。tā búdà ~ zài nàr. It's hardly probable that he will be there. *Il est peu probable qu'il soit là.*

可是 kěshì G, H4, S1 **but, yet, however,** *mais, cependant, pourtant, néanmoins* 她回家时很累，~很高兴。tā huíjiā shí hěn lèi, ~ hěn gāoxìng. She came home tired but happy. *Elle est rentrée fatiguée mais heureuse.*

~有其他更重要的事情。~ yǒu qítā gèng zhòngyào de shìqing. There are more important matters, however. *Il y a des problèmes plus importants, pourtant.*

可以 kěyǐ G, N, H2, S1 **can, may,** **passable, awful,** *pouvoir, passable, assez* *bien, vraiment* 我~进来吗？--- 当然~。wǒ ~ jìnlái ma? -- dāngrán ~. May I come in? – Of course you may. *Puis-je entrer? – Bien sûr, je vous en prie.*

还~。hái ~. It's passable / adequate. *Ce n'est pas si mauvais / trop mal.* 我今天忙得真~。wǒ jīntiān máng dé zhēn ~. I've had a really busy day. *J'ai eu une journée vraiment occupée.*

课 (課) kè H2, S1 **class, lesson,** **course,** *cours m, leçon f* 我现在去上~。wǒ xiànzài qù shàng ~. I'm going to take a class now. *Je vais prendre un cours maintenant.* 她给我们上~。tā gěi wǒmen shàng ~. She teaches us. *Elle nous donne des cours.*

这一~我还不太懂。zhè yí ~ wǒ hái bú tài dǒng. I haven't assimilated the lesson yet. *Je n'ai pas encore bien assimilé la leçon.*

yuan 块 (塊) kuài H1, S1 **, [classifier],** *yuan, [classificateur m]* 多少钱? --- 五~七毛三。duōshǎo qián? -- wǔ ~ qī máo sān. How much is it? -- Five yuan seven mao and three (centimes). *Combien ça coûte? – Cinq yuan sept mao et trois (centimes).* 我要一~面包。wǒ yào yí ~ miànbāo. I'd like to have a piece of bread. *Je voudrais (avoir) un morceau de pain.*

谁朝他扔第一~石头? shéi cháo tā rēng dìyī ~ shítou? Who's going to be the one to cast the first stone at him? *Qui lui jetera la première pierre?*

快 kuài H2, S1 **fast, quick, almost,** *vite,* *vite, rapidement* !你走得很~。nǐ zǒu dé hěn ~. You're a fast walker. *Tu marches vite.* 我尽~做。wǒ jìn ~ zuò. I'll do it as quick as possible. *Je le ferai aussi vite que possible.*

她很~地看了看今天的晨报。tā hěn ~ de kàn le kan jīntiān de chénbào. She had a quick look at the papers this morning. *Elle a lu rapidement les* journaux de ce matin. 我~做完了。wǒ ~ zuò wán le. I've almost finished. *J'ai bientôt fini.*

快乐（快樂）kuàilè H2, S1 **happy, merry, cheerful, joyful,** *joyeux, gai, de bonne humeur* 圣诞快乐! shèngdàn ~! Merry Christmas! *Joyeux Noël!* 生日~! shēngrì ~! Happy birthday! *Joyeux anniversaire!*

她总那么 ~ / 快快乐乐的。tā zǒngshì nàme ~ / kuàikuài lèlè de. She's always cheerful. *Elle est toujours de bonne humeur.* 那是件很~的事儿。nà shì jiàn hěn ~ de shì. That was a joyful event. *C'était un événement joyeux.*

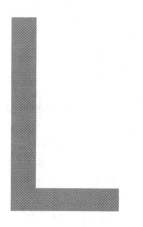

来（來）lái D, H1, S1 **come,** *venir* 到这儿~。dào zhèr ~. Come here. *Venez ici.* 我~了! wǒ ~ le! (I'm) Coming! *J'arrive!*

我跑~跑去忙了一整天。tā pǎo ~ pǎo qù máng le yì zhěng tiān. I've been rushed off my feet all day. *J'ai passé ma journée à courir à droite et à gauche.*

老师（老師）lǎoshī G, H1, S1 **teacher,** *enseignant(e), professeur m* 他是数学~。tā shì shùxué ~. He is a maths teacher. *Il est professeur de maths.* 她是我的法文~。tā shì wǒ de fǎwén ~. She's my French teacher. *Elle est mon professeur de français.*

他当~了。tā dāng ~ le. He has become a teacher. *Il est entré dans l'enseignement.*

了 le D, H1, S1 (1), **at the end of a sentence: expressing a change;** *à la fin d'une phrase: exprimer un changement* 下雨~! xià yǔ ~. It's raining! *Il pleut!* 别说~! bié

shuō ~! Be quiet! / Shut up! *Tais-toi! / Taisez-vous!*
(2), **after a verb: a finished action,** *après un verbe: une action finie* 我问~他一个问题。wǒ wèn~ tā yígè wèntí. I've asked him a question. *Je lui ai posé une question.* 她走~，我没有走。tā zǒu ~, wǒ méiyǒu zǒu. She has gone, but I haven't. *Elle est partie, mais pas moi.*

冷 lěng H1, S1 **cold,** *froid* 我很~。wǒ hěn ~. I'm cold. *J'ai froid.* 她手~。tā shǒu ~. Her hands are cold. *Elle a les mains froides.*

我脚~。wǒ jiǎo ~. My feet are cold. *J'ai froid aux pieds.* 这儿太~了，咱们生火吧。zhèr tài ~ le, zánmen shānghuǒ ba. It's cold here. Let's make a fire. *Il fait froid ici. On fera du feu.*

离（離）lí H2, S1 **be away from, leave, [distance or period :] off, away, from,** *quitter, [distance ou durée:] de, dans* 她~家已经三年了。tā ~ jiā yǐjīng sān nián le. She's been away from home for three years. *Elle a quitté sa famille depuis trois ans.*

车站~这儿(有)两公里。The railway station is two kilometres from here. *La gare est à deux kilomètres d'ici.* ~元旦只有十天了。~ yuándàn zhǐ yǒu shí tiān le. The New Year's Day is only ten days away. *Le Nouvel An sera seulement dans dix jours.*

里（裡）lǐ G, H1, S1 **li: a Chinese unit of length (= ½ kilometre); in, into,** *li: unité chinoise de longueur (= ½ kilomètre); dans, à* 一公里等于二~。yì gōnglǐ děngyú èr ~. A kilometre is equal to two li. *Un kilomètre est égale à deux li.*

她回到了屋~。tā huídào le wū~. She went back into her room. *Elle est rentrée dans sa chambre.* 他手~拿着一本书。tā shǒu ~ ná zhe yì běn shū. He's holding a book in his hand. *Il tient un livre à la main.*

理 lǐ D, S1 **be reasonable, truth, have reason,** *être raisonnable, vrai, avoir raison* 你没有~。nǐ méiyǒu ~. You're being unreasonable. *Tu n'es pas raisonnable.*

他说的有些~。nǐ shuō de yǒuxiē ~. There's some truth in what he says. *Il y a du vrai dans ce qu'il dit.* 我们有~由怀疑他撒谎。wǒmen yǒu ~yóu huáiyí tā sāhuǎng. We have reason to believe he is lying. *Nous avons de bonnes raison de croire qu'il ment.*

两（兩）liǎng (数) (1) H2, S1 **two, *deux*** 有~个。yǒu ~ gè. There are two (of them). *Il y en a deux.* 这样我们就是~个人。zhèyàng wǒmen jiù shì ~ gè rén. That makes two of us. *On est deux.*

我想讲~句。wǒ xiān jiǎng ~ jù. I'd like to say a few words. *J'ai deux mots à dire.* 他爷爷参加了~万五千里长征。tā yéye cānjiā le ~wàn wǔqiān lǐ chángzhēng. His grandpa took part in the Long March of 25,000 li (or 12,500 kilometres). *Son grand-père a participé à la Longue Marche de 25 000 li (ou 12 500 kilomètres).*

两（兩）liǎng (量) (2) H2, S1 **liang: a Chinese unit of weight (= 50 grams), *liang: une unité chinoise de poids (= 50 grammes)*** 他喝了二~白酒。He's drunken two liang (100 grams) of alcohol. *Il a bu deux liang (100 grammes) d'alcool.*

两个（兩個）liǎnggè G **two, both, *deux*** 这~我都要。zhè ~ wǒ dōu yào. I'll take both. *Je vais prendre les deux.*

你不孤单，加我咱们~人。nǐ bù gūdān, jiā wǒ zánmen ~. That makes two of us. *Vous n'êtes pas le seul, c'est pareil.* 那~学校在同一个村里。nà ~ xuéxiào zài tóng yígè cūnlǐ. Both schools are in the same village. *Les deux écoles sont dans le même village.*

两国（兩國）liǎngguó N **two countries, *deux pays*** 我们~关系 紧张 / 友好。wǒmen ~ guānxì jǐnzhāng / yǒuhǎo. Relations between our two countries are strained / friendly. *Les relations entre nos deux pays sont tendus / amicales.*

~总理签订了一个商业条约。~ zǒnglǐ qiāndìng le yígè shāngyè tiáoyuē. The prime ministers of the two countries signed a commercial treaty. *Les premiers ministres des deux pays ont signé un traité commercial.*

领导（領導）lǐngdǎo N, H5, S1 **manage, lead, *diriger, mener, chef m*** 她很容易~。tā hěn róngyì ~. She is easily led. *Elle va comme on la mène.*

这个事业他~得不好。zhè gè shìyè tā ~ dé bùhǎo. He mismanaged the business. *Il a mal dirigé l'entreprise.* 他是党的~人。tā shì dǎng de ~rén. He leads the party. *Il est chef du parti.*

六 liù H1, S1 **six, *six*** 我们~点去。wǒmen ~ diǎn qù. We'll go at six (o'clock). *On y va à six heures.*

这个人~亲不认。zhè gè rén ~qīn búrèn. That man repudiates all family connections. *Cet homme renie toute la parenté.*

陆（陸）lù T **land, *terre f*** 他们离船登~了。tāmen lí chuán dēng ~ le. They disembarked from the ferry. *Ils ont débarqué du ferry.*

水~交通都很频繁。shuǐ ~ jiāotōng dōu hěn pínfán. Both land and water communications are intense. *Toute la communication par eau et par terre est intense.* 诺曼底登~发生在 1944 年。nuòmàndǐ dēng~ fāshēng zài 1944 nián. The Normandy landing took place in 1944. *Le Débarquement en Normandie eut lieu en 1944.*

乱（亂）luàn T, H4, S1 **mess, go wrong, noise, disorder, *désordre m, mal tourner, bruit m*** 屋子里怎么这么~! wūzi lǐ zěnme zhème ~! What a mess in the bedroom! *Quel désordre dans cette chambre!* 出~子了。chū ~zi le. Things have gone wrong. *Les choses ont mal tourné.*

后面~呼呼的，让我讲不下去! hòumiàn ~hūhū de, ràng wǒ jiǎng bú xiàqù! I hate explaining something against a background of noise! *J'ai horreur d'expliquer quelque chose dans le bruit!* 现在(是)天下大~。xiànzài (shì) tiānxià dà~. There is great disorder under heaven now. *Le désordre règne sous le ciel maintenant.*

略 luè T **brief, slight, bold, *résumé m, léger, stratégie f*** 我~述一下大意。wǒ ~ shù yíxià dàyì. I'll give a brief account. *Je ferai un résumé.*

两种解释~有出入。liǎng zhǒng jiěshì ~ yǒu chūrù. The explications vary slightly. *Les explications divergent légèrement.* 那个人雄才大~。nà gè rén xióngcái dà~. That's a person of great talent and bold vision. *C'est quelqu'un de grand talent qui a une stratégie audacieuse.*

旅游（旅遊）lǚyóu H2, S1 **tour, tourism, *tourisme m*** 他们到爱尔兰~过。tāmen dào ài'ěrlán ~ guo. They went touring round Ireland. *Ils ont fait du tourisme en Irlande.* 请问，~局怎么走? qǐng wèn, ~jú zěnme zǒu? Can you suggest me a tourism agency? *Pouvez-vous m'indiquer une agence de tourisme?*

今年~大丰收。jīnnián ~ dà fēngshōu. It's been a bumper year for tourism. *Ça a été une année exceptionnelle pour le tourisme.* 长城是一个~胜地。chángchéng shì yígè ~ shèngdì. The Great Wall is a famous scenic spot. *La Grande Muraille est un site réputé.* 上个月我们参加了去意大利有组织的~。shànggè yuè wǒmen cānjiā le qù yìdàlì yǒu zǔzhī de ~. We went on a tour of Italy last month. *Nous avons fait une visite guidée de l'Italie le mois dernier.*

妈妈 | 妈（媽媽 | 媽）māma | mā H1, S1 **ma, mum, mummy, mother,** *maman f, mère f* 约翰，你~在哪儿? yuēhàn, nǐ ~ zài nǎr? Where's your mum(my), John? *Où est ta maman, John?* 马克的~病了。mǎkè de ~ bìng le. Mack's mum / mom is ill. *La maman de Mark est malade.*

大家的~都(被)邀请了。dàjiā de ~ dōu (bèi) yāoqǐng le. All mums are invited. *Toutes les mamans sont invitées.*

麻 má T **rough, pockmark,** *rugueux, variolé* 这个平面不光滑, 很~。zhègè píngmiàn bù guānghuá, hěn ~. This surface isn't smooth, but very rough. *Cette surface n'est pas lisse, mais très rugueuse.*

他是~脸。tā shì ~ liǎn. His face is covered with pockmarks. *Il a le visage grêlé / variolé.* 我腿发~。wǒ tuǐ fā ~. I have pins and needles in my legs. *J'ai des fournis dans les jambes.*

马（馬）mǎ T, H3, S1 **horse,** *cheval m* 我喜欢骑~。wǒ xǐhuan qí ~. I like riding a horse. *J'aime monter à cheval.*

他从~(背)上摔下来了。tā cóng ~ (bèi) shàng shuāi xiàlái le. He fell off his horse. *Il a fait une chute de cheval.* 这是匹很有柔情的~。zhèshì pī hěn yǒu róuqíng de ~. It's a very affectionate horse. *C'est un cheval très affectueux.*

骂（罵）mà T, H5, S2 **insult, call names, swear,** *insulter, injurier, insulte f* 他~我了。tā ~ wǒ le. He insulted me / called me names. *Il m'a insulté.*

他~她~个没完。tā ~ tā ~gè méiwán. He's always insulting her. *Il n'arrête pas de l'injurier.* 他们对~个不停。tāmen duì ~ gè bùtíng. They were slinging insults at each other. *Ils se lançaient des insultes.* 别在孩子们面前~人。bié zài háizi men miànqián ~ rén. Don't swear in front of the children. *Ne dis pas de gros mots devant les enfants.*

吗（嗎）ma H1, S1 **[a question word, placed at the end of a sentence],** *[un mot de question, mis à la fin d'une phrase]* 你认识他~? nǐ rènshi tā ~? Do you know him? *Est-ce que tu le connais?*

这条裙子我穿合适~? zhè tiáo qúnzi wǒ chuān héshì ~? Does this dress suit me? *Cette robe me va?* 您现在点菜~? nín xiànzài diǎn cài ~? Do you wish to order? *Voulez-vous commander?* 很有意思，不是~? hěn yǒuyìsi, bú shì ~? It was interesting, wasn't it? *C'était très intéressant, n'est-ce pas?*

买（買）mǎi H1, S1 **buy, purchase,** *acheter* 我去~东西。wǒ qù ~ dōngxi. I'll do some shopping. *Je vais faire des courses.*

这个用钱~不来。zhègè yòng qián ~ bùlái. Money cannot buy it. *Cela ne se paie pas.* 这个我~得很便宜。zhègè wǒ ~ dé hěn piányi. I bought it cheap. *Je l'ai acheté (à) bon marché.*

卖（賣）mài H2, S1 **sell,** *vendre* 这个他~得很贵 / ~得很便宜。zhè gè tā ~ dé hěn guì / ~ dé hěn piányi. He sold it dear / cheap. *Il l'a vendu cher / (à) bon marché.* 李子 怎么~ / ~多少钱? lǐzi zěnme ~ / ~ duōshǎo qián? What are plums selling at? *Combien se vendent les prunes?*

高级轿车~不出去了。gāojí jiàochē ~ bù chūqù le. Big cars don't sell anymore. *Les grosses voitures ne se vendent plus.*

麦 mài T **wheat,** *blé m* 他们在地里种了~子。tāmen zài dìlǐ zhòngle ~zi. They've planted land with wheat. *Ils ont planté une terre en blé.*

这里的农夫主要种小~。zhèlǐ de nóngfū zhǔyào zhòng xiǎo~. Farmers often grow wheat here. *Les agricultures cultivent surtout du blé ici.*

慢 màn H2, S1 **slow, *lent, retarder*** 这个表~了。zhè gè biǎo ~ le. This watch is slow. *Cette montre retarde.*

他工作得很~ / ~~地工作。tā gōngzuó dé hěn ~ / ~~ de gōngzuò. He's a slow worker. *Il travaille lentement.* 且~! 让我考虑一下。qiě ~! ràng wǒ kǎolǜ yíxià. Just a moment! Let me think it over. *Attendez ! Laissez-moi réfléchir un peu.*

忙 máng H2, A1 **busy, hurry, rush off one's feet, *occupé, précipitation f, courir à gauche et à droite*** 现在不行, 我很~。xiànzài bùxíng, wǒ hěn ~. Not now – I'm busy. *Pas maintenant – je suis occupé.*

她~得把钥匙都忘(带)了。tā ~ dé bǎ yàoshi dōu wàng(dài) le. In her hurry, she forgot her keys. *Dans sa précipitation elle a oublié ses clés.* 我跑来跑去~了一天。wǒ pǎolái pǎoqù ~ le yìtiān. I've been rushed off my feet all day. *J'ai passé ma journée à courir à droite et à gauche.*

猫 (貓) māo H1, S2 **cat, *chat m, chatte f*** 我们有一只~、两只狗。wǒmen yǒu yìzhī ~、liǎngzhī gǒu. We have a cat and two dogs. *Nous avons un chat et deux chiens.*

看这只温柔的小~。kàn zhè zhī wēnróu de xiǎo ~. Look at the little pussy cat. *Regarde le petit chat.* 他们像~和狗一样, 在一起总争个没完。tāmen xiàng ~ hé gǒu yíyàng, zài yìqǐ zǒng zhēng gè méiwán. They always quarrel like cat and dog. *Ils s'entendent toujours comme chien et chat.*

么 (麼) me D **[particle], *[particule f]*** 不让你去~, 你又要去。bú ràng nǐ qù ~, nǐ yòu yào qù. If we don't permit you to go there, you will insist on going there. *Si on ne te permet pas d'y aller, tu insisteras de le faire.*

这些蛋糕很好吃~! zhè xiē dàngāo hěn hǎo chī ~! These cakes are really delicious! *Ces gâteaux sont vraiment délicieux!*

没 (沒) méi D, H1, S1 **(1), not have, *ne pas avoir*** 他~(有)钱。tā ~ (yǒu) qián. He has / He's got no money. *Il n'a pas d'argent.* 她~工作。tā ~ gōngzuò. She has no job. *Elle n'a pas de travail.*

(2), not have done, *ne pas avoir fait* 你还~做吗? nǐ hái ~ zuò ma? Haven't you done it yet? *Tu ne l'as pas encore fait?*

我~看见他。wǒ ~ kànjiàn tā. I didn't see him. *Je ne l'ai pas vu.* 他~想跟他们去

---

tāmen qù. He hadn't wanted to go with them. *Il n'avait pas voulu y aller avec eux.*

没关系 (沒關係) méi guānxi H1, S1 **it doesn't matter, it's nothing, that's all right, never mind, *il n'y a pas de quoi, peu importe, de rien*** 这~。zhè ~. It doesn't matter. *Peu importe.*

这丝毫~。zhè sīháo ~. It doesn't matter a bit. *Cela n'a pas la moindre importance.* 对我来说, 天冷不冷~。duì wǒ láishuō, tiān lěng bù lěng ~. I don't mind cold. *Le froid ne me gêne pas.*

没有 (沒有) méi yǒu G, N, S1 (= 没 méi) **have not, have not done, *ne pas avoir, ne pas avoir fait*** 他~朋友。tā ~ péngyou. He has no friends. *Il n'a pas d'amis.* 我的箱子上~(写)名字。wǒde xiāngzi shàng ~ (xiě) míngzi. My bag has no name on it. *Ma valise ne porte pas de nom.* 那个行人~看见汽车来了。nàgè xíngrén ~ kànjiàn chē lái le. The pedestrian didn't see the car coming. *Le piéton n'a pas vu arriver la voiture.* 他在会上一句话也~说。tā zài huì shàng yíjù huà yě ~ shuō. He didn't say a word at the meeting. *Il n'a pas dit un mot pendant la réunion.*

每 měi (代) (1) H2, S1 **every, each, per, *chaque, chacun*** 她~天都来。tā ~ tiān dōu lái. She comes every day. *Elle vient tous les jours.*

~个人都有生存的权力。~ gè rén dōu yǒu shēngcún de quánlì. Every person has the right to live. *Chacun a le droit de vivre.* 他说的~一句话都是谎言。tā de ~ yí jù huà dōu shì huǎngyán. Every word he says is a lie. *Tout ce qu'il dit est mensonge.*

每 měi (副) (2) H2, S1 **as many times as, *autant de fois que*** 我~剪一次头发都花八欧元。wǒ ~ jiǎn yícì tóufa dōu huā bā ōuyuán. It costs me €8 a time to have my hair cut. *Une coupe de cheveux me coûte huit euros.*

我~提个建议你怎么都要反对? wǒ ~ tí gè jiànyì nǐ zěnme dōu yào fǎnduì? Why do you disagree each time I propose something? *Pourquoi tu t'y oppose chaque fois que je propose quelque chose?*

美国 (美國) měiguó N **the United States [of America] (U.S., U.S.A.), America, *les Etats-Unis [d'Amérique] (EU), Amérique f*** 我那个朋友在~。wǒ nàgè péngyou zài ~. That friend of mine is in America. *Cet ami à moi est en Amérique.*

~和欧洲一样大。~ hé ōuzhōu yíyàng dà. The United States is as large as Europe. *Les Etats-Unis sont aussi grands que l'Europe.* 《 今日~ 》是读者最多的全国大报。"jīnrì ~" shì dúzhě zuìduō de quánguó dàbào. USA Today is a national US newspaper read by more people than any other. *USA Today est le journal national le plus lu des journaux aux Etats-Unis.*

妹妹 | 妹 mèimei | mèi H2, S1 **little sister, younger sister,** *jeune sœur, sœur cadette* 她是我~. tā shì wǒ ~. She is my little sister / younger sister. *Elle est ma petite sœur / sœur cadette.* 我有一个姐姐、一个~。wǒ yǒu yígè jiějie、yígè ~. I have an elder sister and a little sister. *J'ai une grande sœur et une petite sœur.*

门（門）mén H2, S1 **door, [classifier],** *porte f, [classificateur m]* 她走进了~. tā zǒujìn le ~. She walked through the door. *Elle a franchi la porte.* 我去按~铃。wǒ qù àn ~líng. I'll ring the (door) bell. *Je vais sonner à la porte.*
公交车在我家~前停。gōngjiāochē zài wǒjiā ~ qián tíng. The bus stops at my (front) door? *Le bus me descend à ma porte.* 他现在考四~课。tā xiànzài kǎo sì ~ kè. He's taking exams in four subjects. *Il passe des examens dans quatre matières.*

...们（...們）...men D, S1 **[a plural suffix],** *[le suffixe de pluriel]* 我~是中国人。你~是哪国人? wǒ~ shì zhōngguórén. nǐ~ shì nǎguórén? We're Chinese. What's your nationality? *Nous sommes Chinois. Quelle est votre nationalité?*
孩子~，起床的时间到了! háizi~, chǐfàn de shíjiān dào le! Children, it's time to get up! *Enfants, c'est l'heure de se lever!* 朋友~，欢迎你~! péngyǒu~, huānyíng nǐ~. My friends, you're welcome! *Mes amis, soyez les bienvenus!*

米饭（米飯）mǐfàn H1, S1 **(cooked) rice,** *riz (cuit)* 我们可以做~和鱼吃。wǒmen kěyǐ zuò ~ hé yú chī. We could do some rice with the fish. *On pourrait faire du riz avec le poisson.*

面 miàn (名) D, S1 **face, surface, noodles,** *face f, surface f, nouilles fpl* 他~部受伤。tā ~bù shòushāng. He has injured to the face. *Il a des blessures à la face.* 我们吃~。wǒmen chī ~. We'll have noodles. *On va manger des nouilles.*

池塘水~冻冰了。chítáng shuǐ~ dòngbīng le. The surface of the pond is frozen. *La surface de l'étang est gelée.* 这座房子~向南。zhè zuò fángzi ~ xiàng nán. The house faces south. *La maison est orientée au sud.*

面 miàn (量) D, S1 **[classifier],** *[classificateur m]* 那~镜子很脏。nà ~ jìngzi hěn zāng. The mirror is very dirty. *Le miroir est très sale.*
我们需要几~彩旗。wǒmen xūyào jǐ ~ cǎiqí. We need a few coloured flags. *Il nous faut quelques drapeaux de couleur.*

明白 míngbai G, H3, S1 **understand, clear, be franc,** *comprendre, clair, dire la vérité* ~不~ / 明不~ / ~没(有)~? ~ bù ~ / míng bù ~ / ~ méi(yǒu) ~? Do you understand? *Est-ce que tu comprends?*
这句话的意思很~。zhè jù huà de yìsi hěn ~. The meaning of the sentence was clear. *Le sens de la phrase était clair.* 我看你跟我讲得不~. wǒ kàn nǐ gēn wǒ jǐng dé bù ~. I don't think you're being frank with me. *Je ne crois pas que tu me dises la vérité.*

明天 míngtiān H1, S1 **tomorrow,** *demain* ~见! ~ jiàn! See you tomorrow! *A demain!* ~等待我们的是什么? ~ děngdài wǒmen de shì shénme? Who knows what tomorrow holds? *Qui sait ce que demain nous réserve?*
今天能做的事儿不要拖到~. jīntiān néng zuò de shìr búyào tuō dào ~. Never put off till tomorrow you can do today. *Il ne faut pas remettre au lendemain ce qu'on peut faire le jour même.*

名字 míngzi H1, S1 **be called, name,** *s'appeler, nom m* 你姐姐叫什么~? nǐ jiějie jiào shénme ~? What's your elder sister called? *Comment s'appelle ta grande sœur?*
名单上没有你的~. míngdān shàng méiyǒu nǐde ~. Your name isn't on the list. *Ton nom ne figure pas sur la liste.* 您可以在名单上把我的~划掉 。nín kěyǐ zài míngdān shàng bǎ wǒde ~ huádiào. You can take me off the list. *Vous pouvez me rayer sur la liste.*

母亲（母親）mǔqin G, H4, S1 **mother,** *mère f* 她当了~. tā dāngle ~. She's become a mother. *Elle est devenue mère.*
这是位有四个孩子的~. zhèshì wèi yǒu sì gè háizi de ~. She is a mother of 4 children. *Elle est mère de 4 enfants.* 她就像我的~. tā jiù xiàng wǒde ~.

She was like a mother to me. *Elle était une vraie mère pour moi.*

目前 mùqián N, H5, S1 **at present, at the moment,** *à présent, à l'heure actuelle, actuellement* ~的形势令人鼓舞。 ~ de xíngshì lìngrén gǔwǔ. The present situation is encouraging. *La situation actuelle est encourageante.* ~还够。 ~ hái gòu. That's enough for the present. *Ça suffit pour le moment.*

根据~的情况我们要 等着瞧 / 采取等待的政策 。 gēnjù ~ de qíngkuàng wǒmen yào děng zhe qiáo / cǎiqǔ děngdài de zhèngcè. Given the present circumstances we must wait and see / take a wait-and-see policy. *Etant donné les circonstances actuelles il faudra voir / prendre la politique attentiste.*

哪 nǎ H1, S1 **which, what,** *quel, lequel* ~个人是你父亲? ~ gè rén shì nǐ fùqin? Who's your father? *Qui est ton père?* 您要~本书? nǐ yào ~ běn shū? Which book would you like to have? *Quel livre voudriez-vous avoir?* 他对我~有那么坏? tā duì wǒ ~ yǒu nàme huài? He isn't so nasty to me. *Il n'est pas si méchant avec moi.*

哪里（哪裡） nǎli S1 **where,** *où* 你去~? nǐ qù ~? Where are you going? *Où vas-tu?* 您是从~来的? nín shì cóng ~ lái de? Where are you from? *D'où venez-vous?*

我~知道他要来? wǒ ~ zhīdào tā yào lái? How do I know (that) he will come? *Qui me dit qu'il viendra?* 干得真棒! --- ~, ~。 gàn dé zhēn bàng!

-- ~, ~. Well done! – It was nothing. *Bravo! – C'est peu de chose.*

哪儿（哪兒） nǎr H1, S1 (= 哪里 nǎli: where, *où*)

那 nà (代) (1) D, H1, S1 **that, ce, cela, celui-là** ~是什么? ~ shì shénme? What's that? *Qu'est-ce que c'est que ça?* ~是谁? ~ shì shéi? Who is that? *Qui est-ce, celui-là / celle-là?*

~(一)天下雨。 ~ (yì) tiān xià dàyǔ. It was raining that day. *Il pleuvait ce jour-là.* ~一点我们都同意。 ~ (yì) diǎn wǒmen dōu tóngyì. We all agree on that point. *Nous sommes tous d'accord là-dessus.* 他不是~种不付款就走的人。 tā búshì ~ zhǒng bú fùkuǎn jiù zǒu de rén. It's not like him to leave without paying. *Partir sans payer, ce n'est pas son genre.*

那 nà (连) (2) D, H1, S1 **then, in that case, alors, en ce cas** ~, 我们就等着吧。 ~, wǒmen jiù děngzhe ba. In that case, it's best to wait. *En ce cas, il vaut mieux attendre.*

要是不在我的手提包里，~就看看柜子里。 yàoshì bú zài wǒde shǒutíbāo li, ~ jiù kànkan guìzi lǐ. If it's not in my bag, then look in the cupboard. *Si ce n'est pas dans mon sac, regarde dans le placard.*

那个（那個） nàge G, S2 **that, how, ce...là, celui-là, comme...! trop** ~是什么? ~ shì shénme? What's that? *Qu'est-ce que c'est que ça?* ~人是谁? ~ rén shì shéi? Who's that? *Qui est-ce, celui-là / celle-là?*

瞧她~漂亮呀! qiáo tā ~ piàoiang ya! See how pretty she is! *Regardez comme elle est jolie!* 他的脾气也太~了。 tāde píqi yě tài ~ le. He's in a temper a little too – you know what I mean. *Il est d'une humeur un peu trop – tu sais ce que je veux dire.*

那么（那麼） nàme G, S1 **like, that, so, comme, tellement** 他像父亲~说话。 tā xiàng fùqin ~ shuōhuà. He talks like his father. *Il parle comme son père.*

我不~疼。 wǒ bú ~ téng. It doesn't hurt that much. *Je n'ai pas tellement mal.* 他~爱她。 tā ~ ài tā. He loves her so much. *Il l'aime tellement.*

那儿（那兒） nàr H1, S1 **that place, there, là, là-bas** 她还在~。 tā hái zài ~. She's still there. *Elle est encore là.* 钥匙不在~。 yàoshi bú zài ~. The keys aren't there. *Les clefs ne sont pas là.*

他在~工作吗? tā zài ~ gōngzuò ma? Does he work in that place? *C'est là-bas / dans cet endroit-là qu'il travaille?*

那些 nàxiē G, S1 **those, *ces...là, ces*** ~人

是谁? ~ rén shì shéi? Who are those people? *Qui sont ces gens-là?*

~是我的东西 / ~东西是我的。 ~ shì wǒde dōngxi / ~ dōngxi shì wǒde. Those are my things. *Ce sont mes affaires.*

那样（那樣) nàyàng G, S1 **of that kind, like that, such, so, *comme, ainsi, de la sorte, tel*** 他不像她~聪明。 tā bú xiàng tā ~ cōngming. He's is not as clever as she is. *Il n'est pas aussi intelligent qu'elle.*

我了解不少~的人。 wǒ liǎojiě bùshǎo ~ de rén. I know plenty of people like that. *Je connais pas mal de gens comme ça.*

南方 nánfāng S1 **south, the southern part of China, the Midi (the South of France), *sud m, le Sud de la Chine, le Midi*** 我们去~度假。 wǒmen qù ~ dùjià. We're going south for our holidays. *Nous allons passer nos vacances dans le sud.* 他们住在~。 tāmen zhù zài ~. They live down south. *Ils habitent dans le sud.* 小王是~人。 xiǎo wáng shì ~ rén. Xiao Wang is a southerner. *Xiao Wang est du sud.*

男人 nánrén (1) H2, S1 **man, *homme m*** (你)是个~就站出来! (nǐ) shì gè ~ jiù zhàn chūlái! Step outside if you're a man! *Sors si t'es un homme.*

你到底是个~还是只老鼠? nǐ dàodǐ shì gè ~ háishì zhī lǎoshǔ? What are you, a man or a mouse? *Alors, t'es un homme (ou un lâche)?*

男人 nánren (2) [口] H2, S1 **husband, *homme m, mari m*** 你~很会开玩笑。 nǐ ~ hěn huì kāi wánxiào. Your husband is very funny. *Ton mari est très drôle.*

他是个持家的好~。 tā shì gè chíjiā de hǎo ~. He's a real family man. *C'est un vrai père de famille.* 她又有了个~。 tā yòu yǒu le gè ~. There's a new man in her life. *Il y a un nouvel homme dans sa vie.*

呢 ne H1, H1, S1 **[particle], *[particule m]*** 我要学汉语。你~? wǒ yào xué hànyǔ. nǐ ~? I'm learning Chinese. And you? *Je vais apprendre le chinois. Et toi?*

看连环画有什么不好的~? kàn liánhuánhuà yǒu shénme bùhǎo de ~? What's wrong with reading comics? *Qu'est-ce qu'il y a de mal à lire des bandes dessinées?* 为什么这么急急忙忙的~? wèishénme zhème jíjí-mángmáng de ~? What's all the rush for? *Qu'est-ce qui presse tant?*

能 néng D, H1, S1 **can, energy, *pouvoir, énergie f*** 您~帮我一把吗? nín ~ bāng wǒ yìbǎ ma? Can you help me? *Pouvez-vous m'aider?*

她再也不~走路了 / 再也走不了路了。 tā zài yě bù ~ zǒu lù le / zàiyě zǒu bùliǎo lù le. She can no longer walk. *Elle ne peut plus marcher.* 你们做了哪些节~的事儿? nǐmen zuòle nǎxiē jié ~ de shìr? What things have you done to save energy? *Quelles choses avez-vous faites pour faire des économies d'énergie?*

你 nǐ D, H1, S1 **you (second person singular), *tu, te, toi*** 是~。 shì ~. It's you. *C'est toi.* ~对。 ~ duì. You are right. *Tu as raison.*

~没有要求。 ~ méiyǒu yāoqiú. You didn't ask. *Tu n'as pas demandé.* ~要我做什么? ~ yào wǒ zuò shénme? What do you expect me to do? *Que veux-tu que je fasse?*

你们（你們) nǐmen G, S1 **you (second person plural), *vous (deuxième personne au pluriel)*** ~都听着! ~ dōu tīng zhe! Listen, all of you! *Ecoutez-moi tous!* 她控告~三个人。 tā kònggào ~ sān gè rén. She accused all three of you. *Elle vous a accusés tous les trois.*

~这些专家什么事儿都不干。 ~ zhèxiē zhuānjiā shénme shìr dōu bú gàn. You're the specialists and you're not doing anything. *Vous (autres), les spécialistes, vous ne faites rien.*

年 nián D, H1, S1 **year, *an m, année f*** 新~好! xīn ~ hǎo! Happy New Year! *Bonne année!* 我认识他有十~了。 wǒ rènshi tā yǒu shí ~ le. I have known him for ten years. *Je le connais depuis dix ans.*

您 nín H2, S1 **you (courteous appellation), *vous (appellation courtoise, vouvoiement)*** 见到~很高兴! jiàndào ~ hěn gāoxìng! Please to meet you! *Enchanté de faire votre connaissance!* 我认识~! wǒ rènshi ~. I know you! *Je vous connais, vous!*

是~亲口跟我说的。 shì ~ qīnkǒu gēn wǒ shuō de. You told me so yourself. *C'était vous-même qui me l'avez dit.* 这是~的像片儿。 zhè shì ~ de xiàngpiàr. Here's a photo of you. *Voilà une photo de vous.*

牛奶 niúnǎi H2, S1 **milk, *lait m*** 这是鲜~。zhè shì xiān ~. It's milk fresh from the cow. *C'est du lait fraîchement trait.*

我每天早上都喝~。wǒ měitiān zǎoshang dōu hē ~. I drink milk every morning. *Je bois du lait tous les matins.*

女儿（女兒）nǚ'ér H1, S1 **daughter, *fille f*** 他们有一个儿子、两个~。tāmen yǒu yígè érzi、liǎnggè ~. They have one son and two daughters. *Ils ont un fils et deux filles.*

我们的~十七岁了。wǒmen de ~ shíqī suì le. Our daughter is 17 years old. *Notre fille est âgée de 17 ans.*

女人 nǚrén (1) G, H2, S1 **woman, womenfolk npl, *femme f, les femmes fpl*** 她变成~了。tā biànchéng ~ le. She's becoming a woman. *Elle devient femme.*

有个~每星期来为他们做一次家务。yǒu gè ~ měi xīngqī lái wèi tāmen zuò yícì jiāwù. They have a woman in once a week to do the cleaning. *Ils ont quelqu'un qui vient faire leur ménage une fois par semaine.*

女人 nǚren (2) [口] G, H1, S1 **wife, *femme f*** 她是他~。tā shì tā ~. She's his woman. *C'est sa femme.*

我最好还是问问我~是不是想来。wǒ zuìhǎo háishì wènwen wǒ ~ shìshíshì xiǎng lái. I'd better ask the wife if she wants to come. *Je ferais mieux de demander à ma bourgeoise si elle veut venir.*

O, P

欧元（歐元）ōuyuán * **euro, *euro m*** 我想把一百~换成人民币。wǒ xiǎng bǎ yìbǎi ~ huànchéng rénmínbì. I'd like to change a hundred euros into RMB (RenMin Bi). *Je voudrais changer cent euros en RMB (RenMin Bi).*

旁边（旁邊）pángbiān H2, S1 **side, *côté m*** 我在他~坐了下来。wǒ zài tā ~ zuò le xiàlái. I sat down at his side. *Je me suis assis à ses côtés.*

这个套房在花园~。zhè gè tàofáng zài huāyuán ~. It's a flat overlooking the garden. *C'est un appartement côté jardin.*

跑步 pǎo//bù H2, S2 **run, running, *courir, course f*** 我每天早上都去公园~。wǒ měitiān zǎoshàng dōu qù gōngyuán ~. I run every morning in the park. *Je cours tous les matins dans le parc.*

他~跑得累极了。tā ~ pǎo dé lèi jí le. He was exhausted from his running. *Il a été épuisé par sa course.*

朋友 péngyou G, H1, S1 **friend, *ami(e)*** 小田是我的好~。Xiao Tian is a good friend of mine. *Xiao Tian est un grand ami à moi.* 他是家里的~。He's a friend of the family. *C'est un ami de la famille.*

我们只是好~而已。We're just good friends. *Nous sommes bons amis, c'est tout!* 我们作为好~分手吧。Let us part friends. *Séparons-nous (en) bons amis.*

便宜 piányi H2, S1 **cheap, *bon marché*** 这很~。zhè hěn ~. It's cheap. *C'est bon marché.*

那个店主东西卖得很~。nà gè diànzhǔ dōngxi mài dé hěn ~. That shopkeeper is very cheap. *Ce commerçant n'est pas cher.* 那都是些低质量的~家具。nà dōu shì xiē dī zhìliàng de ~ jiājù. The furniture was cheap and nasty. *Ces meubles pas chers étaient de très mauvaise qualité.*

瓶 píng T, S1 **bottle, vase, _bouteille f,_ _vase m_** 一~多少钱? yì ~ duōshǎo qián? How much is it for a bottle? _C'est combien la bouteille?_

我们要了一~葡萄酒。wǒmen yào le yì ~ pútao jiǔ. We ordered a bottle of wine. _Nous avons commandé une bouteille de vin._ 这个花~真漂亮! zhè gè huā ~ zhēn piàoliang! What a beautiful vase! _Comme ce vase est joli!_

婆 pó T **husband's mother, a woman in a certain occupation, _mère du mari, femme dans certaine occupation_** 她是我~~。tā shì wǒ ~~. She's my husband's mother. _C'est la mère de mon mari._

她喜欢当媒~儿。tā xǐhuan dáng méi~r. She loves matchmaking. _Elle adore jouer les marieuses._ 别那么~~妈妈的! bié nàme ~~ māmā de! Don't be too sentimental! _Ne sois pas trop sentimental(le)!_

普通话 (普通話) pǔtōnghuà H3, S1 **Mandarin Chinese, common speech of Chinese, _chinois mandarin, langue chinoise commune_** 他(的)~说得很漂亮。tā (de) ~ shuō dé hěn piàoliang. He speaks beautiful Mandarin Chinese. _Il parle très bien le chinois mandarin._ ~ 是标准发音的中文。~ shì biāozhǔn fāyīn de zhōngwén. Mandarin / "common speech" is the standard Chinese. _Le mandarin / "le parlé commun" est le chinois standard._

七 qī H1, S1 **seven, _sept_** 火车行程(是)~个小时。huǒchē xíngchéng (shì) ~ gè xiǎoshí. The train journey takes seven hours. _Le voyage en train dure sept heures._

她心里~上八下，不知道如何是好。tā xīnlǐ ~ shàng bā xià, bùzhī rúhé shìhǎo. She was so agitated that she didn't know what to do. _Elle était tellement agitée qu'elle ne savait que faire._ 他已经~老八十了。tā yǐjīng ~ lǎo bā shí le. He's already very old. _Il est déjà très âgé._

妻子 qīzi H2, S2 **wife, _épouse f, femme f_** 这位是马丁先生和他的~。zhè wèi shì mǎdīng xiānsheng hé tā de ~. That's Mr Martin and his wife. _Ce sont M. Martin et son épouse._ 他有一个好~。tā yǒu yígè hǎo ~. She's been a good wife to him. _Elle a été une bonne épouse pour lui._

其 qí {书} D, S2 **his (her, its, their), he (she, it, they), _son, (leur), il(s) (elle[s], cela)_** 她是我同学，~父亲是商人。tā shì wǒde tóngxué, ~ fùqin shì shāngren. She's my schoolmate, her father is a businessman. _Elle est ma camarade de classe, son père est un homme d'affaires._

端这个盘子，将~放到桌子上。duān zhè gè pánzi, jiāng ~ fàngdào zhuōzi shàng. Take this plate and put it on the table. _Prenez cette assiette et mettez-la sur la table._

起 qǐ D, S1 **get up, rise, arouse, _se lever, éveiller_** ~床了! ~ chuáng le! Get up! _Lève-toi!_ ~

风了。~ fēng le. The wind is rising. *Le vent se lève.*

那个人奇怪的行为使她~了疑心。nàgè rén qíguàn de xíngwéi shǐ tā ~ le yíxīn. That man's strange behaviour aroused her suspicion(s). *Le comportement étrange de cet homme a éveillé ses soupçons.*

起床 qǐ chuáng H2, S1 **get up, *se lever*** ~ 了! le! Get up! *Lève-toi!* 我一般七点~。wǒ yìbān qī diǎn ~. I usually get up at seven. *J'ai l'habitude de me lever à sept heures.*

他周末不~，睡懒觉。tā zhōumò bù ~, shuì lǎnjiào. He doesn't get up, and stay in bed (very) late at / on the weekend. *Il ne se lève pas et fait la grasse matinée le week-end.*

起来（起來） qǐlái D, H5, S1 **stand up, get up, *se lever*** 请站~! qǐng zhàn ~! Stand up, please! *Levez-vous, s'il vous plaît!*

她站了~要要把位子让给我。tā zhànle ~ yào bǎ wèizi ràng gěi wǒ. She stood up to offer me her seat. *Elle s'est levée pour m'offrir sa place.* 他周末不~，睡懒觉。tā zhōumò bù ~, shuì lǎn jiào. He doesn't get up, and stay in bed (very) late at / on the weekend. *Il ne se lève pas et fait la grasse matinée le week-end.*

企业（企業） qǐyè N, H5, S2 **firm, company, business, *entreprise f, société f, entreprise f*** 这是一个制造~。zhè shì yígè zhìzào ~. It's a manufacturing firm. *C'est une entreprise de fabrication.* 这家~破产了。zhè jiā ~ pòchǎn le. The company has been put into liquidation. *La société a été mise en liquidation.*

他拥有一个小的汽车修理~。tā yōngyǒu yígè xiǎo de qìchē xiūlǐ ~. He owns a small car repair business. *Il a une petite entreprise de réparation de voitures.* 这一计划完全是私人~提供的资金。zhè yí jìhuà wánquán shì sīrén ~ tígōng de zījīn. The project is completely funded by private enterprises. *Le projet est totalement financé par des fonds privés.*

气（氣） qì (名) (1) T, S1 **gas, air, breath, *gaz m, air m, souffler, soulagement m*** 他用 煤~ / 天然~ 做饭。tā yòng méi~ / tiānrán~ zuòfàn. He uses gas for cooling. *Il fait la cuisine au gaz.* 让我先喘口~呀。ràng wǒ xiān chuǎn kǒu ~ ya. Give me time to draw breath. *Donne-moi le temps de souffler.*

这让人松了口~。zhè ràng rén sōngle kǒu ~. This was somewhat of a relief. *C'était en quelque sorte un soulagement.* 他一口~(没停)就说完了。

他一口 ~ (méi tíng) jiù shuōwán le. He said it all in one breath. *Il l'a dit d'un trait.*

气（氣） qì (动) (2) T, S1 **make angry, enrage, annoy, *furieux, taquiner, mettre hors de soi*** 我~得走开了。wǒ ~ dé zǒukāi le. Enraged, I left. *Furieux, je suis parti.* 别老~你妹妹。bié lǎo ~ nǐ mèimei. Stop annoying your little sister. *Cesse de taquiner ta petite sœur.*

他的无礼把我~坏了。tā de wúlǐ bǎ wǒ ~ huài le. His insolence made me very angry. *Son insolence m'a mis hors de moi.*

汽车（汽車） qìchē S1 **automobile, motor vehicle, car, *voiture f, automobile f, auto f*** 上~! shàng ~! Take your seats! *En voiture!* 咱们开~去。zánmen kāi ~ qù. We'll go by car. *Nous y allons en voiture.* ~在车库里。~ zài chēqù lǐ. The car is in the garage. *La voiture est dans le garage.*

千 qiān T, H2, S1 **thousand, *mille*** 这个要两~欧元。zhè gè yào liǎng~ ōuyuán. It costs two thousand euros. *Ça vaut deux mille euros.*

当时有数~人。dāngshí yǒu shù~ rén. There were thousands of people. *Il y avait des milliers de personnes.* 我喜欢看 "一~零一夜"。wǒ xǐhuan kàn "yì~ líng yī yè". I like reading the "Arabian Nights". *J'aime lire "Les Mille et une Nuits".*

签证（簽證） qiānzhèng H4, S2 **visa, *visa m*** 去中国需要~。qù zhōngguó xūyào ~. You need a visa to go to China. *Il faut un visa pour aller en Chine.* 他提出了申请去美国的~。tā tíchū le qù měiguó de ~. He has applied for an American visa. *Il a demandé un visa pour l'Amérique.*

钱（錢） qián H1, S1 **money, cash, *argent m*** 他(很)有~。tā (hěn) yǒu ~. He's got money. *Il a de l'argent.* 我身上从不带很多~。wǒ shēn shàng cóng bú dài hěnduō ~. I never carry much cash. *Je n'ai jamais beaucoup d'argent sur moi.*

你~也花得太多了。nǐ ~ yě huā dé tài duō le. You spent too much money. *Tu as dépensé trop d'argent.* 这个我们得花一大笔~。zhè gè wǒmen děi huā yí dà bǐ ~. It's going to cost us a considerable sum. *Ça va nous coûter très cher.*

前 qián D, S1 **front, ahead, ago, precedent, *devant, il y a + durée, précédent*** 往~看! wǎng ~ kàn! Look in front of you. *Regardez devant vous!* 一直朝~走! yìzhí wǎng ~ zǒu! Walk straight ahead! *Marchez tout droit devant vous!*

他们十年~搬到了这儿。tāmen shínián ~ bāndào le zhèr. They moved here ten years ago. *Ils ont emménagé ici il y a dix ans.* 这没有~例。zhè mèiyǒu ~lì. There's no precedent for it. *Il n'y en a point de précédent.*

前面 qiánmiàn H1, S1 **in front, ahead,** *devant,* 往~看! wǎng ~ kàn. Look in front of you. *Regardez devant vous!*

她在电视~坐着。tā zài diànshì ~ zuòzhe. She was sitting in front of the TV. *Elle était assise devant la télé.* 一直朝~走! yìzhí wǎng ~ zǒu. Walk straight ahead! *Marchez tout droit devant vous!*

晴 qíng H2, S2 **fine, clear (up),** *beau,* *(temps) se lever* 明天天~。míngtiān tiān ~. It will be fine tomorrow. *Il fera beau demain.* 天转~了。tiān zhuǎn ~ le. It's clearing up. *Le temps se lève.*

情况 (情況) qíngkuàng N, H4, S1 **situation,** *situation f, cas m* 他的~相似。He is in the same situation. *C'est également son cas.*

我的经济~不佳。wǒde jīngjì ~ bùjiā. My financial situation is none too healthy. *Ma situation financière n'est pas brillante.* 那得看~而定。nà děi kàn ~ ér dìng. That depends. *Ça dépend.*

请 (請) qǐng H1, S1 **please,** *s'il te / vous plait, veuille(z), je t'en prie / je vous en prie* ~进。~ jìn. Come in, please. *Entrez, s'il vous plaît.* ~坐。~ zuò. Please sit down. *Veuillez-vous asseoir.*

~不要插话! ~ búyào chā huà. Please don't interrupt! *Veuillez bien ne pas nous interrompre!* 我可以吗？--- ~吧! wǒ kěyǐ ma? -- ~ ba! May I? – Please do. *Vous permettez? – Je vous en prie!*

去 qù D, H1, S1 **go,** *aller* 我们~西班牙。wǒmen ~ xībānyá. We're going to Spain. *Nous allons en Espagne.* 他到一个朋友家~了。tā dào yígè péngyou jiā ~ le. He went to a friend's house. *Il est allé chez un ami.*

我们是 开车~的 / 走着~的。wǒmen shì kāichē ~ de / zǒuzhe ~ de. We went by car / on foot. *Nous sommes allés en voiture / à pied.* 上~! shàng ~! Going up! *On monte!* 咱们进~! zánmen jìn ~! Let's go in! *Entrons!* 让他睡觉~。ràng tā shuìjiào ~! Let him sleep / Leave him to sleep. *Laisse-le dormir.*

去年 qùnián H2, S1 **last year,** *l'année dernière* 公司是~成立的。gōngsī shì ~ chénglì de. The company was set up last year. *La société a été établie l'année dernière.*

我是~年初开始学习中文的。wǒ shì ~ niánchū kāishǐ xué zhōngwén de. I began to learn Chinese at the beginning of last year. *J'ai commencé à apprendre le chinois au début de l'année dernière.*

全国 (全國) quánguó N, S1 **the whole country, nationwide,** *tout le pays, la nation tout entière* 他下月参加~运动会。tā xiàyuè cānjiā ~ yùndònghuì. He'll take part in the national games next month. *Il participera aux jeux nationaux le mois prochain.*

~人仍在问谁是杀人犯。~ rén réng zài wèn shéi shì shārénfàn. The whole country's still wondering who the murder might be. *Tout le pays se demande encore qui est l'assassin.* 这一讲话是在~播放的。zhè yí jiǎnghuà shì zài ~ bō fàng de. The speech was broadcast nationwide. *Le discours a été diffusé dans tout le pays.*

群众 (群眾) qúnzhòng N, H6, S1 **the masses,** *les masses fpl* 大多数~ / ~的大多数拥护这一(个 / 项)政策。dà duōshù ~ / ~ de dà duōshù yōnghù zhè yí (gè / xiàng) zhèngcè. The mass of the people are in favour of this policy. *La majorité des gens est favorable à cette politique.*

38

Personne n'est parfait. 他正是我需要的~。 tā zhèng shì wǒ xūyào de ~. He's just the man for me. *C'est l'homme qu'il me faut.*

人家 rénjia G, H6, S1 **everybody else,** *tous les autres* 这件事~都知道。 zhè jiàn shí ~ dōu shīdao. Everybody else knows that. *Tous les autres le savent.*

我(去)把椅子还给~去。 wǒ (qù) bǎ yǐzi huángěi ~ qù. I'll give the chair back to him / her / them. *Je lui / leur rendrai la chaise.* 你把~吓了一大跳! nǐ bǎ ~ xià le yí dà tiào. You gave me a terrible fright! *Tu m'as vraiment fait peur!*

人民 rénmín N, S1 **people,** *peuple m* 权利属于~。 quánlì shǔyú ~. Power belongs to the people. *Le pouvoir revient au peuple.* 这是一个~的政府。 zhèshì yígè ~ de zhèngfǔ. It's a government by the people. *C'est un gouvernement par le peuple.*

他声称代表~的声音。 tā shēngchēng dàibiǎo ~ de shēngyīn. He claims to be the voice of the people. *Il se fait passer pour la voix du peuple.*

人民币（人民幣） rénmínbì H4, S1 **Renminbi (RMB) / Chinese Yuan (CNY),** *Renminbi (RMB) / Yuan chinois (CNY)* 你们接受~吗? nǐmen jiēshòu ~ ma? Do you accept Renminbi (RMB)? *Vous acceptez Renminbi (RMB)?* 姚女士为这一事业捐赠了五十万元~ / 五百千元~。 yáo nǚshì wèi zhè yí shìyè juānzèng le wǔshí-wàn yuán ~ / wǔbǎi qiān yuán ~. Ms Yao contributed 500 000 yuan (CNY) to the cause. *Mme Yao a versé 500 000 yuan (CNY) au profit de la cause.*

人员（人員） rényuán H5, S1 **staff,** *personnel m* 工作~有多少? gōngzuò ~ yǒu duōshao? How many people are there on the staff? *Combien de personnes le personnel compte-t-il?*

他去年成了工作~。 tā qùnián chéng le gōngzuò ~. He joined the staff last year. *Il est entré dans le personnel l'année dernière.*

认识（認識） rènshi H1, S1 **know, meet, understand,** *connaître, connaissance f, (se) comprendre* ~您很高兴! ~ nín hěn gāoxìng. Very pleased to meet you! *Très heureux de faire votre connaissance!*

他小的时候我就~他了。 tā xiǎo de shíhòu wǒ jiù ~ tā le. I knew him when he was a child. *Je l'ai connu tout petit.* 对这个有不同的~(方式)。 duì zhège yǒu bùtóng de ~ (fāngshì). This can be

然 rán D **right, correct, like that,** *juste, correct, comme cela* 我(对他)不以为~。 wǒ (duì tā) bù yǐ wéi ~. I don't agree (with him). *Je ne suis pas d'accord (avec lui).*

这个人知其~, 不知其所以~。 zhè gè rén zhī qí ~, bù zhī qí suǒyǐ ~. That person knows the hows, but not the whys. *Cette personne sait le comment, mais non le pourquoi.*

然后（然後） ránhòu G, H3, S1 **then, afterwards,** *puis, ensuite* (你)先向右拐, ~向左拐。 (nǐ) xiān xiàng yòu guai, ~ xiàng zuǒ guǎi. Turn right (and) then left. *Tourne à droite puis à gauche.*

~他们回家去了。 ~ tāmen huíjiā qù le. Afterwards they went home. *Ils sont rentrés ensuite chez eux.*

热（熱） rè H1, S1 **hot, warm,** *chaud, plein (de cœur)* 今天很~。 jīntiān hěn ~. It's hot today. *Il fait très chaud aujourd'hui.* 你的茶不够~。 nǐ de chá bú gòu ~. Your tea is barely warm. *Ton thé est à peine chaud.*

她是个~心人。 tā shì gè ~xīn rén. She is very warm-hearted. *Elle est pleine de cœur.*

人 rén D, H1, S1 **human being, man, person, people,** *homme m, être humain, personne f, gens mpl* 她~很好。 tā ~ hěn hǎo. She's very nice. *Elle est très sympa.*

他不可能是十全十美的~。 tā bù kěnéng shì shíquán shíměi de ~. He's only human / Nobody's perfect. *Il est humain, après tout /*

understood in several ways. *Cela peut se comprendre de plusieurs façons.*

认为 (認為) rènwéi N, H3, S1 **think, consider, *penser, croire*** 说这种事儿她~不好。 shuō zhèzhǒng shìr tā ~ bùhǎo. She considers it wrong to say such thing. *Elle pense qu'il est mauvais de dire de telles choses.*

最好就此为止，您不这样~吗? zuì hǎo jiùcǐ wéizhǐ, nǐ bú zhèyàng ~ ma? It's better, don't you think, to get it over? *Il vaut mieux en finir, vous ne croyez pas?*

日 rì H1, S1 **sun, day, *soleil, m, journée f***

~出了 / 落了。 ~ chū le / luò le. The sun is rising / setting. *Le soleil se lève / se couche.*

我们在海边过了一~。 wǒmen zài hǎibiān guò le yí~. We had a day at the seaside. *Nous sommes passés une journée au bord de la mer.* 来~见! lái ~ jiàn! *See you later! A bientôt!*

日报 (日報) rìbào S1 **daily paper, daily, *quotidien m*** 我常常 看 / 读 这个~。 wǒ chángcháng kàn / dú zhège~. I often read this daily (paper). *Je lis souvent ce quotidien.*

这是一家全国~。 zhèshì yìjiā quánguó ~. It's a (major) national daily. *C'est un grand quotidien.*

日本 rìběn N **Japan, *Japon m*** ~首都是东京。 ~ shǒudū shì gōngjīng. The capital of Japan is Tokyo. *La capitale du Japon est Tokyo.*

我母亲明天从~回来。 wǒ mǔqin míngtiān cóng ~ huílái. My mother is coming back from Japan tomorrow. *Ma mère reviendra du Japon demain.* 我喜欢吃~饭。 wǒ xǐhuan chī ~ fàn. I love Japanese cuisine. *J'adore la cuisine japonaise.*

如 rú D, S2 **as good as, obedience, for example, *aussi bien que, au doigt et à l'œil, par exemple*** 我不~他。 wǒ bù ~ tā. I'm not as good as he is. *Je ne suis pas aussi bien que lui.*

人对他事事~命。 rén duì tā shìshì ~ mìng. He commands strict obedience. *On lui obéit au doigt et à l'œil.* 愿万事~意。 yuàn wàn shì ~ yì. All good wishes / Every good wish. *Tous mes vœux.* 这一地区有猛兽，~狮子。 zhèyí dìqū yǒu měngshòu, ~ shīzi. There are big cats in the region, for example the lion. *Il y a des fauves dans la région, par exemple le lion.*

如果 rúguǒ G, H3, S1 **if, *si*** 你~陪着我就去。 nǐ ~ péizhe wǒ jiù qù. I'll go if you come with me. *J'irai si tu m'accompagnes.*

我~事先知道，本来就去看他们了。 wǒ ~ shìxiān zhīdao, běnlái jiù qù kàn tāmen le. If I had known, I would have visited them. *Si j'avais su, je leur aurais rendu visite.*

三 sān H1, S1 **three, *trois*** 今天~月十~号。 jīntiān ~ yuè shíyī hào. Today is March 13th. *Aujourd'hui est le 13 mars.*

他~点~十走。 tā ~ diǎn sānshí zǒu. He leaves at thirty past three. *Il part à trois heures trente.* 别~心二意了! bié ~ xīn èr yì le! Stop shilly-shallying (around)! *Décide-toi enfin!*

商店 shāngdiàn H1, S1 **shop, *magasin m*** 她出门去~了。 tā chūmén qù ~ le. She's gone out to the shops. *Elle est allée au magasin faire des courses.*

你能为我管几个小时~吗? nǐ néng wèi wǒ guǎn jǐgè xiǎoshí ~ ma? Would you mind keeping the shop for me for a few hours? *Est-ce que tu veux bien me tenir le magasin pendant quelques heures?*

上 shàng (动) (1) D, H4, S1 **go up, be at (school), put down, begin, just, *monter, être à (une école), sur, commencer, de justesse*** 我~床睡觉。 wǒ ~ chuáng shuì jiào. I'm going up to bed. *Je monte me coucher.* 咱们坐电梯~楼。 zánmen zuò diàntī ~ lóu. Let's go up in the lift. *On va monter par l'ascenseur.* 他在~大学。 tā zài ~ dàxué. He's now at college. *Il est maintenant à l'université.*

她摆~了一个花瓶。 tā bǎi ~ le yígè huāpíng. She has put down a flower vase. *Elle y a posé un vase.* 不久就下~雨了。 bù jiǔ jiù xià ~ yǔ le. It soon began to rain. *Il n'a pas tardé à pleuvoir.* 我到底赶~了 / 差一点儿没赶~。wǒ dàotǐ gǎn~ le / chà yìdiǎr méi gǎn ~. I caught it just in time. *Je l'ai rattrapé de justesse.*

上 shàng (名) (2) D, H4, S1 **last, first, above, dernier, premier, au-dessus de** 他们是~星期一来的。tāmen shì ~ xīngqī yī lái de. They came last Monday. *Ils sont venus lundi dernier.* 他~半年病了。tā ~ bànnián bìng le. He was ill during the first six months. *Il a été malade durant les six premiers mois.* 她是中~水平。tā shì zhōng~ shuǐpíng. She's above the average. *Elle est au-dessus du moyen.*

上班 shàngbān H2, S1 **go to work, start work, be on duty, aller au travail / au bureau** 我每天骑车~。wǒ měitiān qíchē ~. I cycle to work every day. *Je vais au travail en vélo tous les jours.* 她星期三不~。tā xīngqī sān bú ~. She has Wednesdays off. *Elle a congé / Elle ne travaille pas le mercredi.*

上午 shàngwǔ H1, S1 **morning, matinée f, matin m** 我整个(一)~都没看见他。wǒ zhěnggè (yí) ~ dōu méi kànjiàn tā. I haven't seen him all morning. *Je ne l'ai pas vu de toute la matinée.* 邮递员每天~过。yóudìyuán měitiān ~ guò. The postman comes every morning. *Le facteur passe tous les matins.* ~有一个航班。~ yǒu yígè hángbān. There's a flight in the morning. *Il y a un vol dans la matinée.*

上学 (上學) shàngxué S1 **go to school, attend school, be at school, aller à l'école, être à l'école** 你在哪个学校~? nǐ zài nǎgè xuéxiào ~? Which school do you go to? *Quelle école fréquentes-tu?* 我还在~。wǒ hái zài ~. I'm still at school. *Je vais encore à l'école.* 今天不~。jīntiān bú ~. There's no school today. *Il n'y a pas (d')école aujourd'hui.* 我~时跟他同班。wǒ ~ shí gēn tā tóngbān. I was in the same class with him when I was at school. *J'étais dans la même classe avec lui quand j'étais à l'école.*

少 shǎo H1, S1 **few, little, less, lack of, peu, peu nombreux, manquer** 我们人很~。wǒmén rén hěn ~. We are few (in number). *Nous sommes peu nombreux.* 她因为睡得太~所以很累。tā yīnwéi shuì dé tài ~ suǒyǐ hěn lèi. She was tired from lack of sleep. *Elle était fatiguée de n'avoir pas assez dormi.* 他们什么都不~。tāmen shénme dōu bù ~. They lack for nothing. *Ils ne manquent de rien.*

社会 (社會) shèhuì N, H4, S1 **society, société f** 这对~造成了危险。zhè duì ~ zàochéng le wēixiǎn. It is a danger to society. *Cela constitue un danger pour la société.* 我们生活在一个多元文化的~里。wǒmen shēnghuó zài yígè duōyuán wénhuà de ~ lí. We live in a multicultural society. *Nous vivons dans une société multiculturelle.*

谁 (誰) shéi//shuí H1, S1 **who, someone, anyone, qui, quelqu'un, quiconque** 他是~? tā shì ~? Who is he? *Qui est-ce, lui?* ~跟你去? ~ gēn nǐ qù? Who's going with you? *Qui est-ce qui t'accompagne?* 你把自己当成~了? nǐ bǎ zìjǐ dāngchéng ~ le? Who do you think you are? *Tu te prends pour qui?* ~把雨伞忘了。~ bǎ yǔsǎn wàng le. Somebody has left their umbrella behind. *Quelqu'un a oublié son parapluie.* 我的两个兄弟~也不能来。wǒde liǎnggè xiōngdì ~ yě bù néng lái. Neither of my brothers can come. *Aucun de mes deux frères ne peut venir.*

身份证 (身份證) shēnfènzhèng S1 **identity card, carte d'identité** 您有~吗? nín yǒu ~ ma? Have you got any ID? *Est-ce que vous avez une pièce d'identité?* 我能看一下您的~吗? wǒ néng kàn yíxià nín de ~ ma? (Can I see) your identity card, please. *(Puis-je voir) votre carte d'identité, s'il vous plaît.*

身体 (身體) shēntǐ G, H2, S1 **body, health, santé f** 您~好吗? nín ~ hǎo ma? How are you? *Comment allez-vous?* 他~总是很(虚)弱。tā ~ zǒngshì hěn (xū)ruò. His health has never been good. *Il a toujours été fragile.* 抽烟会损坏你的~。chōuyān huì sǔnhuài nǐ de ~. Smoking is bad for your health. *Le tabac est mauvais pour ta santé.*

什么 (什麽) shénme G, H1, S1 **(1) what, something, que, quoi, quel; (2)** 什么都 (没 / 不) **everything (nothing), tout (rien)** 这是~? zhè shì ~? What's that? *Qu'est-ce que c'est (que ça)?* 告诉我发生了~事。gàosù wǒ fāshēng le ~ shì. Tell me what's happened. *Dites-moi ce qui s'est passé.* 我给你带来了点儿~来。wǒ gěi nǐ dàilái le diǎr ~ lái. I've brought you a little something. *Je t'ai apporté un petit quelque chose.* ~都没决定。~ dōu méi juédìng. Nothing has been decided. *Rien n'a été décidé.* 他们~都卖。tāmen ~ dōu mài. They sell everything. *Ils vendent de tout.*

生病 shēng bìng H2, S1 **fall ill, *tomber malade*** 她~了。tā ~ le. She's ill. *Elle est malade.* 去年他生了一场大病。qùnián tā shēng le yìchàng dà bìng. He was seriously ill last year. *Il a fait une grave maladie l'année dernière.* 你没有~还是怎么了? nǐ méiyǒu ~ hái shì zěnme le? Are you sick in the head or something? *Tu n'es pas un peu malade ?*

生产（生產）shēngchǎn N, H5, S1 **production, produce, output, *fabriquer, production f, produire*** 我在~线上工作。wǒ zài ~ xàn shàng gōngzuò. I work on a production line. *Je travaille à la chaîne.*

我们工厂~洗衣机零件。wǒmen gōngchǎng ~ xǐyījī língjiàn. Our factory produces spare parts for washing machines. *Notre usine fabrique des pièces détachées pour machines à laver.* 我们的~赶不上我们的需要。wǒmen de ~ gǎn búshàng wǒmen de xūyào. Our output is lower than our needs. *Notre production est inférieure à nos besoins.*

生日 shēngrì H2, S1 **birthday, *anniversaire m*** ~快乐! ~ kuàilè! Happy birthday! *Joyeux anniversaire!*

他们为我的~要搞一个聚会。tāmen wèi wǒ de ~ yào gǎo yígè jùhuì. They're giving me a birthday party. *Ils organisent une fête pour mon anniversaire.*

声音（聲音）shēngyīn G, H3, S1 **sound, voice, *son m, bruit m, voix f*** 听得出是你的~。tīng dé chū shì nǐde ~. It recognizes the sound of your voice. *On reconnaît le son de ta voix.* 别出~! bié chū ~. Don't make noise! *Ne fais pas de bruit!*

今晚我们将听到世界最美的~之一。jīnwǎn wǒmen jiāng tīngdào shìjiè zuìměi de ~ zhīyī. Tonight we welcome one of the finest voices in the world. *Nous accueillons ce soir une des plus belles voix du monde.*

十 shí H1, S1 **ten, *dix*** 我在~号房间。wǒ zài ~ hào fángjiān. I'm in the room number 10. *Je suis dans la chambre N° 10.*

[3 X 10 = 30] 三乘以~等于三~。sān chéngyǐ ~ děngyú sānshí. Three tens are thirty. *Trois fois dix font trente.* 她的演出达到了~全~美(的境地)。tā de yǎnchū dádào le ~ quán ~ měi (de jìngdì). Her performance attained the acme of perfection. *Son interprétation est arrivée à la perfection même.*

时（時）shí D, S1 **hour, when, time, presently, *heure f, quand, moment m, actuellement*** 我们上午八~出发。wǒmen shàngwǔ bā ~ chūfā. We're leaving at 8 o'clock in the morning. *On part à 8 heures du matin.*

他二十岁~离开了城市。tā èrshí suì ~ líkāi le chéngshì. He left town when he was twenty. *Il a quitté la ville quand il avait vingt ans.* 那~我根本不知道。nà~ wǒ gēnběn bù zhīdào. I didn't know it at the time. *Je n'en savais rien à ce moment-là.* ~下她在写一部新小说。~xià tā zài xiě yíbù xīn xiǎoshuō. She's presently working on a new novel. *Elle travaille actuellement à un nouveau roman.*

时候（時候）shíhou H1, S1 **time, when, *temps m, quand, lorsque*** 你用了多少~啦! nǐ yòng le duōshǎo ~ la? You took your time about it! *Tu en as mis du temps!* 现在是什么~了? xiànzài shì shénme ~ le? What time is it now? *Quelle heure est-il maintenant?*

我十八岁的~离开了城市。wǒ shíbā suì de ~ líkāi le chéngshì. I left town when I was eighteen. *J'ai quitté la ville quand j'avais dix-huit ans.* 他就是疼的~也不说。tā jiùshì téng de ~ yě bù shuō. Though he is in pain, he says nothing. *Même lorsqu'il souffre, il ne le dit pas.*

时间（時間）shíjiān N, G, H2, S1 **(how) long, time, *temps m*** 他在这儿多长~了? tā zài zhèr duōcháng ~ le? How long has he been here? *Depuis combien de temps est-il ici?* ~过得太快了! ~ guò dé tài kuài le. Doesn't time fly! *Comme le temps passe vite!*

这是和~赛跑。zhè shì hé ~ sàipǎo. It's a race against time. *C'est une course contre le temps.*

实（實）shí D **straight, honest and sincere, solid, actual, real, *franc, honnête et sincère, au fond, exact, réel*** ~说! ~ shuō! Talk straight! *Parle franchement!* 他人很~。tā rén hěn ~. He's honest and sincere. *Il est honnête et sincère.*

池塘结冰结得很~。chítáng jiébīng jié dé hěn ~. That's a pond frozen solid. *C'est un étang gelé jusqu'au fond.* 这是个~数。zhè shì gè ~shù. That's the actual number / a real number. *C'est le nombre exact / un nombre réel.*

实习（實習）shíxí H5, S1 **internship, training, *stage m*** 他在一家公司~。He is doing an internship in a company. *Il fait un stage en entreprise.* 我们将进行三个月的~。

We'll do a three-month training period. *Nous ferons un stage de trois mois.*

是 shì D, H1, S1 **be, *être*** 他们~谁? tāmen ~ shéi? Who are they? *Qui sont-ils?* 她~我妹妹。tā ~ wǒ mèimei. She's my little sister. *Elle est ma petite sœur.*

他穿的~蓝(色)的。tā chuān de ~ lán(sè) de. He is dressed in blue. *Il est habillé en bleu.* 她这样做完全~一片好心。tā zhèyàng zuò wánquán ~ yípiàn hǎoxīn. She acted with the best and most honourable intentions. *Elle a agi en tout bien (et) tout honneur.* 桌子上 ~ / 有 几本书。zhuōzi shàng ~ / yǒu jǐběn shū. There are some books on the table. *Il y a des livres sur la table.*

是不是 shì bu shì S1 (= 是否 shìfǒu) **whether or not, whether, if, *oui ou non, si*** 你~同意? nǐ ~ tóngyì? Do you agree? *Es-tu d'accord?* 小王~来过了? xiǎo wáng ~ lái guò le? Did Xiao Wang come earlier? *Est-ce que Xiao Wang était déjà venu?* 我去看看她~起床了。wǒ qù kànkan tā ~ qǐchuáng le. I'll see if she's up yet. *Je vais voir si elle est levée.*

市场 (市場) shìchǎng N, H4, S1 **market, *marché m*** 咱们 到 / 上 ~去。zánmen dào / shàng ~ qù. Let's go to (the) market. *Allons au marché.*

这是~上最经济的汽车。zhè shì ~ shàng zuì jīngjìde qìchē. It's the most economical car on the market. *C'est la voiture la plus économique dans le marché.* 这些产品没有~。zhè xiē chǎnpǐn méiyǒu ~. There's no market for these products. *Ces produits ne se vendent pas.*

世界 shìjiè N, H3, S1 **world, *monde m, planète f*** 她想改变~。tā xiǎng gǎibiàn ~. She wants to change the world. *Elle veut changer le monde.*

这个消息震动了全~。zhège xiāoxi zhèndòng le quán ~. The news shook the world. *La nouvelle a ébranlé le monde entier.* 我们生活在不同的~上。wǒmen shēnghuó zài bùtóng de ~ shàng. We live in different worlds. *Nous ne vivons pas sur la même planète.*

事 shì S1 **matter, affair, thing, accident, case, *chose f, histoire f, accident m, affaire f*** 我有~(儿) / 事情。wǒ yǒu ~(r) / shìqing. I'm busy. *Je suis occupé.* ~(儿) / 事情 不要紧。~(r) / shìqing bú yàojǐn. 这是小~(儿) / 小事情 一桩。zhè shì xiǎo~(r) / shìqing yìzhuāng. It's no great matter. *Ce n'est pas grand-chose.*

~很糟糕。~ hěn zāogāo. It was a sorry affair. *C'était une histoire lamentable.* 你把~(儿) / 事情看得太重了。nǐ bǎ ~r / shìqing kàn dé tài zhòng le. You take things too seriously. *Tu prends les choses trop au sérieux.* 她儿子开车出~了。tā érzi kāichē chū~ le. Her son had a car accident. *Son fils a eu un accident de voiture.* 案子里也有他的~吗? ànzi lǐ yě yǒu tā de ~ ma? Was he involved in the case too? *Etait-il aussi impliqué dans l'affaire?*

事情 shìqing G, H5, S1 (= 事 shì) **matter, affair, thing, accident, case, *chose f, histoire f, accident m, affaire f*** 小~一桩。Xiǎo ~ yìzhuāng. It's no great matter. *Ce n'est pas grand-chose.*

~看来很糟糕。~ kànlái hěn zāo. It seemed a sorry affair. *Il semblait une histoire lamentable.* 你把~(儿) / 事情 看得太重了。nǐ bǎ ~r / shìqing kàn dé tài zhòng le. You take things too seriously. *Tu prends les choses trop au sérieux.* 她开车出~了。tā kāichē chū~ le. She had a car accident. *Elle a eu un accident de voiture.*

手表 (手錶) shǒubiǎo H2, S1 **wrist watch, *montre-bracelet*** 我的~十二点了。wǒ de ~ shí'èr diǎn le. By my watch it's midday. *A ma montre, il est midi.*

你的~慢了。nǐ de ~ màn le. Your watch is slow. *Ta montre retarde.* 您的~快了十分钟。nín de ~ kuài le shí fēnzhōng. Your watch is / You are 10 minutes fast. *Votre montre avance / Vous avancez de 10 minutes.*

手机 (手機) shǒujī H2, S1 **mobile, mobile phone, *portable m*** 打他~。Call him on his mobile. *Appelle-le sur son portable.* 我打(给)你的~。I'll call you on your mobile phone. *Je t'appellerai sur ton portable.*

手续 (手續) shǒuxù H5, S1 **formality, *formalité f*** ~很简单。~ hěn jiǎndān. It's a mere formality. *C'est une simple formalité.* 我去办理必要的~。wǒ qù bànlǐ bìyào de ~. I'll go through required formalities. *Je vais régler toutes les formalités requises.*

书 (書) shū H1, S1 **book, *livre m*** 我喜欢看~。wǒ xǐhuan kàn ~. I like reading. *J'aime la lecture.* 这是一本中文~。zhèshì yìběn zhōngwén ~. It's a book in Chinese. *C'est un livre en chinois.*

你看这本~了吗? (写得)好极了。nǐ kàn zhè běn ~ le ma? (xiě dé) hǎo jí le. Have you read this book? It's great. *Tu as lu ce livre? Il est génial.*

书记 (書記) shūji G, H6 **clerk, secretary, *employé(e), secrétaire nmf*** 他在公司当~。He clerks in the company. *Il travaille comme employé de bureau dans l'entreprise.*

老李是党委~。Lao Li is the secretary of the Party committee. *Lao Li est le secrétaire du comité du parti.* 联合国总~会见了我国总理。liánhéguó zǒng ~ huìjiàn le wǒguó zǒnglǐ. The General Secretary of the United nations met our prime minister. *Le Secrétaire général des Nations-Unies a rencontré notre premier ministre.*

刷 shuā T, S2 **scour, whitewash, eliminate, *récurer, blanchir, éliminer*** 好好地~一~平底锅。hǎohāo de ~ yì ~ píngdǐguō. Give the pans a good scour. *Récurez bien les casseroles.*

这个周末我得~墙。zhè gè zhōumò wǒ děi ~ qiáng. I'll whitewash the walls this week-end. *Je vais blanchir les murs à la chaux ce week-end.* 他们到 / 在 半决赛给~了下来。tāmen dào / zài bàn juésài gěi ~ le xiàlái. They were eliminated in the semifinal. *Ils ont été éliminés en demi-finale.*

双 (雙) shuāng T, H3, S1 **two, pair, double, *deux, paire f, double m*** 这是条~向马路。zhè shì tiáo ~xiàng mǎlù. It's a two-way street. *Ça marche dans les deux sens.* 这~手套是我的。zhè ~ shǒutào shì wǒ de. The pair of gloves are mine. *La paire de gants est à moi.*

他要是干夜班就能拿~份儿工资。tā yàoshì gàn yèbān jiù néng ná ~ fèr gōngzī. They pay him double if he works nights. *On le paie (au tarif) double s'il travaille la nuit.*

水 shuǐ H1, S1 **water, *eau f*** 这儿的~ / 这种 ~ 可以喝吗? zhèr de ~ / zhè zhǒng ~ kěyǐ hē ma? Is the water safe to drink? *Est-ce que l'eau est potable?* 我喝了(杯)~。wǒ hē le (bēi) ~. I took a drink of water. *J'ai bu de l'eau / un verre d'eau.*

我鞋子进~了。wǒ xiézi jìn ~ le. My shoes let in water. *Mes chaussures prennent l'eau.* 我流口~了。wǒ liú kǒu ~ le. My mouth is watering. *J'en ai l'eau à la bouche.*

水果 shuǐguǒ H2, S1 **fruit, *fruit m*** 您想吃(个)~吗? nǐ xiǎng chī (gè) ~ ma? Would you like some fruit? *Prendrez-vous un fruit?*

递给我一个~。dì gěi wǒ yígè ~. Pass me a piece of fruit. *Passe-moi un fruit.* 这个~有核儿。zhè gè ~ yǒu hér. It's a stone fruit. *C'est un fruit à noyau.* 多吃些~! duō chī xiē ~! Eat more fruit! *Mangez plus de fruits!*

睡 shuì T, S1 **sleep, *dormir, se coucher*** 好好~! hǎohāo ~! Sleep tight! *Dors bien!* ~得好吗? ~ dé hǎo ma? Did you sleep well? *Tu as bien dormi?*

是我不让你~吗? shì wǒ bú ràng nǐ ~ ma? Am I keeping you up? *Je t'empêche de te coucher?* 我只~了两个小时。wǒ zhǐ ~ le liǎnggè xiǎoshí. I only had two hours' sleep. *Je n'ai dormi que deux heures.* 她~得很沉。tā ~ dé hěn chén. She slept through the storm. *La tempête ne l'a pas réveillée.*

睡觉 (睡覺) shuìjiào H1, S1 **sleep, *dormir, se coucher*** ~的时间到了。~ de shíjiān dào le. It's bedtime. *Il est l'heure d'aller se coucher.* 她在~。tā zài ~. She's asleep. *Elle dort.*

别在办公桌上~! 把腰挺直! bié zài bàngōngzhuō shàng ~! bǎ yāo tǐngzhí! Don't slouch over your desk! Set up straight! *Ne te couche pas sur ton bureau! Tiens-toi droit!* 我周末常常睡懒觉。wǒ zhōumò chángcháng shuì lǎn jiào. I often have a long lie (on) weekends. *Je fais souvent la grasse matinée le week-end.*

顺 (順) shùn T, S2 **down, follow, polish, yield to, yours..., *au fil de, suivre, poli, céder, veuillez agréer...*** 小船~流而下。xiǎochuán ~ liú ér xià. The boat drifted downstream. *La barque dérivait au fil de l'eau.* ~着箭头走。~ zhe jiàntóu zǒu. Follow the arrows. *Suivez les flèches.*

他的举止需要~一~。tā de jǔzhǐ yào ~ yí ~. His style needs polishing. *Son style manque de poli.* 这一点我只能~着他们了。zhè yì diǎn wǒ shǐ néng ~zhe tāmen le. I had to yield to them on that point. *J'ai dû leur céder sur ce point.* ~致崇高的敬意。~ zhì chónggāo de jìngyì. Yours faithfully / sincerely / truly. *Veuillez agréer mes sentiments distingués.*

说 (說) shuō D, S1 **speak, talk, say, *parler, dire*** 大 / 小 点儿声~。dà / xiǎo diǎr shēng ~. Speak louder / Don't speak so loud. *Parle plus fort / Parle moins fort.*

整个晚上她一句话也没跟我~。zhěnggè wǎnshang tā yíjù huà yě méi gēn wǒ ~. She never talked to me the whole evening. *Elle ne m'a pas dit un mot de la soirée.* 您只要~一句话

就是了。nǐ zhǐyào ~ yíjù huà jiù shì le. You have only to say the word. *Vous n'avez qu'à le dire.* 这个很容易~明白。zhège hěn róngyì ~ míngbai. That is easily explained. *Cela s'explique facilement.* 他撒谎叫母亲~了(他)一顿。tā sāhuǎng jiào mǔqin ~ le (tā) yīdùn. He got a good scolding from this mother for lying. *Il s'est fait attraper par sa mère pour avoir menti.*

说话（說話）shuōhuà H1, S1 **speak, talk, say, *parler, dire*** 别~! bié ~! Do not speak! *Ne parlez pas!* 她来说了~。tā lái shuōle ~. She came over for a chat. *Elle est venue bavarder un peu.*

不要听别人说闲话。búyào tīng biérén shuō xiánhuà. Don't listen to gossip. *N'écoutez pas les racontars.*

四 sì H1, S1 **four, *quatre*** ~五二十。~ wǔ èrshí. Four fives are twenty. *Quatre fois cinq font vingt.*

我这是第~次给你打电话。wǒ zhèshì dì~ cì gěi nǐ dǎ diànhuà. It's the fourth time I've called you. *C'est la quatrième fois que je t'appelle.* 我们~点半喝茶。wǒmen ~diǎn bàn hēchá. We have tea at half past four. *Nous prenons le thé à quatre heures et demie.*

送 sòng H2, S1 **see sb off, give, deliver, *dire au revoir, offrir, livrer*** 她来火车站~了我。tā lái huǒchēzhàn ~ le wǒ. She came to see me off at the station. *Elle est venue à la gare me dire au revoir.*

小李生日时我们~他一个光盘吧。xiǎo lǐ shēngrì shí wǒmen ~ tā yígè guāngpán ba. We could give Xiao Li a CD for his birthday. *On pourrait offrir un CD à Xiao Li pour son anniversaire.* 您想叫人把报纸~上门吗? nín xiǎng jiào rén bǎ bàozhǐ ~ shàng mén ma? Do you want your newspaper (to be) delivered? *Est-ce que vous voulez qu'on vous livre votre journal?*

虽（雖）suī S2 S2 **although, though, *quoique, bien que*** 他~阔，但不大方。Although rich, he was hardly generous. *Quoique riche, il n'était guère généreux.*

她~不漂亮，但很可爱。tā ~ bú piàoliang, dàn hěn kě'ài. Though not handsome, she was attractive. *Sans être belle, elle avait du charme.* 她房子~小，但很舒适。tā fángzi ~ xiǎo, dàn hěn shūshì. Small though it is, her house is nice. *Sa maison, bien que petite, est agréable.*

岁（歲）suì T, H1, S1 **year of age, *âge m, an m*** 小朋友, 你几~了? xiǎo péngyou, nǐ jǐ ~ le? The boy / The girl, how old are you? *Le petit / La petite, quel âge as-tu?* --- 他多大了? --- 他 22 ~了。-- tā duōdà le? -- èrshí'èr ~ le. -- How old is he? -- He is 22 (years old). -- *Quel âge a-t-il? -- Il a 22 ans.*

他们是五十~开外的人。tāmen shì wǔshí ~ kāiwài de rén. They're people over the age of 50. *Ce sont les gens de plus de 50 ans.*

所 suǒ T, H5, S1 **place, [classifier], [auxiliary word], *lieu m, [classificateur m], [mot auxiliaire]*** 这是我的住~。zhè shì wǒde zhù ~. It's my place of residence. *C'est le lieu de résidence que j'ai.* 那是一~儿童医院。nà shì yì ~ értóng yīyuàn. That's a children's hospital. *Là c'est un hôpital pour enfants.*

她被他的体贴~感动。tā bèi tā de tǐtiē ~ gǎndòng. She was touched by his thoughtfulness. *Elle est touchée par sa délicatesse.* 我要把这个交给税务~。wǒ yào bǎ zhègè jiāo gěi shuìwù~. I have to send this to the tax office. *Je dois envoyer ça au centre des impôts.*

所以 suǒyǐ G, H2, S1 **that's why, therefore, *c'est pourquoi, donc*** 我觉得不舒服, ~我没有去。wǒ juéde bù shūfu, ~ wǒ méiyǒu qù. I didn't feel well. That's why I didn't go. *Je ne me sentais pas bien. C'est pourquoi je n'y suis pas allé.*

您是他的朋友, ~也是我的朋友。nín shì tā de péngyou, ~ yě shì wǒ de péngyou. You are his friend and therefore mine. *Vous êtes son ami et donc vous êtes aussi le mien.*

walk with it. *Va chercher le chien et on va se balader avec (lui).*

(是)小王做的那个东西，并把~拿到了晚会上。(shì) xiǎo wáng zuò de nàgè dōngxi, bìng bǎ ~ ná dào le wǎnhuì shàng. Xiao Wang made the object and brought it to the party. *Xiao Wang a fait l'objet et l'a apporté à la soirée.*

它们（它們） tāmen S1 **they (animals or objects),** *ils (des animaux ou des objets)* 把那些母鸡招来，喂~吃的。bǎ nàxiē mǔjī zhāo lai, wèi ~ chīde. Fetch the hems and give them to eat. *Va chercher les poules et donne-leur à manger.*

台湾（臺灣） táiwān N **Taiwan,** *Taiwan* ~工业化程度很高。 ~ gōngyèhuà chéngdù hěn gāo. Taiwan is highly industrialized. *Taiwan est hautement industrialisé.*

我们下个月去~旅游。wǒmen xiàgè yuè qù ~ lǚyóu. We're going to go sightseeing in Taiwan next month. *Nous allons faire du tourisme à Taiwan le mois prochain.*

太 tài H1, S1 **too, very,** *trop, très* 她干得~累了。tā gàn dé ~ lèi le. She works too hard. *Elle travaille trop.* ~感谢你了！~ gǎnxiè nín le. Thank you very much indeed! *Merci infiniment!*

比萨饼好吃吗？--- 很好吃 / 不~好吃。bǐsàbǐng hǎochī ma? -- hěn hǎochī / bú ~ hǎochī. Was the pizza good? – Very / Not very. *La pizza était-elle bonne? – Très / Pas très.*

太太 tàitai G, H5, S1 **Mrs, madam, lady,** *madame f* 王~，您好吗? wáng ~, nín hǎo ma? Mrs. Wang, how are you? *Mme Wang, comment allez-vous?*

这是位令人尊重的~。zhè shì wèi hěn lìngrén zūnzhòng de ~. She's a real lady. *C'est une femme très comme il faut.* 那是个很傲慢的~。She's a bit of madam / She's really stuck-up. *C'est une pimbêche / Elle s'y croit vraiment. .*

谈判（談判） tánpàn H5, S1 **negotiate, negotiation, talks,** *débattre, négocier, négociations* 这个价格需要~。zhègè jiàgé xūyào ~. It's a price to be negotiated. *C'est un prix à débattre.* 他们拒绝~。tāmen jùjué ~. They refuse to negotiate. *Ils refusent de négocier.* 他们开始了和平~。tāmen kāishǐ le hépíng ~. They have begun peace talks. *Ils ont commencé des négociations de la paix.*

T

他 tā D, H1, S1 **he, il** ~来了! tā ~ le. There he is! *Le voilà!* 她比~大。~ bǐ tā dà. She is older than he is. *Elle est plus âgée que lui.*

~说什么呢? ~ shuō shénme ne? What is he saying? *Que dit-il?* ~这个人很怪。~ zhègè rén hěn guài. He's a strange man. *C'est un homme étrange.*

他们（他們） tāmen G, N, S1 **they, ils, elles** ~还不知道。~ bù shīdào. They still don't know about it. *Ils l'ignorent encore.*

~要对此负责。~ yào duì cǐ fùzé. They are the ones who are responsible. *Ce sont eux les responsables.*

她 tā D, H1, S1 **she, elle** ~在干什么呢? ~ zài gàn shénme ne? What's she doing? *Qu'est-ce qu'elle fait?*

~个子很高。~ gèzi hěn gāo. She's tall. *Elle est grande.* 这个~可做不了。zhègè ~ kě zuò bù liǎo. SHE can't do it. *Elle ne peut pas le faire.*

她们（她們） tāmen S1 **they (female sex),** *elles* ~是护士。~ shì hùshì. They're nurses. *Elles sont des infirmières.* 你可以信任~。nǐ kěyǐ xìnrèn ~. You can have complete confidence in them. *Vous pouvez avoir confiance en elles.* 找~俩去问。zhǎo ~ liǎ qù wèn. Ask both of them. *Adressez-vous à toutes les deux.*

它 tā H2, S1 **it (an animal or object),** *il (an animal ou un objet)* 把那条狗叫来，咱们带~散步去。bǎ nà tiáo gǒu jiào lái, zánmen dài ~ sànbù qù. Fetch the dog and we'll go for a

踢足球 tī zúqiú H2 **play football,** *jouer au football* 他们喜欢~。tā xǐhuan ~. They like playing football. *Ils aiment jouer au football.* 他们每星期六都~。tāmen měi xīngqī liù dōu ~. They play football every Saturday. *Ils jouent au football tous les samedis.*

提出 tíchū N, S1 **put forward, advance,** *présenter, avancer* 他~了一个建议。tā tíchū le yígè ~. He made a proposal. *Il a fait une proposition.* 她拒绝了他~结婚的建议。tā jùjué le tā ~ jiéhūn de jiànyì. She refused his proposal. *Elle a refusé sa demande en mariage.* 这是向你~的一个警告。zhèshì xiàng nǐ ~ de yígè jìnggào. Let that be a warning to you. *Que cela te serve d'avertissement.*

提高 tígāo N, H3, S1 **improve, raise,** *améliorer, élever* 产品质量~了。chǎnpǐn zhìliàng ~ le. The quality of products has been improved. *La qualité des produits a été améliorée.* 我们的目标是~全面的水平。wǒmen de mùbiāo shì ~ quánmiàn de shuǐpíng. Our aim is to raise overall standards. *Notre but est d'élever le niveau global.*

题 (題) tí H2, S1 **subject, question, topic,** *sujet, question* 咱们回到正~上来吧。zánmen huídào zhèng~ shànglai ba. Let's get back to the subject. *Revenons à nos moutons.* 考~是什么? kǎo~ shì shénme? What was the examination question? *Quel a été le sujet d'examen?* 今晚的辩论~是失业。jīnwǎn de biànlùn ~ shì shīyè. Tonight's topic for debate is unemployment. *Le débat de ce soir porte sur le chômage.* 这是小~大做。zhè shì xiǎo ~ dà zuò. It was a tempest in a teapot. *C'est une tempête dans un verre d'eau.*

天 tiān D, S1 **sky, day,** *ciel m, jour m* ~亮了。~ liàng le. It's getting light already. *Il commence déjà à faire jour.* 我每~工作八个小时。wǒ měi~ gōngzuò bāgè xiǎoshí. I work an eight-hour day. *Je travaille huit heures par jour.* 我干这个花了三~。wǒ gàn zhègè huā le sān ~. It took me three days to do it. *Ça m'a pris trois jours pour le faire.* ~哪! ~ na! Good Heavens! *Mon Dieu!*

天气 (天氣) tiānqì H1, S1 **weather,** *temps m* 今天~怎么样? jīntiān ~ zěnme yàng? What's the weather (like) today? *Quel temps fait-il aujourd'hui?* ~很好 / 很糟。~ hěn hǎo / hěn zāo. It's beautiful / terrible weather. *Il fait beau / mauvais.*

跳舞 tiào wǔ H2, S1 **dance,** *danser* 你想~吗? nǐ iǎng ~ ma? Do you want to dance? *Tu veux danser?* 我下一轮可以跟您~吗? wǒ xià yìlún kěyǐ gēn nín ~ ma? May I have the next dance? *Voulez-vous m'accorder la prochaine danse?*

铁路 (鐵路) tiělù S1 **railway, railroad,** *chemin m de fer, voie ferrée* 他们下星期六开始~旅行。tāmen xià xīngqī liù kāishǐ ~ lǚxíng. They're beginning to travel by railroad next Saturday. *Ils commenceront à voyager en chemin de fer samedi prochain.* 我从没在俄国~旅行过。wǒ cóngméi zài éguó tiělù ~ lǚxíng guò. I'd never travelled by Russian railway. *Je n'avais jamais pris le train en Russie.*

听 (聽) tīng H1, S1 **listen, hear,** *écouter, entendre* 注意~! zhùyì ~! Listen carefully! *Ecoutez-bien!* 你~新闻了吗? nǐ ~ xīnwén le ma? Did you listen to the news? *As-tu écouté les informations?* 我要是~母亲的话就好了。wǒ yàoshi ~ mǔqin de huà jiù hǎo le. If only I'd listened to my mother! *Si seulement j'avais écouté ma mère.* 我说的你~进去了吗? wǒ shuō de nǐ ~ jìnqù le ma? Do you hear me? *Tu entends ce que je te dis?*

听力 (聽力) tīnglì S1 **oral comprehension,** *compréhension orale* 我英语~不很好。wǒ yīngyǔ ~ bù hěn hǎo. I'm not very good at English oral comprehension. *Je ne suis pas très fort en compréhension orale d'anglais.* 我们要多搞~训练。wǒmen yào duō gǎo ~ xùnliàn. We must do more listening comprehension training. *Nous devons faire plus d'entraînement à la compréhension orale.*

听说 (聽說) tīngshuō S1 **be told, hear of,** *entendre dire, entendre parler de* 我是听(人)说的。wǒ shì tīng (rén) shuō de. I know it by hearsay. *Je le sais par ce qu'on entendre dire.* 我~他走了。wǒ ~ tā zǒu le. I heard that he had left. *J'ai entendu dire qu'il était parti.* 我这是第一次~。wǒ zhèshì dì yīcì ~. That's the first time I've heard of it. *C'est la première fois que j'entends (dire) ça.*

停车 (停車) tíng chē S1 **stop, pull up, s'arrêter** 我们没找到~的地方。wǒmen méi zhǎodào ~ de dìfang. We didn't find room to park. *Nous n'avons pas trouvé de place pour nous garer.* 这里禁止~。zhèlǐ jìnzhǐ ~. Parking is prohibited here. *Le parking est interdit.*

停车场 (停車場) tíngchē chǎng S1 **car park, parking lot, parking area, parc m de stationnement, parking** 你把车停在~里了吗? nǐ bǎ chē tíng zài ~ lǐ le ma? Have you put your car in the car park? *As-tu mis ta voiture au parking?*

通过 (通過) tōngguò N, H4, S1 **pass through, get by, passer, réussir** 他顺利地~了检查。tā shùnlì de ~ le jiǎnchá. He passed through the checkpoint without any trouble. *Il a passé le poste de contrôle sans encombre.*

这儿太窄通不过(去)。zhèr tài zhǎi tōng bú guò(qù). There isn't enough room to get by. *Il n'y a pas assez de place pour passer.* 你笔试~了吗? nǐ bǐshì ~ le ma? Did you pass your written exam? *As-tu réussi ton examen écrit?*

同时 (同時) tóngshí N, H5, S1 **at the same time, meanwhile, entretemps, en même temps** 我们是~到的。wǒmen shì ~ dào de. We arrived at the same time. *Nous sommes arrivés en même temps.*

在这~，又有两千人失去了工作。zài zhè ~, yòu yǒu liǎngqiān rén shīqù le gōngzuò. Meanwhile, another 2,000 people have lost their jobs. *Entre-temps, 2 000 personnes de plus ont perdu leur emploi.*

同学 (同學) tóngxué H1, S1 **schoolmate, classmate, camarade d'école, camarade de classe** 他们是我的~，小王是我同班~。tāmen shì wǒ de ~, xiǎo wáng shì wǒ de tóngbān ~. They're my schoolmates, and Xiao Wang is my classmate. *Ce sont mes camarades d'école, et Xiao Wang est mon camarade de classe.*

同意 tóngyì H3, S1 **agree, approve, être de l'avis de qn, être d'accord avec** 我~您的意见。wǒ ~ nín de yìjiàn. I agree with you. *Je suis de votre avis.* 我不~这个计划。wǒ bù ~ zhège jìhuà. I don't approve of the plan. *Je ne suis pas d'accord avec ce projet.*

投资 (投資) tóuzī N, H5, S2 **investment, invest, investir, placer l'argent dans** 那家公司在世界各地都有~。nà jiā gōngsī zài shìjiè gèdì dōu yǒu ~. The company has investments all over the world. *La société a des capitaux investis dans le monde entier.*

他把所有钱向一家机械企业~了。tā bǎ suǒyǒu de qián xiàng yìjiā jīxiè qǐyè ~ le. He invested all his money in an engineering business. *Il a placé tout son argent dans une entreprise de mécanique.*

突然 tūrán D, H3, S1 **abrupt, sudden(ly), unexpected, brutalement, inattendu, soudainement** 天气~变了。tiānqì ~ biàn le. There was an abrupt change in the weather. *Le temps a changé brutalement.*

这实在很~。zhè shízài hěn ~. This is all very sudden / It is completely unexpected. *C'est plutôt inattendu / On ne s'y attend pas du tout.* 她~改变的主意。tā ~ gǎibiàn le zhǔyì. She very suddenly changed her mind. *Elle a changé d'avis très soudainement.*

liǎngmén ~. He speaks two foreign languages fluently. *Il parle deux langues étrangères couramment.* 姐妹俩都学~。jiěmèi liǎ dōu xué ~. Both sisters are studying a foreign language / foreign languages. *Toutes les sœurs étudient une langue étrangère / des langues étrangères.* 这个职位要求至少会讲三门~。zhègè zhíwèi yāoqiú zhìshǎo huì jiǎng sānmén ~. You have to speak at least three foreign languages for this post. *Il faut parler au moins trois langues étrangères pour ce poste.*

完 wán H2, S1 **finish, be over, be through, run out of,** *finir, ne plus avoir* 您~没有~? nǐ ~ méiyǒu ~? Are you through? *Avez-vous fini?* 他(把)钱都用~了。tā (bǎ) qián dōu yòng~ le. He's run out of money. *Il n'a plus d'argent.* 晚会开~了。The party's over. *La fête est finie.*

请让我把话说~。qǐng ràng wǒ bǎ huà shuō~. Please let me finish [speaking]. *S'il te plaît, laisse-moi finir (de parler).*

玩 wán H2 **play,** *jouer* 他们在~扑克。tāmen zài ~ pūkè. They are playing poker. *Ils jouent au poker.*

这个人跟我~了个手段。zhègè rén gēn wǒ ~ le gè shǒuduàn. That man played a trick on me. *Cet homme m'a joué un tour.*

晚安 wǎn'ān S1 **good night,** *bonne nuit* --- 我去睡觉。--- ~! I'll go to bed. -- Good night! *– Je vais dormir. -- Bonne nuit!*

晚上 wǎnshang H2, S1 **night, evening,** *soir m, nuit f* 女士们、先生们，~好，欢迎你们！nǚshì men、xiānsheng men, ~ hǎo, huānyíng nǐmen! Good evening, ladies and gentlemen, and welcome! *Bonsoir, mesdames et messieurs, soyez les bienvenus!*

我们有几个礼拜~都没出去了。wǒmen yǒu jǐgè lǐbài ~ dōu méi chūqù le. It's weeks since we had a night out. *Ça fait des semaines que nous ne sommes pas sortis le soir.*

委员 (委員) wěiyuán N, H6 **committee member,** *membre m d'un comité / d'une commission* ~会中有七名~。~ huì zhōng yǒu qī míng ~. There are seven members in the committee. *Il y a sept membres dans le comité.*

王先生是(~会)~. wáng xiānsheng shì (~ huì) ~ Mr Wang is a committeeman. *M. Wang est membre du comité.* 李夫人是(~会)(女)~。lǐ fūren shì (~ huì) (nǚ) ~ Ms Li is a

---

外 wài H2, S1 **out, stranger,** *étranger* 我从窗户往~看。wǒ cóng chuānghù wǎng ~ kàn. I'm looking out of the window. *Je regarde par la fenêtre.*

她每天都换~衣。tā měitiān dōu huàn ~yī. She appears in a new outfit every day. *Elle porte une tenue différente chaque jour.* 我在她眼里成了个~人。wǒ zài tā yǎnlǐ chéng le gè ~rén. I'm like a stranger to her now. *Je suis devenu un étranger pour elle.*

外国 (外國) wàiguó S1 **foreign country,** *pays étranger* 他去~了。tā qù ~ le. He went abroad. *Il est allé à l'étranger.* 这是从~来的。tā shì cóng ~ lái de. It comes from abroad. *Ça vient de l'étranger.* 她能说三门~语。tā néng shuō sān mén ~ yǔ. She can speak three foreign languages. *Elle peut parler trois langues étrangères.*

外国人 (外國人) wàiguórén S1 **foreigner,** *étranger(ère)* 我在这儿觉得是个~。wǒ zài zhèr juédé shì gè ~. I feel like a foreigner here. *Je me sens étranger ici.* ~没有权利投票。~ méiyǒu quánlì tóupiào. Foreigners are not allowed to vote. *Les étrangers n'ont pas le droit de voter.*

外文 wàiwén S1 (= 外语 wàiyǔ) **foreign language,** *langue étrangère*

外语 (外語) wàiyǔ S1 (= 外文 wàiwén) **foreign language,** *langue étrangère* 他能流利地说两门~。tā néng liúlì de shuō

committeewoman. *Mme Li est membre (femme) du comité.*

喂 wèi (动) (1) H1, S1 **feed, *donner à manger*** 我每天~母鸡。wǒ měitiān ~ mǔjī. I feed the hens every day. *Je donne à manger aux poules tous les jours.*

那个母亲给娃娃~瓶奶。nà gè mǔqin gěi wáwa ~ píng nǎi. The mother is giving her baby its bottle. *La mère donne le biberon à son bébé.*

喂 wèi (叹) (2) H1, S2 **hey, hello, *hé, holà, allô*** ~! 停下(来)! ~! Tíng xià(lái)! Hey! Stop it! *Hé! Arrêtez!*

~! 起床了! ~! qǐ chuáng le! Hello there, wake up! *Holà! Debout!* ~, 是小王吗? ~, shì xiǎo wáng ma? Hello, is that Xiao Wang? *Allô, c'est Xiao Wang?*

为 (為) wèi D, H3, S1 **for, *à, pour*** ~我去。~ wǒ qù. Go for me / instead of me. *Allez-y pour moi.* 我~他行事。wǒ ~ tā xíngshì. I'll act on his behalf. *J'agirai pour lui.*

这个按钮是~什么的? --- ~调节音量的。zhègè ànniǔ shì ~ shénme de? -- ~ tiáojié yīnliàng de. What's the knob for? – It's for adjusting the volume. *A quoi sert ce bouton ? – Ça sert à régler le volume.* 他们~孩子才没有分手。tāmen ~ háizi cái méiyǒu fēnshǒu. They stayed together for the sake of the children. *Ils sont restés ensemble à cause des enfants.*

为了 (為了) wèile H3, S1 **so as (not) to, for, *pour, à cause de*** 这是~我吗? zhè shì ~ wǒ ma? Is it for me? *C'est pour moi?* 我~他行事。wǒ ~ tā xíngshì. I'll act on his behalf. *J'agirai pour lui.* 我~不迷路买了张地图。wǒ ~ bù mílù mǎi le zhāng dìtú. I bought a map so as not to get lost. *J'ai acheté une carte pour ne pas me perdre.*

为什么 (為什麼) wèi shénme H2, S1 **why, why / how is it that, *pourquoi, pour quelle raison, dans quel but*** 他~从不打电话? tā ~ cóng bù dǎ diànhuà? Why is it that he never phones? *Pourquoi est-ce qu'il ne téléphone jamais?*

这一点您~没有说? zhè yìdiǎn nǐ ~ méiyǒu shuō? Why (ever) didn't you say so? *Pourquoi ne l'avez-vous pas dit?* ~不呢? ~ bù ne? Why not? *Pourquoi pas?* ~难过呢? ~ nánguò ne? Why get upset? *A quoi bon se rendre malade?* 我不知道~。wǒ bù zhīdào ~. I don't know the reason why. *Je ne sais pas le pourquoi.* 我告诉你~。wǒ

gàosù nǐ ~. I'll tell you why. *Je vais te dire pourquoi.*

文化 wénhuà N, H3, S1 **civilization, culture, literacy, *civilisation f, cultivé, lire et écrire*** 中国~迷住了他。zhōngguó ~ mízhù le tā. The Chinese civilization fascinates him. *La civilisation chinoise le passionne.*

她是个有~的人。tā shì gè yǒu ~ de rén. She is a person of culture. *C'est une personne cultivée.* 我甚至开始怀疑他学没学过~。wǒ shènzhì kāishǐ huáiyí tā xuéméixué guò ~. I am beginning to doubt even his literacy. *Je commence même à douter qu'il sache lire et écrire.*

文明 wénmíng H5, S1 **civilization, civilized, *civilisation f, bien élevé, convenable(ment)*** 中国和印度一样是两个~古国。zhōngguó hé yìndù yíyàng shì liǎnggè ~ gǔguó. China and India are both a country with an ancient civilization. *La Chine et l'Inde sont tous les deux un pays de civilisation ancienne.* 真是个懂~的小姑娘。zhēn shì gè dǒng ~ de xiǎo gūniáng. The little girl is really quite civilized. *La petite fille est très bien élevée.* 你吃饭不能~点儿吗? nǐ chīfàn bù néng ~ diǎr ma? Can't you eat in a civilized manner? *Tu ne peux pas manger convenablement?*

文学 (文學) wénxué H5, S1 **writing, literature, *littérature f*** 他搞~(这一行)。tā gǎo ~ (zhè yì háng). He makes a career in writing. *Il fait carrière dans la littérature.* 这一(个)题材有大量的~作品。zhè yí (gè) tícái yǒu dàliàng de ~ zuòpǐn. There's a wealth of literature on this subject. *Il existe une abondante littérature sur ce sujet.*

文字 wénzì S1 **characters, writing, *caractères mpl, écriture f*** 中文是一种表意~。zhōngwén shì yìzhǒng biǎoyì ~. Chinese is a kind of ideographic writing. *Le chinois est une écriture idéographique.* 欧洲语言是拼音(化)~。ōuzhōu yǔyán shì pīnyīn(huà) ~. European languages are alphabetic writing. *Les langues européennes sont des écritures alphabétiques.* 你(写)的~叫人看不懂。nǐ xiě de ~ jiào rén kàn bùdǒng. I can't read your writing. *Je ne peux pas déchiffrer ton écriture.*

问 (問) wèn H2, S1 **ask, inquire, responsible for, *poser une question, demander, responsable de*** 我能~您一个问题吗? wǒ néng ~ nín yígè wèntí ma? May I ask you a question? *Puis-je vous poser une question?* 她~

您的消息。tā ~ nín de xiāoxi. She asked after you. *Elle a demandé de vos nouvelles.*

这个事故从法律上看可能唯他是~。zhè gè shìgù cóng fǎlǜ shàng kàn kěnéng wéi tā shì ~. He can be held legally responsible for the accident. *Il est peut-être légalement responsable de l'accident.*

问题 (問題) wèntí G, N, H2, S1
question, problem, issue, *question f, problème m, affaire f* 我能问您几个~吗? wǒ néng wèn nín jǐgè ~ ma? May I ask you some questions? *Puis-je vous poser quelques questions?*

这可能会是个小~。zhè kěnéng huì shì gè xiǎo ~. That's going to be a bit of a problem. *Ça va poser un petit problème.* 你现在真有~了! nǐ xiànzài zhēn yǒu ~ le. You're really in trouble now! *Tu es dans de beaux draps maintenant!*

我 wǒ G, H1, S1 **I, *je*** ~到了。~ dào le. Here I am. *Me voici.* ~喜欢滑冰。~ xǐhuān huábīng. I like skiing. *J'aime skier.*

是~找到的，不是你。shì ~ zhǎodào de, bú shì nǐ. I found it, not you. *C'est moi qui l'ai trouvé, pas toi.* ~说什么来着? ~ shuō shénme lái zhe? What have I said? *Qu'ai-je dit?*

我们 (我們) wǒmen G, N, H1, S1
we, *nous* ~俩谢谢您。~ liǎ xièxie nín. We both thank you. *Nous vous remercions tous (les) deux.*

~是英国人，他们是法国人。~ shì yīngguó rén, tāmen shì fǎguó rén. We are British, and they are French. *Nous, nous sommes britanniques, eux, ils sont français.*

五 wǔ H1, S1 **five, *cinq*** 他~点离开办公室。tā ~ diǎn líkāi bàngōngshì. He leaves his office at five. *Il quitte son bureau à cinq heures.*

我们要一张~个人的桌子。wǒmen yào yìzhāng ~ gè rén de zhuōzi. We'd like a table set for five. *Nous voudrions une table de cinq couverts.* 这是个~星宾馆。zhèshì gè ~ xīng bīnguǎn. It's a five-star hotel. *C'est un palace.*

午饭 (午飯) wǔfàn S1 **lunch, *déjeuner m*** 我每天十二点半吃~。wǒ měitiān shí'èr diǎn bàn chī ~. I have lunch at 12.30 every day. *Je déjeune à 12:30 tous les jours.*

武术 (武術) wǔshuì H5, S1 **martial art, *arts martiaux*** 我练~。wǒ liàn ~. I do martial art. *J'exerce des arts martiaux.* 那个老头儿很会~。nàgè lǎotóur hěn huì ~. That old man knows how to practice martial arts quite well.

Cette vieille personne sait bien pratiquer les arts martiaux. ~是打拳和使用兵器的技术，几千年前起源于中国。~ shì dǎquán hé shǐyòng bīngqì de jìshù, jǐ qiān nián qián qǐyuán yú zhōngguó. Martial arts are styles of unarmed and armed combat, which were originated in China thousands years ago. *Les arts martiaux sont des styles de combats non-armés et armés dont la naissance fût en Chine il y a des milliers d'années.*

西餐 xīcān S1 **Western-style food, *cuisine occidentale*** 您吃~还是(吃)中餐? nǐ chī ~ háishì (chī) zhōngcān? Which food would you prefer, Western-style food or Chinese? *Quelle cuisine préfériez-vous, occidentale ou chinoise?*

西方 xīfāng S1 **the west, the West, the Occident, *ouest m, Occident m*** 太阳升于东方，落于~。tàiyáng shēng yú dōngfāng, luò yú ~. The sun rises in the east and sets in the west. *Le soleil se lève à l'est et se couche à l'ouest.* 我对中~关系很感兴趣。wǒ duì zhōng ~ guānxì hěn gǎn xìngqu. I'm interested in the Sino-Western relations. *Je suis intéressé aux relations sino-occidentales.*

西瓜 xīguā H2, S2 **watermelon, *pastèque f, melon m d'eau*** 他们夏天常吃~。tāmen xiàtiān cháng chī ~. They often have watermelon in summer. *Ils mangent souvent de la pastèque en été.*

西医 (西醫) xīyī S1 **Western medicine, *médecine occidentale*** 您学的是~还是中医? nǐ xué de shì ~ háishì zhōngyī? Did

you study Western medicine or Chinese? *Avez-vous étudié la médecine occidentale ou celle chinoise?*

希望 xīwàng H2, S1 **hope, wish, expect,** *espérer, vœu m, s'y attendre* (我)~能(和您)重新见面。(wǒ) ~ néng (hé nín) chóngxīn jiànmiàn. I hope to see you again. *J'espère vous revoir.*

我们~能有最好的结果。wǒmen ~ néng yǒu zuìhǎo de jiéguǒ. We'll just have to hope for the best. *Nous n'avons plus qu'à espérer que tout aille pour le mieux.* 你的~将得以实现。nǐ de ~ jiāng déyǐ shíxiàn. Your wish will come true. *Ton vœu se réalisera.* 电影比我~的还要好。diànyǐng bǐ wǒ ~ de háiyào hǎo. The movie was better than I expected (it to be). *Le film était meilleur que je ne m'y attendais.*

洗 xǐ H2, S1 **wash,** *laver* 去~~手。qù ~~ shǒu. Go and wash your hands. *Va te laver les mains.*

我刚~了脸。wǒ gāng ~ le liǎn. I just washed my face. *Je viens de me laver la figure.* 她把头发~了。tā bǎ tóufa ~ le. She washed her hair. *Elle s'est lavé les cheveux.*

洗手间（洗手間）xǐshǒujiān H3, S1 **toilet,** *toilette f* ~在哪儿? ~ zài nǎr? Where's the toilet? *Où sont les toilettes?* 他在~把东西扔掉了。tā zài ~ bǎ dōngxi nēngdiào le. He threw it down the toilet. *Il l'a jeté dans les toilettes.*

喜欢（喜歡）xǐhuan H1, S1 **like, be fond of, be keen on,** *aimer, préférer, être friand de, enchanter* 我~跳舞。wǒ ~ tiàowǔ. I like dancing / to dance. *J'aime danser.* 我最~老李。wǒ zuì ~ lǎo lǐ. I like Lao Li best. *C'est Lao Li que je préfère.*

她特别~甜食。tā tèbié ~ tiánshí. She's very fond of sweet things. *Elle est très friande de sucreries.* 这个主意我不大~。zhègè zhǐyì wǒ búdà ~. I'm not so keen on the idea. *L'idée ne m'enchante pas vraiment.*

下 xià (动) (1) D, H1, S1 **get off, go dawn, fall,** *descendre, tomber* 我们下一站~车。wǒmen xià yízhàn ~ chē. We get off at the next stop. *On descend au prochain arrêt.*

我总是走楼梯~楼。wǒ zǒngshì zǒu lóutī ~ lóu. I always go down by stairs. *Je descends toujours par l'escalier.* 雪~得很大。xuě ~ dé hěn dà. The snow is falling heavily. *Il neige à gros flocons.* 昨天~了冰雹。zuótiān ~ le bīngbáo. It hailed yesterday. *Il est tombé de la grêle hier.*

下 xià (名) (2) D, H1, S1 **next, in,** *prochain, à* ~星期一是节假日。~ xīngqī yī shì jiéjiàrì. Next Monday is a public holiday. *Lundi prochain est férié.* 不要总呆在太阳~。búyào zǒng dāi zài tàiyáng ~. Don't stay in the sun too much. *Ne reste pas trop au soleil.*

下 xià (量) (3) D, H1, S1 **[classifier],** *[classificateur m]* 吃一口尝一~。chī yì kǒu cháng yí ~. Just a mouthful to taste. *Juste une bouchée pour goûter.* 她敲了三~门。tā qiāo le sān ~ mén. She gave three knocks on the door. *Elle a frappé trois fois à la porte.*

我对形势仔细地考虑了一~。wǒ duì xíngshì zǐxì de kǎolǜ le yí ~. I've done some serious thinking about the situation. *J'ai sérieusement réfléchi à la situation.*

下车（下車）xià chē S1 **get off, (help) down,** *descendre* 咱们在下一站~。zánmen xià yí zhàn ~. We're getting off at the next station. *On descend à la prochaine station.* 帮女病人~。bāng nǚbìngrén ~. Help the patient down. *Fais descendre la malade.*

下课（下課）xià kè S1 **get out of class, finish class,** *terminer un cours, sortir de classe* 现在~了，再见! xiànzài ~ le, zàijiàn! That's all for today. Goodbye! *C'est tout pour aujourd'hui. Au revoir!* ~后再来吧。~ hòu zài láibe. Come when you've finished your class. *Viens quand tu auras terminé ton cours.*

下来（下來）xiàlai G, S1 **come down, [verb+下来: from high to low, from far to near or from the past till now],** *descendre, [verbe+下来: de haut en bas, de loin à près ou du passé au présent]* 从树上~! cóng shù shàng ~! Come down from that tree! *Descends de cet arbre!* 风静~了。fēng ~ xiàlái le. The wind grew quiet. *Le vent s'est apaisé.*

你讨价还价的话，他还可以降~几欧元。nǐ tǎojià huánjià de hua, tā hái kěyǐ jiàng ~ xiàlái jǐ ōuyuán. He'll come down a few euros if you bargain. *Il baissera son prix de quelques euros si tu marchandes.* 这个习俗是从罗马人那里传~的。zhègè xísú shì cóng luómǎrén nàlǐ chuán ~ de. This custom comes down from the Romans. *Cette coutume vient des Romains.*

下去 xiàqu G, S1 **go down, get off, [verb+下去: from high to low, from near to**

far or from now till future], *descendre,* **[verbe+下去: de haut en bas, de près à loin ou du présent au futur]** ~开门。~ kāi mén. Go down and answer the door. *Descends ouvrir.* 咱们在下一站~。zánmen zài xià yízhàn ~. We're getting off at the next station. *On descend à la prochaine station.*

洪水退~了。hóngshuǐ tuì ~ le. The flood has receded. *L'inondation s'est retirée.* 我们要坚持~! wǒmen yào jiānchí ~! We must stick it out! *Nous devons tenir le coup jusqu'au bout!*

下午 xiàwǔ H1, S1 **afternoon,** *après-midi* ~好! ~ hǎo! Have a nice afternoon / Good afternoon! *Bon après-midi!* 我明天~来。wǒ míngtiān ~ lái. I'll come tomorrow afternoon. *Je viendrai demain dans l'après-midi.*

~三点了。~ sāndiǎn le. It's three in the afternoon / It's 3 p.m. *Il est trois heures dans l'après-midi.* 她每星期去两个~。tā měi xīngqī qù liǎnggè ~. She goes there two afternoons a week. *Elle y va deux après-midis par semaine.*

下雨 xià yǔ H1, S1 **rain,** *pleuvoir* 好象要~了。hǎoxiàng yào ~ le. It looks like rain. *On dirait qu'il va pleuvoir.* ~了。It rains / It is raining. *Il pleut.* 正在下大雨。zhèngzài xià dà yǔ. It is raining hard. *Il pleut à verse.*

当时下着小雨。dāngshí xiàzhe xiǎo yǔ. A light rain was falling. *Il tombait une pluie fine.*

下周 xiàzhōu S1 **next week,** *la semaine prochaine* ~见! ~ jiàn! See you next week! *A la semaine prochaine!* 我~去看她。wǒ ~ qù kàn tā. I'll go and see her next week. *J'irai la voir la semaine prochaine.*

先 xiān T, H3, S1 **before, earlier,** *d'abord, d'avance* (进门时) 您~进。nǐ ~ jìn. After you (going through door). *Après vous (par la porte).* 他~到了五分钟。tā ~ dào le wǔ fēnzhōng. He arrived five minutes (too) earlier. *Il est arrivé avec cinq minutes d'avance.*

我是最~看见的! wǒ shì zuì ~ kànjiàn de! I saw it first! *C'est moi qui l'ai vu le premier!* 我们只得~付了两个星期的钱。wǒmen zhǐdé ~ fù le liǎnggè xīngqī de qián. We had to pay two weeks in advance. *Il a fallu qu'on paie deux semaines d'avance.*

先生 xiānsheng G, H1, S1 **mister (Mr), gentleman, sir,** *monsieur m* 王~, 您好! wáng ~, nín hǎo! Good morning Mr Wang! *Bonjour Monsieur Wang!* ~们, 请安静! ~men, qǐng

ānjìng! Gentlemen, would you please be quiet! *Messieurs, un peu de silence s'il vous plaît.*

小朋友, 可以把笔借给~用一下吗? xiǎopéngyou, kěyǐ bǎ bǐ jiè gěi ~ yòng yíxià ma? Boy, could you lend the gentleman your pen for a minute? *Mon petit, peux-tu prêter un instant ton style à Monsieur?* 总统~, 通货膨胀情况如何? zǒngtǒng ~, tōnghuò péngzhàng qíngkuàng rúhé? Mr President, what about inflation? *Monsieur le Président, et l'inflation?*

鲜 (鮮) xiān T, S2 **fresh, bright, tasty,** *frais, vif, savoureux* 这是从菜园刚摘的~蔬菜。zhèshì cóng càiyuán gāng zhāi de ~ shūcài. The vegetables are fresh from the garden. *Les légumes (frais) viennent directement du jardin.*

这块布颜色太~。zhè kuài bù yánsè tài ~. This cloth is too bright. *La couleur de cette étoffe est trop vive.* 这个菜(肴)真~。zhè gè cài (yáo) zhēn ~. It's a tasty dish. *C'est un plat savoureux.*

现 (現) xiàn D, T **show, present,** *se montrer, actuel* 这里他不会再~了。zhèlǐ tā bú huì zài ~ le. He won't show his face here again. *Il ne se montrera plus ici.* 她~了原形。tā ~ le yuánxíng. She showed her true colours. *Elle s'est montrée sous son vrai jour.*

~阶段还没有更好的办法。~ jiēduàn hái méiyǒu gènghǎo de bànfǎ. At the present stage we still can't find a better solution. *Dans l'étape actuelle on ne pourra pas encore trouver une meilleure solution.*

现金 (現金) xiànjīn H5, S1 **cash,** *espèces fpl, argent m* 我付~。wǒ fù ~. I'll pay by cash. *Je paye en espèces.* 我从不带很多~。wǒ cóng bú dài hěn duō ~. I never carry mush cash. *Je n'ai jamais beaucoup d'argent sur moi.*

现在 (現在) xiànzài G, N, H1, S1 **now, for the present, today,** *maintenant, pour le moment, aujourd'hui* 我们~干什么? wǒmen ~ gàn shénme? What shall we do now? *Qu'est-ce qu'on fait maintenant?* ~够了。~ gòu le. That's enough for the present. *Ça suffit pour le moment.*

她~要比十年前受欢迎。tā ~ yào bǐ shínián qián shòu huānyíng. She's more popular today than she was 10 years ago. *Elle est plus populaire aujourd'hui qu'il y a 10 ans.*

香 xiāng H4, S1 **perfume, scented,** *parfumé, odorant* 她(~水洒得)很~。tā (~shuǐ xǎ dé) hěn ~. She's wearing perfume. *Elle est parfumée.* 这个梨(味儿)真~。zhègè lí (wèir) zhēn ~. It's a deliciously scented pear. *C'est une poire délicieusement parfumée.*

香港 xiānggǎng N **Hong Kong,** *Hong Kong*

他们在~。 tāmen zài ~. They are in Hong Kong. *Ils sont à Hong Kong.*

~中文的意思是"芬芳的港口"。 ~ zhōngwén de yìsi shì "fēnfāng de gǎngkǒu". Hong Kong means a "sweet-smelling harbour" in Chinese. *Hong Kong signifie un "port odorant" en chinois.*

想 xiǎng D, H1, S1 **think,** *réfléchir, penser*

让我~(一)~。 ràng wǒ ~ (yì) ~. Let me think. *Laisse-moi réfléchir.*

我反复~了后才接受的。 wǒ fǎnfù ~ le hòu cái jiēshòu de. I thought twice before accepting. *J'ai réfléchi à deux fois avant d'accepter.* 您~他们会不会同意? --- 我~大概会的。 nín ~ tāmen huì bú huì tóngyì? -- wǒ xiǎng dàgài huì de. Do you think they'll agree? – I should think so. *Croyez-vous qu'ils accepteront? – Je pense que oui.*

想到 xiǎngdào G, S1 **think of,** *y penser, avoir l'idée de* 这个主意是谁~的? zhègè zhǔyì shì shéi ~ de? Who thought of the idea? *Qui a eu cette idée?*

你为什么没打个电话? --- 我没~。 nǐ wèishénme méi dǎ gè diànhuà? --- wǒ méi ~. Why didn't you telephone? – I didn't think of it. *Pourquoi n'as-tu pas téléphoné? – Je n'y ai pas pensé.*

向 xiàng (名) T, H3, S1 **direction, aspiration, intention,** *direction f, aspiration f, intention f* 风~变了。 fēng ~ biàn le. The wind is changing. *Le vent tourne.*

这是些有政治志~的年轻人。 zhèshì xiē yǒu zhèngzhì zhì~ de niánqīngrén. They are young people with political aspirations. *Ce sont des jeunes qui ont des aspirations politiques.* 我绝没有在这里过一辈子的意~。 wǒ jué méiyǒu zài zhèlǐ guò yíbèizi de yì~. I have absolutely no intention of spending my life here. *Je n'ai aucune intention de passer ma vie ici.*

向 (嚮) xiàng (副) T **face, for, to, towards,** *orienté à, à* 这是~南的房子。 zhè shì ~ nán de fángzi. The house faces south. *La maison est orientée au sud.*

她~往着爱情。 tā ~wǎng zhe àiqíng. She yearned for love / to be loved. *Elle aspirait à l'amour / Elle avait très envie d'être aimée.* 我们~天津开去。 wǒmen ~ tiānjīn kāiqù. We headed towards Tianjin. *Nous avons pris la direction de Tianjin.*

小 xiǎo D, S1 **minor, small, little, young(er), petty,** *petit, secondaire, jeune*

这是个~问题。 zhè shì gè ~ wèntí. It's a minor question. *C'est une question secondaire.* 他办(着)一个~农场。 He's a farmer in a small way. *Il tient une petite exploitation agricole.*

我们现在有了自己的~房子。 wǒmen xiànzài yǒu le zìjǐ de ~ fángzi. We've got our own little house now. *Nous avons notre petite maison à nous maintenant.* 她比我~。 tā bǐ wǒ ~. She is younger than I am. *Elle est plus jeune que moi.* 他们是~资产者。 tāmen shì ~ zīchǎnzhě. They're petty bourgeois. *Ce sont des petits-bourgeois.*

小姐 xiǎojiě H1, S1 **Miss,** *mademoiselle f* 李~，谢谢您。 lǐ ~, xièxie nín. Thank you, Miss Li. *Merci, mademoiselle Li.* ~们，你们好。 ~ men, nǐmen hǎo. Good morning, young ladies. *Bonjour Mesdemoiselles.*

~，您把什么东西落下了。 ~, nín bǎ shénme dōngxi làxià le. Excuse me Miss, you've forgotten something. *Mademoiselle, vous avez oublié quelque chose.*

小时 (小時) xiǎoshí H2, S1 **hour,** *heure f* 这出剧(演 / 要)一个~。 zhè chū xì (yǎn / yào) yígè ~. The play is an hour long. *La pièce dure une heure.* 我们等了几个~了。 wǒmen děng le jǐgè ~ le. We've been waiting for hours. *Ça fait des heures que nous attendons.*

每~正点都有一列火车。 měi ~ zhèngdiǎn dōu yǒu yíliè huǒchē. There's a train every hour, on the hour. *Il y a un train toutes les heures à l'heure juste.*

小学 (小學) xiǎoxué S1 **primary school,** *école primaire* 中学比~难。 zhōngxué bǐ ~ nán. It's more difficult at secondary school than at primary school. *C'est plus difficile à l'école secondaire qu'à l'école primaire.* 我是~老师。 wǒ shì ~ lǎoshī. I'm a primary school teacher. *Je suis instituteur / institutrice.*

小学生 (小學生) xiǎoxuéshēng S1 **pupil, schoolchild, schoolboy / schoolgirl,** *écolier(ère), élève du primaire* 一个班有三十个~。 yígè bān yǒu sānshí gè ~. There are 30 pupils in a class. *Il y a 30 élèves dans une classe.* 史密斯小姐给~上私人课, 教唱歌和弹钢琴。 shǐmìsī xiǎojiě gěi ~ shàng sīrén kè, jiāo chànggē hé tán gāngqín. Miss Smith takes private schoolchildren in singing and piano-playing. *Mlle Smith donne des cours privés de chant et de piano aux élèves d'école primaire.*

笑 xiào H2, S1 **smile, laugh, laugh at sb,** *rire, se moquer de* 别~! bié ~! Don't smile! *Ne ris pas!* 没什么可~的。méi shénme kě ~ de. It's not funny. *Ce n'est pas drôle.* 你(别)让我~死了! nǐ (bié) ràng wǒ ~ sǐ le! Don't make me laugh! *Laisse-moi rire!* 你带着那顶帽子真好~。nǐ dài zhe nà dǐng màozi zhēn hǎo~. You looked so funny in that hat. *Tu étais si amusant avec ce chapeau.* 人们要~她的。rénmen yào ~ tā le. People will laugh at her. *Les gens vont se moquer d'elle.*

写 (寫) xiě H1, S1 **write,** *écrire* 他~得一手好字。tā ~ dé yìshǒu hǎo zì. He writes a good hand. *Il a une belle écriture.* 这不是我~的。zhè búshì wǒ ~ de. This was not written by me. *Cela n'est pas écrit de ma main.* 他中文说得不很好，但是能~。tā zhōngwén shuō dé bù hěn hǎo, dànshì néng ~. He can't speak Chinese very well, but he can write it. *Il ne parle pas très bien le chinois, mais il peut l'écrire.*

谢谢 (謝謝) xièxie H1, S1 **thanks, thank you,** *merci m, remercier* ~您了! Thanks / Thank you. *Merci / Je vous remercie.* 对您(为我)所做的，我不知道怎么谢(谢)才好。duì nín (wèi wǒ) suǒ zuò de, wǒ bù zhīdào zěnme xiè(xie) cái hǎo. I can't thank you enough for what you've done. *Je ne sais comment vous remercier pour ce que vous avez fait pour moi.* 你安然无事，~老天爷了! nǐ ānrán wúshì, ~ lǎotiānyé le! Thank heaven(s) you're safe! *Dieu merci tu es sain et sauf!*

新 xīn H2, S1 **new,** *nouveau, récent, nouveau, neuf* 这是最~消息。zhè shì zuì ~ xiāoxi. It's the latest news? *C'est une nouvelle toute récente.* 这条连衣裙不是~的。zhè tiáo liányīqún bú shì ~ de. This dress isn't new. *Ce n'est pas une nouvelle robe.* 我们搬进了(一所)~房子。wǒmen bānjìn le (yìsuǒ) xīn fángzi. We've moved to a new house. *Nous avons emménagé dans une maison neuve.* 他第一次穿上了那套~西服。tā dìyī cì chuānshàng le nàjiàn ~ xīzhuāng. He's wearing his new suit for the first time. *Il porte son nouveau costume pour la première fois.*

新年 xīnnián S1 **New Year,** *nouvel an, nouvelle année* ~好! ~ hao! Happy New Year! *Bonne année!* 我们~除夕来了个吃饱喝足的。wǒmen ~ chúxī lái le gè chībǎo hēzú de. We had too much to eat and drink on New Year's Eve. *Nous avons trop bien réveillonné.*

新闻 (新聞) xīnwén H3, S1 **news,** *nouvelle f, information f* 我错过了(听 / 看)~。wǒ cuòguò le (tīng / kàn) ~. I missed the news. *J'ai raté les informations.* 您有他的~吗? nǐ yǒu tā de ~ ma? Have you any news of him? *Avez-vous de ses nouvelles?* 我有~要告诉你。wǒ yǒu ~ yào gàosù nǐ. I've got news for you. *J'ai du nouveau à t'annoncer.* 没有~就是好~。méi yǒu ~ jiùshì hǎo ~. No news is good news. *Pas de nouvelles, bonnes nouvelles.*

心 xīn D, S2 **heart, sense, mean, thought,** *cœur m, se sentir, intention f, esprit m* 他~非常好 / 非常狠。tā ~ fēicháng hǎo / fēicháng hěn. He has a big heart / a heart of gold // a heart of stone. *Il a un très bon cœur / un cœur d'or // un cœur de pierre.* 她有羞耻之~。tā yǒu xiūchǐ zhī ~. She felt a sense of shame. *Elle s'est sentie honteuse.* 我们有~取胜。wǒmen yǒu ~ qǔshèng. We mean to win. *Nous avons (bien) l'intention de gagner.* 对不起，我~不在这儿。duìbùqǐ, wǒ ~ búzài zhèr. Excuse me, my thoughts were elsewhere. *Excusez-moi, j'avais l'esprit ailleurs.*

信 xìn (名) (2) H3, S1 **letter, message,** *lettre f, message m* 我收到了他(写的)一封~。wǒ shōudào le tā (xiě de) yìfēng ~. I've had a letter of him. *J'ai reçu une lettre de lui.* 您要给他留个~(儿)吗? nín yào gěi tā liú gè ~® ma? Would you like to leave a message for him? *Voulez-vous lui laisser un message?*

信息 xìnxī H5, S1 **information,** *se renseigner, information f* 恐怕您的~有误。kǒngpà nín de ~ yǒu wù. I'm afraid your information is wrong. *Je crains qu'on vous ait mal renseigné.* 他们讨论了我们这个时代~的重要性。tāmen tǎolùn le wǒmen zhègè shídài ~ de zhòngyàoxìng. They discussed the importance of information in our time. *Ils ont parlé de l'importance de l'information à notre époque.*

信用卡 xìnyòngkǎ H4, S1 **bank card, credit card, Visa card,** *carte bancaire, carte de crédit, carte bleue, carte Visa* 你们接受~吗? nǐmen jiēshòu ~ ma? Do you accept bank cards / credit cards / Visa Card? *Acceptez-vous les cartes bancaires / les cartes de crédit / la Carte Bleue / la carte Visa?*

星期 xīngqī H1, S2 **week,** *semaine f* 今天~几? --- ~二。What day is it today? – (It's) Tuesday. *Quel jour sommes-nous aujourd'hui? –*

(C'est) mardi. 今天十三号~五。jīntiān shísān hào ~ wǔ. Today is Friday the thirteenth. *Aujourd'hui c'est vendredi treize.*

我一个~后回来。wǒ yígè ~ hòu huílái. I'll be back in a week('s time). *Je serai de retour dans une semaine.* 我有几个~都没看见她了。wǒ yǒu jǐgè ~ dōu méi kànjiàn tā le. I haven't seen her for weeks. *Je ne l'ai pas vue depuis des semaines.*

行 xíng D, H4, S1 **go on foot, all right, perform, *aller à pied, d'accord, agir*** 我步~去。wǒ bù ~ qù. I'll go on foot. *J'y irai à pied.*

以后再说，~吗? --- ~。yǐhòu zài shuō, ~ ma? -- ~. We'll speak about it later, all right? – All right. *Nous en reparlerons plus tard, d'accord? – D'accord.* 质量上有人~骗。zhìliàng shàng yǒurén ~ piàn. The quality hasn't been described accurately. *Il y a tromperie sur la qualité.*

行李 xíngli S1 **bag, luggage, baggage m, *bagage m*** 打~的时间到了。dǎ ~ de shíjiān dào le. It's time to pack our bags. *C'est le moment de plier bagage.* 我~很多。wǒ ~ hěn duō. I have lots of luggage. *J'ai beaucoup de bagages.* 他有两件~。He has two pieces of luggage. *Il a deux bagages.*

姓 xìng H2, S1 **surname, family name, *nom m de famille*** (您)贵~? (nín) guì ~? What's your (venerable) family name? *Quel est votre (vénérable) nom de famille?* 您~什么叫什么? nín ~ shénme jiào shénme? What are your surname and first name? *Quels sont vos nom et prénom?*

王、李、张是中国人的常用(家)~。wáng、lǐ、zhāng shì zhōngguórén de chángyòng (jiā) ~. Wang, Li and Zhang are common Chinese surnames. *Wang, Li et Zhang sont des noms de famille chinois usuels.*

熊猫 (熊貓) xióngmāo H3 **panda, *panda m*** ~生活在中国森林中，食用竹子。~ shēnghuó zài zhōngguó sīnlín zhōng, shíyòng zhúzi. Pandas live in forests in China and eat bamboo. *Les pandas vivent dans des forêts en Chine et mangent du bambou.*

休息 xiūxi H2, S1 **have / take a rest, rest, *se reposer, prendre du repos*** 咱们~一会儿。zánmen ~ yíhuìr. Let's have a rest for a while. *Allons-nous reposer un instant.* 你去~一个小时。nǐ qù ~ yígè xiǎoshí. Go and rest for an hour. *Va te reposer une heure.*

蒸气浴使你觉得是~。zhēngqì yù shǐ nǐ juédé shì ~. A sauna is restful. *Ça repose, le sauna.*

学 (學) xué D, S1 **study, learn, imitate, *étudier, apprendre, imiter*** 她~医 / 历史。tā ~ yī / lìshǐ. She's studying medicine / history. *Elle fait des études de médecine / d'histoire.*

活到老，~到老。huó dào lǎo, ~ dào lǎo. It's never too late to learn. *Il n'est jamais trop tard pour apprendre.* 他很会~同事的样子。tā hěn huì ~ tóngshì de yàngzi. He does a good imitation of his colleagues. *Il imite très bien ses collègues.*

学生 (學生) xuésheng N, H1, S1 **student, pupil, *élève nmf, étudiant(e)*** 他还只是个~。tā hái zhǐ shì gè ~. He's only a schoolchild. *Ce n'est qu'un écolier.* 他女儿是班上最好的~。tā nǚ'ér shì bānshàng zuì hǎo de ~. His daughter is the best student in the class. *Sa fille est la meilleure élève de la classe.*

那里有一群高中~ / 高中生。nàlǐ yǒu yìqún gāozhōng ~ / gāozhōngshēng. There's a group of secondary school pupils / of high school students. *Là il y a un groupe de lycéens.* 他是学医的(大)~。tā shì xué yī de (dà) ~. He's a medical student. *C'est un étudiant en médecine.* 合法结束~身份的年龄定在十六岁。héfǎ jiéshù ~ shēnfèn de niánlíng zài shíliù suì. The school-leaving age was raised to 16. *L'âge légal de fin de scolarité a été porté à 16 ans.*

学习 (學習) xuéxí H1, S1 **study, learn, *étudier, apprendre*** 我~德文。wǒ ~ déwén. I'm learning German. *J'apprends l'allemand.* 她~拉小提琴。tā ~ lā xiǎotíqín. She's learning the violin. *Elle étudie le violon.*

他把全部时间都用来~。tā bǎ quánbù shíjiān dōu yòng lái ~. He spends all his time in study. *Il consacre tout son temps à l'étude.*

学校 (學校) xuéxiào H1, S1 **school, *école f*** 你上的是哪个~? nǐ shàng de shì nǎge ~? Which school do you go to? *A quelle école vas-tu?* 他今天没有去~。tā jīntiān méiyǒu qù ~. He wasn't at school today. *Il n'était pas à l'école aujourd'hui.*

你离开~以后打算做什么? nǐ líkāi ~ yǐhòu dǎxuàn zuò shénme? What are you going to do when you leave school? *Qu'est-ce que tu comptes faire quand tu auras quitté l'école?*

Y

亚洲（亞洲）Yàzhōu H4 **Asia, *Asie f***

~是最大的洲。~ shì zuìdà de zhōu. Asia is the largest of the continents. *L'Asie est le plus grand des continents.* 我在~工作过两年。wǒ zài ~ gōngzuò guo liǎngnián. I worked in Asia for two years. *J'ai travaillé pendant deux ans en Asie.*

研究 yánjiū N, S1 **study, research, *étudier, (faire des) recherches*** 我需要时间~一下这个问题。wǒ xūyào shíjiān ~ yíxià zhègè wèntí. I want time to study this problem. *J'ai besoin du temps pour étudier ce problème.*

这个~(工作)很杰出。zhègè ~ (gōngzuò) hěn jiéchū. It's an excellent piece of research. *C'est un excellent travail de recherche.* 她~罕见的细菌。tā ~ hǎnjiàn de xìjūn. She's engaged in research into rare viruses. *Elle fait des recherches sur les virus rares.*

研究生 yánjiūshēng H4, S2 **graduate student, postgraduate student, research student, *étudiant(e) chercheur(e), étudiant(e) de deuxième cycle / de troisième cycle*** 她是(我们大学的)~。tā shì (wǒmen dàxué de) ~. She's a postgraduate (student) (at our university). *C'est une étudiante de troisième cycle (dans notre université).* 他去牛津作了~研究犯罪学。tā qù niújīn zuò le ~ yánjiū fànzuìxué. He went to Oxford as a postgraduate to study criminology. *Titulaire de licence, il est allé à Oxford pour étudier la criminologie.*

颜色（顔色）yánsè H2, S1 **colour, color Am, *couleur f*** 他眼睛什么~? tā yǎnjing

shénme ~? What colour are his eyes? *De quelle couleur sont ses yeux?*

你的车是什么~的? nǐ de chē shì shénme ~ de? What colour is your car? *De quelle couleur est ta voiture?* 我喜欢绿~。wǒ xǐhuan lǜ ~. My favourite colour is green. *Ma couleur préférée est le vert.*

眼睛 yǎnjing H2, S2 **eye, *œil m, yeux pl***

她是蓝~。tā shì lán ~. She has blue eyes / Her eyes are blue. *Elle a les yeux bleus / Ses yeux sont bleus.* 他把~睁得大大的。tā bǎ ~ zhēng dé dàdà de. He has opened his eyes wide. *Il a ouvert les yeux tout grands.*

我闭着~也能作。wǒ bì zhe ~ yě néng zuò. I could do it with my eyes closed. *Je pourrais le faire les yeux fermés.*

阳（陽）yáng * **yang, masculine, *yang, masculin*** 所有法语名词或是~性的，或是阴性的。没有英语或汉语中那样的中性词。suǒyǒu fǎyǔ míngcí huòshì ~xìng de, huòshì yīnxìng de. méiyǒu yīngyǔ huò hànyǔ zhōng nàyàng de zhōngxìng cí. All French nouns are either masculine or feminine. There is no neuter as in English or Chinese. *En français, tous les noms sont ou bien masculins ou bien féminins. Il n'y en pas de neutre comme en anglais ou en chinois.* 阴和~是中国哲学领域的两个基本原理。yīn hé ~ shì zhōngguó zhéxué lǐngyù de liǎngjè jīběn yuánlǐ. Yin and yang are the two basic principles in the universe of Chinese philosophy. *Le yin et le yang sont les deux principes fondamentaux dans l'univers de la philosophie chinoise.*

羊肉 yángròu H2 **mutton, lamb, *mouton m*** 我们晚饭吃的是~和豆角。wǒmen wǎnfàn chī de shì ~ hé dòujiǎo. We ate mutton with beans at dinner. *Nous avons mangé du mouton avec des haricots au dîner.*

他们在饭馆儿点了烤~串。tāmen zài fànguǎr diǎn le kǎo ~ chuàn. They ordered lamb kebabs at the restaurant. *Ils ont commandé du mouton en brochettes / des kébabs de mouton au restaurant.*

样（樣）yàng D, S2 **appearance, shape, *forme f, aspect m*** 几年没见，她还是那个(老)~儿。jǐ nián méi jiàn, tā háishì nàgè (lǎo) ~. It's years since I last saw her, but she is exactly the same. *Ça fait des années que je ne l'ai pas vue, mais elle n'a pas changé du tout.*

两个兄弟~儿长的差不多。liǎng gè xiōngdì ~r zhǎng dé chàbùduō. The two brothers are very alike. *Les deux frères se ressemblent beaucoup.*

你喜欢这(个)~的连衣裙吗? nǐ xǐhuan zhè(gè) ~ de liányīqún ma? Do you like this dress pattern? *Aimes-tu le patron de robe?*

邀请 (邀請) yāoqǐng H4, S1 **invite, invitation, *inviter, invitation f*** 她是应我的~来的。tā shì yìng wǒ de ~ lái de. She's here at my invitation. *Elle est venue sur mon invitation.* 老王夫妇~我们去他们家做客。lǎo wáng fūfù ~ wǒmen qù tāmen jiā zuòkè. The Wang have invited us over. *Les Wang nous ont invités chez eux.* 我们~她当主席。wǒmen ~ tā dāng zhǔxí. We invited her to become president. *Nous lui avons demandé de devenir présidente.*

药 (藥) yào H2, S1 **medicine, medication, drug, remedy, *médicament m, remède m*** 现在吃~。xiànzài chī ~. Take your medicine now. *Prends tes médicaments maintenant.*

您目前服什么~吗? nín mùqián fú shénme ~ ma? Are you taking any kind of medication? *Est-ce que vous prenez des médicaments?* 我吃过这种中~。wǒ chī guò zhè zhǒng zhōng~. I've taken this traditional Chinese medicine before. *J'ai déjà pris ce médicament traditionnel chinois auparavant.*

要 yào (动) (1) D, H2, S1 **want, ask, wish, be going to, *vouloir, prier, désirer, aller faire*** 我~一杯咖啡。wǒ ~ yìbēi kāfēi. I want a cup of coffee. *Je voudrais une tasse de café.* ~他等着。~ tā děng zhe. Ask him to wait. *Priez-le d'attendre.*

这个我~人做完。zhè gè wǒ ~ rén zuòwán. I want it to be done. *Je désire que cela soit fait.* 您~见经理吗? nín ~ jiàn jīnglǐ ma? Do you wish to see the director? *Désirez-vous voir le directeur?* ~下雨了。~ xiàyǔ le. It's going to rain. *Il va pleuvoir.*

要 yào (连) (2) D, H2, S2 **if, suppose, in case, *si, supposer, ay cas où*** ~有可能，就在星期四做好。~ yǒu kěnéng, jiù zài xīngqī sì zuòhǎo. Have it done by Thursday, if at all possible. *Faites-le pour jeudi si possible.*

这事~真发生了呢? zhè shì ~ zhēn fāshēng le ne? Just supposing it DID happen. *Supposons que ça se produise.* 万一~下雨, 我还是带上一把伞吧。wànyī ~ xiàyǔ, wǒ háishì dàishàng yìbǎ sǎn ba. I'll take an umbrella, just in case. *Je prends un parapluie au cas où.*

也 yě D, H2, S1 **also, too, as well, either, *aussi, également*** 他~看见了。tā ~ kànjiàn le. He also saw it. *Il l'a vu également.* 这个很有效, ~很便宜。zhè gè hěn yǒuxiào, ~ hěn piányi. It's very efficient and also very cheap. *C'est très efficace et de plus, très bon marché.*

您~(要)来。nín ~ (yào) lái. You're coming too. *Vous venez aussi.* 我~要一个。wǒ ~ yào yígè. I'd like one too. *J'en voudrais un aussi.* 我(即)没见他, ~没见他兄弟。wǒ (jì) méi jiàn tā, ~ méi jiàn yā xiōngdi. I've met neither him nor his brother. *Je n'ai rencontré ni lui ni son frère.* 一个人~没懂。yígè rén ~ méi dǒng. Nobody understood. *Personne n'a compris.*

衣服 yīfu H1, S1 **clothing, clothes, *vêtements mpl, habits mpl*** 他在 穿 / 脱 ~。tā zài chuān / tuō ~. He is putting on / taking off his clothes. *Il s'habille / se déshabille.*

她爱买~。tā ài mǎi ~. She loves buying clothes. *Elle adore acheter des vêtements.* 带足保暖的~。dàizú bǎonuǎn de ~. Take plenty of warm clothing. *Prends beaucoup de vêtements chauds.*

医生 (醫生) yīshēng H1, S1 **doctor, *médecin m, docteur m*** ~说我得休息。~ shuō wǒ děi xiūxi. The doctor said that I should rest. *Le médecin / docteur a dit que je devais me reposer.*

谁是负责您的~? shéi shì fùzé nín de ~? Who is your (regular) doctor? *Qui est votre médecin traitant?* 他是位 军队~ / 军医。tā shì wèi jūnduì ~ / jūnyī. He's a medical officer. *C'est un médecin militaire.*

医院 (醫院) yīyuàn H1, S1 **hospital, *hôpital m*** 她只好去~了。tā zhǐhǎo qu ~ le. She had to go (in) to (the) hospital. *Elle a dû aller à l'hôpital.*

他被(人)送到了~。tā bèi (rén) sòngdào le ~. He was taken to hospital / the hospital. *Il a été emmené à l'hôpital.*

一 yī H1, S1 **one, as soon as, *un, une, dès que*** ~点了。~ diǎn le. It's one o'clock. *Il est une heure.* 只有~个。zhǐ yǒu ~ gè. There is just one. *Il y a un seul.* ~个也没有。~ gè yě méiyǒu. There is not a single one. *Il n'y a pas un seul.*

我们意见不~。wǒmen yìjiàn bù ~. Opinions differ between us. *Les avis sont partagés entre nous.* 咱们大家~(yì)准备好就出发。wǒmen dàjiā ~ zhǔnbèi hǎo jiù chūfā. We'll go (just) as soon as everybody's ready. *Nous partirons dès que tout le monde sera prêt.*

一步 yībù N **step, *pas m*** 这是走上正道的~。zhè shì zǒushàng zhèngdào de ~. It's a step in the right direction. *C'est un pas sur la bonne voie.*

有时退~是必要的。yǒushí tuì ~ shì bìyào de. Sometimes it helps to step back and look at things. *Il est parfois bon de prendre du recul.* 要~~重复(进行)实验。yào ~~ chóngfù (jìnxíng) shíyàn. The experiment must be repeated step by step. *Il faut refaire l'expérience pas à pas.*

一次 yícì G **once, *une fois*** 我已经去过~了。wǒ yǐjīng qùguò ~ le. I've been there once before. *J'y suis déjà allé une fois.*

我每三个月见~她。wǒ měi sāngè yuè jiàn ~ tā. I see her every three months. *Je la vois tous les trois mois.* 这只发生过~。zhè zhǐ fāshēng guò ~. It happened only once. *C'est arrivé une fois seulement.*

一定 yídìng G, H3, S1 **fixed, certainly, surely, necessarily, certain, *fixe, certainement, sûrement, certain, à coup sûr*** 这些都是~的花费。zhè xiē dōu shì ~ de huāfèi. These are all fixed costs. *Ce sont tous des coûts fixes.* 明天~准备好。míngtiān ~ zhǔnbèi hǎo. It will certainly be ready tomorrow. *Cela sera prêt demain sans faute.*

他们~能成功。tāmen ~ néng chénggōng. They will surely succeed. *Ils réussiront sûrement.* 这一点(上)有~程度的混乱。zhè yìdiǎn (shàng) yǒu ~ chéngdù de hùnluàn. There's been a certain amount of confusion over this. *Il y a eu une certaine confusion à ce sujet.*

一个 (一個) yígè N, G **one + noun, *un(e) + nom*** 这是~错儿。zhè shì ~ cuòr. It's a mistake. *C'est une erreur.* 屋子里有~人。wūzi lǐ yǒu ~ rén. There's a man in the room. *Il y a quelqu'un dans la pièce.*

请讲~ / 讲个 故事。qǐng jiǎng ~ / jiǎng gè gùshi. Please tell a story. *Racontez une histoire, s'il vous plaît.* 我去 洗~ / 洗个 澡。wǒ qù xǐ ~ / xǐ gè zǎo. I'll take a bath. *Je vais prendre un bain.* 他走了整(整)~月了。tā zǒu le zhěng(zhěng) ~ yuè le. He went a month ago today. *Il est parti il y a aujourd'hui un mois.*

一路平安 yílù píng'ān H5, S1
祝你 / 您 / 你们 ~! zhù nǐ / nín / nǐmen ~!
Have a pleasant journey! *Bon voyage!*

一切 yíqiè G, H4, S1 **all, every, everything, *tout, toute, tous toutes*** 我有的~都给了。wǒ yǒu de ~ dōu gěi le. I gave all I had. *J'ai donné tout ce que j'avais.*

我们有成功的~机会。wǒmen yǒu chénggōng de ~ jīhuì. There's every chance that we'll succeed. *Nous avons toutes les chances de réussir.* 金钱并非就是~。jīnqián bìngfēi jiùshì ~. Money isn't everything. *Il n'y a pas que l'argent qui compte.*

以 yǐ D, H4 **use, take, in order to, as, *utiliser, parer à, afin de, comme*** 我是~你的毛衣为式样的。wǒ shì ~ nǐde máoyī wéi shìyàng de. I used your sweater as a pattern. *J'ai utilisé ton pull comme modèle.*

我们要~防万一。wǒmen yào ~ fáng wànyī. We must prepare for / guard against any contingency. *Il nous faut parer à toute éventualité.* 我这样做~简化事情。wǒ zhèyàng zuò ~ jiǎnhuà shìqing. I've done it in order to simplify things. *Je l'ai fait afin de simplifier les choses.* ~其人之道，还治其人之身。~ qí rén zhī dào, huán zhì qí rén zhī shēn. Deal with a man as he deals with you. *Traite les gens comme ils te traitent.*

以后 (以後) G, G3, S1 **afterwards, after, *après (que), ensuite, plus tard*** ~见! ~ jiàn. See you later! *A plus tard!*

我在他走了~到了。wǒ zài tā zǒu le ~ dào le. I came after he had left. *Je suis arrivé après qu'il soit parti.* 事情~我又觉得很遗憾。shìqing ~ wǒ yòu juédé hěn yíhàn. I regretted it afterwards. *Par la suite, je l'ai regretté.*

以来 (以來) yǐlái H5, S1 **since, *depuis*** 几天~他觉得不舒服。jǐtiān ~ tā juédé bù shūfu. He hasn't been on form for the past few days. *Il n'est pas en forme depuis quelques jours.* 三个月~我们一直在排戏。sāngè yuè ~ wǒmen yīzhí zài páixì. We've been rehearsing the play for three months. *Nous répétons la pièce depuis trois mois.*

已经 (已經) yǐjīng G, N, H2, S1 **already, *déjà*** ~十点了! ~ shídiǎn le. Ten o'clock already! *Déjà dix heures!* 你~做完了吗? nǐ ~ zuòwán le ma? Have you already finished? *Tu as déjà fini?*

他四岁的时候就~能看书了。tā sìsuì de shíhou jiù ~ néng kànshū le. He already knew how to read at the age of 4. *Il savait déjà lire à l'âge de 4 ans.*

椅子 yǐzi H1, S1 **chair, *chaise f*** 有四把木(头)~。yǒu sì bǎ mù(tou) ~. There're four wooden chairs. *Il y a quatre chaises en bois.*

小王，你坐这把~。xiǎo wáng, nǐ zuò zhè bǎ ~. Xiao Wang, sit down on this chair. *Xiao Wang, assieds-toi sur cette chaise.*

亿（億）yì H4, S1 **a hundred million, *cent millions*** 这个规划花了二十~欧元。zhègè guīhuà huā le érshí ~ ōuyuán. This project cost two billion euros. *Ce projet a coûté deux milliards d'euros.* 全世界有七十~人口。quán shìjiè yǒu qīshí ~ rénkǒu. There are seven billion people in the world. *Il y a sept milliards de personnes dans le monde.*

一点儿（一點兒）yìdiǎnr G, S1 **a bit, a little, the faintest, *un peu, quelque*** 有~贵。yǒu ~ guì. It's a bit more expense. *C'est un peu plus cher.* 我说~法文。wǒ shuō ~ fǎwén. I speak a little French. *Je parle quelques mots de français.*

她比他大~。wǒ bǐ tā dà ~. She's a bit older than he is. *Elle est un peu plus âgée que lui.* 我们打扰您了吗？--- ~也没有。wǒmen dǎrǎo nín le ba? -- ~ yě méiyǒu. Are we bothering you? – Not a bit! *On vous dérange ? – Pas du tout.* 他~赢的机会也没有。tā ~ yíng de jīhuì yě méiyǒu. He hasn't the faintest chance of winning. *Il n'a pas la moindre chance de gagner.*

一起 yìqǐ H2, S1 (= 一块儿 yíkuàir) **one another, together, *ensemble, de concert, être réuni*** 我们很喜欢在~。wǒmen hěn xǐhuan zài ~. We enjoy one another's company. *Nous aimons être ensemble.* 我们~行动。wǒmen ~ xíngdòng. We'll act together. *Nous allons agir de concert.*

我们~去买了东西。wǒmen ~ qù mǎi le dōngxi. We went shopping together. *Nous sommes allés faire des courses ensemble.* 全家圣诞节将聚在~。quánjiā shèngdàn-jié jiāng jù zài ~. The family will all be together at Christmas. *La famille sera réunie à Noël.*

一些 yìxiē N, S1 **some, a number of, a few, a little, *des, un certain nombre, quelques, certains, un peu*** 别忘了买~啤酒。wǒ wàngle mǎi ~ píjiǔ. Don't forget to buy some beer. *N'oublie pas d'acheter de la bière.*

我们只有~人。wǒmen zhǐ yǒu ~ rén. We were few in number. *Nous étions en petit nombre.* 这一点有~混乱。zhè yìdiǎn yǒu ~ hùnluàn. There's

been a certain amount of confusion over this. *Il y a une certaine confusion à ce sujet.*

一直 yìzhí G, H3, S1 **straight, always, *droit, toujours*** 他~朝前看。tā ~ cháoqián kàn. He looked straight ahead. *Il a regardé droit devant lui.*

她~带眼镜。tā ~ dài yǎnjìng. She has always worn glasses. *Elle a toujours porté des lunettes.*

一种 yìzhǒng G **a kind of, a sort of, a type of, *d'un ordre, un drôle de, le genre de*** 这是另~问题。zhè shì lìng ~ wèntí. It's a different kind of problem. *C'est un problème d'un autre ordre.*

那是~很怪的电影。nà shì ~ hěn guài de diànyǐng. That's a strange sort of film. *C'est un drôle de film.* 你知道这(一)种事情。nǐ zhīdào zhè (yì) zhǒng shìqing. You know the type of thing. *Tu vois le genre de choses.*

意思 yì si H2, S1 **meaning, idea, opinion, wish, desire, hint, *vouloir dire, pensée f, dans l'air, un petit cadeau*** 这是什么~? zhè shì shénme ~? What's the meaning of this? *Qu'est-ce que ça veut dire?* 你说的是什么~? nǐ shuō de shì shénme ~? What do you mean? *Qu'est-ce que tu veux dire?*

这没有任何~! zhè méiyǒu rènrén ~. That doesn't mean a thing! *Ça ne veut (strictement) rien dire!* 我的~是你不要说个没完! wǒ de ~ shì nǐ búyào shuō gè méiwán. I wish you wouldn't talk so much! *Tu ne peux pas te taire un peu?* 你既然想知道我的~，那就告诉你。nǐ jìrén xiǎng zhīdào wǒ shuō de ~, nà jiù gàosù nǐ. Well, if you want my honest opinion, I'll tell you. *Puisque tu veux savoir le fond de ma pensée, je vais te le dire.* 这是我给你的一点儿小~。zhè shì wǒ gěi nǐ de yìdiǎr xiǎo ~. I'd like to give a small present. *Je voudrais te faire un petit cadeau.* 有一点儿春天的~了。yǒu yìdiǎr chūntiān de ~ le. There's a hint of spring in the air. *Il y a du printemps dans l'air.*

意义（意義）yìyì H5, S1 **meaning, sense, *sens m*** 我不知道这个字的~。wǒ bù zhīdào zhègè zì de ~. I don't know the meaning of this word. *Je ne connais pas le sens de ce mot.* 我认为我们从实质~上抓住了问题。wǒ rènwéi wǒmen cóng shízhì ~ shàng zhuāzhù le wèntí. I think we have, in a very real sense, grasped the problem. *Je crois que nous avons parfaitement saisi le problème.*

艺术（藝術）yìshù H5, S1 **art, *art m*** 这是个~品。zhè shì gè ~ pǐn. It's a work of art.

C'est une œuvre d'art. 知道怎么做是一门～。 zhīdào zěnme zuò shì yìmén ～. There's an art to doing. *C'est tout un art que de (savoir) faire.* 这种说法实在没什么～口味。 zhè zhǒng shuōfǎ shízài méi shénme ～ kǒuwèi. That wasn't a very tasteful thing to say. *Cette remarque n'était pas de très bon goût.*

阴 (陰) yīn H2, S2 **overcast, lunar, yin, devil, *assombrir, lunaire, yin m, sournois***
天～了下来。 The sky has become overcast. *Le ciel s'est assombri.* ～历对中国农民很重要。 The lunar calendar is very important for Chinese farmers. *Le calendrier lunaire est très important pour les agriculteurs chinois.*
这个家伙很～。 zhègè jiāhuo hěn ～. He's an underhand little devil. *C'est un petit sournois.* ～和阳是中国哲学领域的两个基本原理。 ～ hé yáng shì zhōngguó zhéxué lǐngyù de miǎnggè jīběn yuánlǐ. Yin and yang are the two basic principles in the universe of Chinese philosophy. *Le yin et le yang sont les deux principes fondamentaux dans l'univers de la philosophie chinoise.*

因为 (因為) yīnwèi G, H2, S1
because, for, on account of, *à cause de* ～暴风雨我们没有去。 ～ bàofēngyǔ wǒmen méiyǒu qù. We didn't go on account of there being a storm. *Nous n'y sommes pas allés à cause de la tempête.*
她～很疼而睡不着。 tā ～ hěn téng ér shuì bù zháo. She couldn't sleep for the pain. *Elle ne pouvait pas dormir à cause de la douleur.* ～得病人们让他退休了。 ～ dé bìng rénmen ràng tā tuìxiū le. He has been retired because of his illness. *On l'a mis à la retraite à cause de sa maladie.*

银行 (銀行) yínháng H3, S1 **bank, *banque f*** 附近有～吗? fùjìn yǒu ～ ma? Is there a bank nearby? *Y a-t-il une banque par ici?* 您在哪家～有户头? nín zài nǎjiā ～ yǒu hùtóu? Who do you bank with? *A quelle banque êtes-vous?*

银行卡 (銀行卡) yínhángkǎ S1
bankcard, *carte bancaire* 他有三张～。 tā yǒu sānzhāng ～. He has three bank cards. *Il a trois cartes bancaires.* 你们接受～吗? nǐmen jiēshòu ～ ma? Do you accept bankcard? *Acceptez-vous les cartes bancaires?*

应该 (應該) yīnggāi G, H3, S1
should, ought to, must, *devoir, falloir* 您～马上做。 nín ～ mǎshàng zuò. You should do it at once. *Vous devriez le faire tout de suite.* 你不～笑

话他。 nǐ bù ～ xiàohuà tā. You shouldn't laugh at him. *Tu as tort de te moquer de lui.*
我认为～叫您知道。 wǒ rènwéi ～ jiào nín zhīdào. I thought I ought to let you know about it. *J'ai cru devoir vous en faire part.* 我们现在～做什么? wǒmen xiànzài ～ zuò shénme? What must we do now? *Que devons-nous faire maintenant?*

英国 (英國) yīngguó * **Great Britain, England, *Grande Bretagne, Angleterre f*** 这是她的～护照。 zhè shì tāde ～ hùzhào. That's her British passport. *C'est son passeport britannique.* 皮特是从～来的。 pítè shì cóng ～ lái de. Pitt comes from Great Britain. *Pitt vient de la Grande Bretagne.* 你在学～英语还是美国英语? nǐ zài xué ～ yīngyǔ háishì měiguó yīngyǔ? Are you studying British English or American English? *Est-ce que tu étudies l'anglais britannique ou l'anglais américain?*

英文 yīngwén S1 (英语 = yīngyǔ)

英语 (英語) yīngyǔ S1 (= 英文 yīngwén) **English (language), *anglais m, langue anglaise*** 您讲～吗? nín jiǎng ～ ma? Do / Can you speak English? *Parlez-vous (l')anglais?* 他讲标准～。 tā jiǎng biāozhǔn ～. He speaks the King's / Queen's English. *Il parle l'anglais correct.* 我们是用～ 交谈的 / 对话的。 wǒmen shì yòng ～ jiāotán de / duìhuà de. We spoke (in) English to each other. *Nous nous sommes parlé en anglais.*

用 yòng D, H3, S1 **use, useful, *utiliser, avoir la peine de*** ～～脑袋! ～～ nǎodai! Use your head! *Ne sois pas si bête!* 看, 这个工具～时很不爱护。 kàn, zhè gè gōngjù ～ shí bú àihù. Look, this tool has been roughly used. *Regarde, cet outil a été mal utilisé.*
这本书对我很有～。 zhè běn shū duì wǒ hěn yǒu ～. This book was very useful to me. *Ce livre m'a été très utile.* 讨论一下也没～。 tǎolùn yíxià yě méi～. It's useless even trying to discuss it. *Ce n'est même pas la peine d'essayer d'en discuter.*

邮局 (郵局) yóujú H5, S1 **post office, *bureau de poste*** ～关门了吗? ～ guānmén le ma? Is the post office closed? *La poste est-elle fermée?* 我去～寄这封信。 wǒ qù ～ jì zhè fēng xìn. I'll mail the letter. *Je vais mettre cette lettre à la poste.*

游泳 yóu//yǒng H2, S1 **swim, *nager, se baigner*** 我不会～! wǒ bú huì ～! I can't swim! *Je ne sais pas nager.* 我们每星期三～。 wǒmen měi

xīngqī sān ~. We swim on Wednesdays. *Nous faisons de la natation le mercredi.*

湖水太冷游不了泳。húshuǐ tài lěng yóu bùliǎo yǒng. The lake was too cold to swim in. *Le lac était trop froid pour qu'on s'y baigne.*

有 yǒu D, H1, S1 **have,** *avoir* 您~车吗 / 您~没~车? --- ~, ~两辆。nín ~ chē ma / nín yǒu méi yǒu chē? -- yǒu, yǒu liǎng liàng. Do you have / Have you got a car? – Yes, I do / I have, I have (got) two. *Avez-vous une voiture / des voitures? – Oui, j'en ai deux.*

他~一双大手。tā ~ yìshuāng dà shǒu. He has big hands. *Il a de grosses mains.* 我们明天~客人。wǒmen míngtiān ~ kèrén. We're having visitors tomorrow. *Nous attendons des invités demain.* 她没~朋友。tā meiyǒu ~. She had no friends. *Elle n'avait pas d'amis.*

有点[儿](有點[兒])yǒudiǎr G **some, a little, rather,** *assez, un peu, un tout petit peu, pas très, petit* 这~难。zhè ~ nán. It's somewhat difficult. *C'est assez difficile.* 这~(这有一点点儿)贵。zhè ~ (zhè yǒu yì diǎndiǎr) guì. It's a (little) bit more expensive. *C'est un (tout petit) peu plus cher.*

她长得~一般。tā zhǎng dé ~ yìbān. She is rather plain. *Elle n'est pas très jolie.* 这要花多少钱您必须要~概念。zhè yào huā duōshǎo qián nín bìxū yào ~ gàiniàn. You must have some idea of how much it will cost. *Vous devez avoir une petite idée de combine ça va coûter.*

有关 (有關) yǒuguān N, S2 **concern, bear on, relate to,** *concerner, avoir rapport avec, être en rapport avec* 听一下! 这个讨论跟你~。tīng yíxià, zhè gè tǎolǔn gēn nǐ ~. Listen! This discussion concerns you. *Écoute un peu! Cette discussion te concerne.*

这与事情 ~ / 无关。zhè yǔ shìqing ~ / wúguān. It has a bearing on / It has no bearing on the matter. *Cela a un rapport / n'a aucun rapport avec l'affaire.* 这与我刚才说的~。zhè yǔ wǒ gāngcái shuō de ~. This relates to what I was just saying. *Ceci est en rapport avec ce que je viens de dire.*

有(一)些 yǒu (yì) xiē G, S1 **some,** *un peu, certains, quelques* 这~难。zhè ~ nán. It's somewhat difficult. *C'est un peu difficile.* 我~饿。wǒ ~ è. I'm a bit hungry. *J'ai un peu faim.*

我还~别的。wǒ hái ~ biéde. I've some others. *J'en ai d'autres.* 他们分路走了，~人朝这边走，~人朝那边走。tāmen fēnlù zǒu le, ~ cháo zhèbiān zǒu, ~ cháo nàbiān zǒu. They went off, some one way, some another. *Ils se sont dispersés, les uns d'un côté, les autres de l'autre.*

右边（右邊）yòu bian H2, S1 **the right(-hand) side, the right,** *côté droit, droite f* 这里在~开车。zhèlǐ zài ~ kāichē. You drive on the right-hand side here. *On conduit à droite ici.*

电影院~有一个中国饭馆。diànyǐngyuàn ~ yǒu yígè zhōngguó fànguǎn. To the right of the cinema there's a Chinese restaurant. *A droite du cinéma il y a un restaurant chinois.*

于（於）yú D, S2 **indicating a time, a place, limits, a concerned person or a starting point,** *indiquer un temps, un lieu, des limites, une personne concernée ou le point de départ* 第二次世界大战结束~一九四五年。dì'èrcì shìjiè dàzhàn jiéshù ~ 1945 nián. The Second World War came to an end in 1945. *La Deuxième Guerre mondiale a pris fin en 1945.*

他们年度大会~柏林举行的。tāmen niándù dàhuì ~ bólín jǔxíng de. They held their annual meeting in Berlin. *Ils ont tenu leur assemblée annuelle à Berlin.* 我们在这里求助~人。wǒmen zài zhèlǐ qiúzhù ~ rén. We're asking people for help here. *Ici nous demandons de l'aide aux gens.* 她的成功在~意愿。tā de chénggōng zài ~ yìyuàn. She succeeded by force of will. *Elle a réussi à force de volonté.*

于是 (於是) yúshì G, H4, S2 **thereupon, hence,** *alors, par conséquent* 他被拒绝入内，~离开了。tā bèi jùjué rù nèi, ~ líkāi le. He was refused entry, thereupon he left. *On lui a refusé l'entrée, sur quoi il est parti.*

他圣诞节那天出生，~起的名是诺埃尔。tā shèngdàn-jié nàtiān chūshēng, ~ qǐ de míng shì nuò'āi'ěr. He was born on Christmas Day, hence the name Noël. *Il est né le jour de Noël, d'où son nom.*

语 (語) yǔfǎ T **language, tongue, words,** *langage m, langue f* 俄~是她的母~。é~ shì tā de mǔ~. Russian is her mother tongue. *Le russe est sa langue maternelle.*

昨天的笔~测验比口~测验容易。zuótiān de bǐ~ cèyàn bǐ kǒu~ cèyàn róngyi. The written test was easier than the oral test yesterday. *L'épreuve écrite était plus facile que l'épreuve orale hier.* 他们总是那个口头~。tāmen zǒngshì nàgè kǒutóu ~. With them it's always the same tune. *Avec eux c'est toujours la même rengaine.*

语法 (語法) yǔfǎ H4, S2 **grammar, grammaire f** 这是本德语~(书)。zhè shì běn déyǔ ~ (shū). It's a German grammar (book). *C'est une grammaire / un livre de grammaire allemande.* 他写东西~很糟。tā xiě dōngxi ~ hěn zāo. He writes bad grammar. *Il écrit de façon peu grammaticale.* 你说的不合~。nǐ shuō de bùhé ~. That's not (good) grammar. *Ce que tu dis là n'est pas grammatical.*

语音 (語音) yǔyīn S1 **pronunciation, prononciation f** 他法文~很好 / 很糟。tā fǎwén ~ hěn hǎo / hěn zāo. His French pronunciation is good / bad. *Il a une bonne / mauvaise prononciation en français.* 汉语~的四声西方人觉得比较难。hànyǔ ~ de sìshēng xīfāngrén juéde bǐjiào nán. Westerns find the four tones of Chinese pronunciation quite difficult. *Les Occidentaux trouvent assez difficiles les quatre tons de la prononciation chinoise.*

雨 yǔ T, S1 **rain, pluie f** 下~了。xià ~ le. It is raining. *Il pleut.* 下大~了 / ~下得很大。xià dà ~ le / ~ xià dé hěn dà. It is raining hard. *It pleut à verse.*

他们度假时有一些~天。tāmen dùjià shí yǒu yìxiē ~ tiān. They had some rain during their holiday. *Ils ont eu de la pluie pendant leurs vacances.*

育 yù T **give birth to, raise, educate, donner naissance à, cultiver, éduquer** 她生儿~女了。tā shēng ér ~ nǚ le. She gave birth to children. *Elle a donné naissance à des enfants.* 那个农人在~秧。nà gè nóngrén zài ~ yāng. That peasant is raising rice seedlings. *Le paysan est en train de cultiver les plants de riz.* 德~与智一样重要。dé ~ yǔ zhì ~ yíyàng zhòngyào. Moral education is as important as intellectual one. *L'éducation morale est aussi importante que celle intellectuelle.*

元 yuán T, H4, S1 **yuan, euro, dollar, yuan m, euro m, dollar m** 我昨天在银行存了五千~。wǒ zuótiān zài yánháng cún le wǔqiān ~. I made a deposit of 5000 yuan yesterday. *J'ai déposé 5000 yuan en banque hier.*

我想把一百欧~换成美~。wǒ xiǎng bǎ yībǎi ōu~ huànchéng měi~. I'd like to change a hundred euros into dollars. *Je voudrais changer cent euros en dollars.*

原 yuán T, S2 **original, former, pardon, origine m, même, pardonner** 这个词的~意是

什么？zhè gè cí de ~yì shì shénme? What's the original meaning of the word? *Quel est le sens d'origine du mot?*

这部新电影是~班人马。zhè bù xīn diànyǐng shì ~ bān rénmǎ. The new film has the former staff. *Le nouveau film a la même équipe.* 这是个情有可~的错误。zhè shì gè qíng yǒu kě ~ de cuòwù. It was a pardonable mistake. *C'était une erreur pardonnable.*

园 (園) yuán T, S2 **garden, park, parc m, jardin m, jardinage m** 他周末搞花~(儿)。tā zhōumò gǎo huā~(r). He does the garden at / on the weekend. *Il fait du jardinage le week-end.*

她每天都去公~散步。tā měitiān dōu qù gōng~ sànbù. She goes for a walk in the park every day. *Elle se promène dans le parc tous les jours.* 城里有一个植物~。chénglǐ yǒu yígè zhíwù ~. There is a botanical garden in town. *Il y a un jardin botanique en ville.*

远 (遠) yuǎn T, H2, S1 **far, distant, loin** 他住得很~。tā zhù dé hěn ~. He lives far away. *Il demeure au loin.*

您(是)~道而来的吗？nǐ (shì) ~ dào ér lái de ma? Have you come far? *Etes-vous venu de loin?* 我们从宾馆可以看到~~的海。wǒmen cóng bīnguǎn kěyǐ kàndào ~~ de hǎi. We had a distant view of sea from the hotel. *On pouvait voir la mer au loin depuis l'hôtel.*

院 yuàn T, S1 **yard, court, institute, cour f, tribunal m, institut m** 他在前~等你呢。tā zài qián~ děng nǐ ne. He's waiting for you in the front yard. *Il t'attend dans la cour de devant.*

孩子们在~儿 / ~子里玩儿。háizimen zài ~r / ~zi lǐ wár. The children are playing in the yard. *Les enfants jouent dans la cour.* 我向法~控告了他。wǒ xiàng fǎ~ kònggào le tā. I brought him to court. *Je l'ai traduit devant un tribunal.* 她是商学院院~。tā shì shāngxué~ ~zhǎng. She's the director of the business school. *Elle est la directrice de l'école commerciale.*

怨 yuàn T, S2 **blame, resentment, reproche m, rejeter la responsabilité sur, rancune f** 我~你, 不~她。wǒ ~ nǐ, bú ~ tā. I blame you, not her. *C'est à toi que je fais reproche, pas à elle.*

这不要~我。zhè búyào ~ wǒ. Don't blame me for it! *Ne rejetez pas la responsabilité sur moi!* 我跟那个人结下了~。wǒ gēn nàgè rén jiéxià le ~. I've harboured resentment against that man. *J'ai gardé rancune à cet homme.*

愿（願）yuàn T, S2 **wish, desire, will, *souhaiter, envie f, être prêt*** ~您新年快乐! ~ nín xīnnián kuàilè! I wish you a Happy New Year! *Je vous souhaite une bonne année!*

他丝毫不~来看你。tā sīháo bú ~ lái kàn nǐ. He had not the least / slightest desire to come and see you. *Il n'avait nullement / pas la moindre envie de venir te voir.* 您~不~跟我们合作? nín ~ bú ~ gēn wǒmen hézuò? Are you willing to cooperate with us? *Êtes-vous prêt à collaborer avec nous?*

约（約）yuē T, S1 **invite, appointment, about, *inviter, rendez-vous m, à peu près*** 我 ~了他吃午饭。wǒ ~ le tā chī wǔfàn. I invited him for lunch. *Je l'ai invité à déjeuner.*

我给你~了一个时间去看大夫。wǒ gěi nǐ ~ le yígè shíjiān qù kàn dàifu. I've made an appointment with the doctor for you. *Je t'ai pris un rendez-vous chez le docteur.* 他们~五十人。tāmen ~ wǔshí rén. They're about fifty. *Ils sont à peu près cinquante.*

越 yuè T, H3, S1 **jump, overstep, more...more / less..., *sauter, outrepasser, plus...plus / moins...*** 你能~过篱笆吗? nǐ néng ~ guò líba ma? Can you jump over the hedge? *Peux-tu sauter par-dessus la haie?*

那个人~过了自己的权利范围。nàgè rén ~ guò le zìjǐ de quánlì fànwéi. That man overstepped his authority. *L'homme a outrepassé ses pouvoirs.* 你 ~犹豫, 就~做不成。nǐ ~ yóuyù, jiù ~ zuò bù chéng. The more you think, the less you'll manage to do it. *Plus tu réfléchiras, moins tu y arriveras.*

月 yuè T, H1, S1 **moon, month, *lune f, mois m*** 昨晚 是明~ / ~亮很亮。zuówǎn shì míng ~ / ~liàng hěn liàng. You could see the moon really well last night. *On voyait très bien la lune hier soir.*

她每~挣多少钱? nǐ měi ~ zhèng duōshao qián? How much does she earn a month? *Combien gagne-t-elle par mois?* 我一~去。wǒ yī~ qù. I'll go in January. *J'y irai en janvier.* 我不喜欢二~。wǒ bù xǐhuan èr~. I don't like February. *Je n'aime pas le mois de février.* 两个~以后他就三十岁了。liǎnggè ~ yǐhòu tā jiù sānshí suì le. He will be thirty in two months. *Il aura trente ans dans deux mois.*

云（雲）yún T, H3, S2 **sky, cloud, say, *nuage m, dire*** 看那些乌~, 要下雷阵雨了。kàn nàxiē wū ~, yào xià léizhènyǔ le. Look at those black clouds, there's going to be a thunderstorm. *Regarde ces nuages noirs, il va y avoir un orage.*

下午 有很多~ / ~层密布。xiàwǔ yǒu hěnduō ~ / ~céng mìbù. It clouded over in the afternoon. *Ça s'est couvert dans l'après-midi.* 他人~亦~。tā rén ~ yì ~. He parrots what others say. *Il répète comme un perroquet.*

运（運）yùn T, S2 **carry, supply, *porter, transporter*** 他们把设备~过了桥。tāmen bǎ shèbèi ~guò le qiáo. They carried the equipment across the bridge. *Ils ont porté le matériel de l'autre côté du pont.*

他们 空~ / 水~ 食品。tāmen kōng~ / shuǐ~ shípǐn. They fly / ship food supplied. *Ils transportent des vivres par avion / par bateau.*

运动（運動）yùndòng H2, S1 **sport, campaign, *sport m, campagne f*** 她搞很多(体育)~。tā gǎo hěnduō (tǐyù) ~. She does a lot of sport. *Elle fait beaucoup de sport.*

我是跳高~员。wǒ shì tiàogāo ~yuán. I'm a high jumper. *Je suis sauteur en hauteur.* 他领导反毒品的~。tā lǐngdǎo fǎn dúpǐn de ~. He's conducting a campaign against drugs. *Il mène une campagne contre la drogue.*

les autres sont là. 旅馆~河旁边。lǚguǎn ~ hé pángbiān. The hotel is next to the river. *L'hôtel se trouve près de la rivière.*

这~ / 看 他是否同意。zhè ~ / kàn tā shìfǒu tóngyì. It depends on whether she accepts. *Ça dépend si elle accepte.* 他们~花园里玩儿。tāmen ~ huāyuán lǐ wár. They're playing in the garden. *Ils jouent dans le jardin.* ~红(绿)灯处往左拐。~ hóng(lǜ) dēng chù wǎng zuǒ guǎi. Turn left at the traffic lights. *Tournez à gauche au feu.* 他~胳臂下夹着一份报纸。tā ~ gēbo xià jiāzhe yífèn bàozhǐ. He was carrying a paper under his arm. *Il portait un journal sous le bras.*

在 zài (副) D, T, H1, S1 **be under way, être en train de** 她~唱歌儿。tā ~ chàng gēr. She is singing. *Elle est en train de chanter.* 我~做饭。wǒ ~ zuòfàn. I'm (busy) cooking. *Je suis en train de cuisiner.*

舆论(正)~ 转变。yúlùn (zhèng)~ zhuǎnbiàn. Public opinion is changing. *L'opinion publique est en train d'évoluer.*

再 zài T, H2, S1 **another time, again, once more, encore une fois, de nouveau, à nouveau** 您能~说一遍吗? nín néng ~ shuō yíbiàn ma? Can you say it again? *Pouvez-vous répéter?* ~给我点儿。~ gěi wǒ yìdiǎr. Give me some more. *Donne-moi davantage.*

我不能~等下去了。wǒ bù néng ~ děng xiàqù le. I can't wait any longer. *Je ne peux plus attendre.* (你)先做功课，~看电视。(nǐ) xiān zuò gōngkè, ~ kàn diànshì. Do your homework first than you can watch TV. *Fais d'abord tes devoirs, et ensuite tu pourras regarder la télé.*

再见 (再見) zàijiàn H1, S1 **goodbye, see you, au revoir, à bientôt** ~! zàijiàn Goodbye! *Au revoir!*

希望近期能~! xīwàng jìnqī néng ~! See you soon! *A bientôt!* 我们北京 ~ / 再会! wǒmen běijīng ~ / zàihuì! See you (again) in Beijing! *On se (re)verra à Beijing!*

咱 zán T, S1 **we (including both the speaker and the person or the persons spoken to), nous (qui comprend celui / celle qui parle et ceux / celles qui écoutent)** ~学生钱不多呀! ~ xuésheng qián bù duō ya! We students don't have much money. *Nous, étudiants, on n'a pas beaucoup d'argent.*

~(们)每个人都可能犯错误。~(men) měigè rén dōu kěnéng fàn cuòwù. We all make mistakes. *Tout le monde peut se tromper.*

Z

杂 (雜) zá T, S2 **miscellaneous, odds and ends, different, divers, un bric-à-brac, mélangé** 他们总谈~事儿。tāmen zǒng tán ~shìr. They always make miscellaneous conversation. *Ils font toujours la conversation sur des sujets divers.*

她桌子上总堆满了~七~八的东西。tā zhuōzi shàng zǒng duīmǎn le ~qī ~bā de dōngxi. Her desk is always covered with odds and ends. *Son bureau est toujours encombré de tout un bric-à-brac.* 她常常因为什么~事儿发火。tā chángcháng yīnwéi shénme ~shì fāhuǒ. She often takes offence over nothing. *Elle se fâche souvent pour une bagatelle.* 很多不同的风格都(混)~在一起了。hěnduō bùtóng de fēnggé dōu (hùn)~ zài yìqǐ le. It's a mixture of too many different styles. *On a un peu trop mélangé les genres.*

灾 (災) zāi T, S2 **disaster, flood, adversity, désastre m, inondation f, malheur m** 我们的城市连续受~。wǒmen de chéngshì liánxù shòu ~. Our town has suffered one disaster after another. *Notre ville a subi désastre après désastre.*

庄稼遭了水~。zhuāngjia zāo le shuǐ~. The crops have been ruined by the floods. *Les récoltes ont été perdues à cause des inondations.* 他们遇到了三~八难。tāmen yùdào le sān ~ bā nàn. They met with many adversities. *Ils ont eu bien des malheurs.*

在 zài (动、介) D, T, H1, S1 **be, depend, in, at, être, se trouver, dépendre, dans, à** 他不~，别人都~。tā bú ~, biérén dōu ~. He's not in, and all the others are there. *Il est absent, et tous*

暂（暫）zàn T **temporarily, temporairement** 他~住这里。tā ~ zhù zhèlǐ. He'll stay here temporarily. *Il reste ici temporairement.*

我~不告诉他事实真相。wǒ ~ bú gàosù tā shìshí zhēnxiàng. I kept putting off telling him the truth. *Je continuais à repousser le moment de lui dire la vérité.*

早饭（早飯）zǎofàn S1 **breakfast, petit déjeuner** 我八点吃~。wǒ bādiǎn chī ~. I have breakfast at 8. *Je prends le petit déjeuner à 8 heures.* 你~要吃什么? nǐ ~ yào chī shénme? What do you want for breakfast? *Que veux-tu pour ton petit déjeuner?*

早上 zǎoshang H2, S1 (= 早晨 zǎochen) **morning, matin m** ~好! (Good) morning! *Bonjour!* ~七点了。~ qī diǎn le. It's seven o'clock in the morning. *Il est sept heures du matin.*

~有一个航班。~ yǒu yígè hángbān. There's a flight in the morning. *Il y a un vol le matin.*

怎么（怎麼）zěnme G, H1, S1 **how, why, as, comment, pourquoi, comme** 这个~写? zhège ~ xiě? How do you write it? *Comment est-ce que ça s'écrit?*

他~从不打电话? tā ~ cóng bù dǎ diànhuà? Why is it that he never phones? *Pourquoi est-ce qu'il ne téléphone jamais?* 你觉得~对就~做。nǐ juéde ~ duì jiù ~ zuò. Act as you see fit. *Fais comme bon te semble.*

怎么样（怎麼樣）zěnmeyàng H1, S1 **how (about...?) much, not up to, si on (faisait)...? pas très, pas aussi (bon) que** 最近~? zuìjìn ~? Hi, how's things? *Salut, ça roule?* 我们什么时候去? --- 星期一~? wǒmen shénme shíhou qù? -- xīngqī yī, ~? When shall we go? – What about Monday? *Quand est-ce qu'on y va? – Et si on disait lundi?*

今天晚上出去~? jīntiān wǎnshàng chūqù, ~? How about going out tonight? *Si on sortait ce soir?* 我觉得她不~。wǒ juéde tā bù ~. I don't think much of her. *Je n'ai pas une très haute opinion d'elle.* 跟他水平比他做得不~。gēn tā shuǐpíng bǐ tā zuòdé bù ~. His work is not up to his normal standard. *Son travail n'est pas aussi bon que d'habitude.*

站 zhàn (名) H3, S1 **stand, get up, shelter, être debout, se lever, station, abribus m,**

gare f 他~在门前。tā ~ zài ménqián. He was standing near the door. *Il était debout près de la porte.* 请~起来! qǐng ~ qǐlái! Get up please! *Lève-toi, s'il te plaît!* 你能来公交车~等我吗? nǐ néng lái gōngjiāo chē~ děng wǒ ma? Can you wait for me at the bus shelter? *Peux-tu m'attendre à l'abribus?* 我到车~接你。wǒ dào chē~ jiē nǐ. I'll meet you at the station. *Je te retrouverai à la gare.* 火车进~了。huǒchē jìn ~ le. The train came into the station. *Le train est entré en gare.*

张（張）zhāng (量) H2, S1 **[classifier], [classificateur m]** 我们预定了一~桌子。wǒmen yùdìng le yì ~ zhuōzi. We've booked a table. *Nous avons retenu une table.*

给我一~纸，我把地址记下来。gěi wǒ yì ~ zhǐ, wǒ bǎ dìzhǐ jì xiàlái. Pass me a piece of paper, I'm going to write the address down. *Passe-moi un papier, je vais noter l'adresse.* 我们要了(一个)有两~床的房间。wǒmen yàole (yìgè) yǒu liǎng~ chuáng de fángjiān. We asked for a room with two beds. *Nous avons demandé une chambre à deux lits.*

张（張）zhāng (动) H2, S1 **open, spread, ouvrir, voilier** 他~开了双臂。tā ~ kāi le shuāngbì. He's opened his arms. *Il a ouvert les bras.*

~开嘴呼吸。~ kāi zuǒ hūxī. Breathe through your mouth. *Respirez par la bouche.* 现在是你们自己~开翅膀的时候了。xiànzài shì nǐmen zìjǐ ~ kāi chìbàng de shíhou le. It's time you spread your wings. *Il est temps que vous voiliez de vos propres ailes.*

丈夫 zhàngfu H2, S2 **husband, mari m** 他们是~、妻子关系吗? tāmen shì ~、qīzi guānxì ma? Are they husband and wife? *Sont-ils mari et femme?*

玛丽的~很会开玩笑。mǎlì de ~ hěn huì kāi wánxiào. Mary's husband is very funny. *L'époux de Marie est très drôle.*

找 zhǎo H2, S1 **looking for, seek, want to see, chercher, vouloir voir** 你~(人)打架吗? nǐ ~ (rén) dǎjià ma? Are you looking for fight? *Tu cherches la bagarre?* 我们最好~人帮助。wǒmen zuìhǎo ~ rén bāngzhù. We'd better seek help. *Il vaut mieux aller chercher de l'aide.*

有人~你。yǒu rén ~. Someone wants to see you. *Quelqu'un veut te voir.* ~我有什么事儿? ~ wǒ yǒu shénme shì? What can I do for you? *Que puis-je vous être utile?*

这（這）zhè / zhèi D, H1, S1 **this, *ce, cela, ceci*** ~是我(的)母亲。 ~ shì wǒ (de) mǔqin. This is my mother. *Je vous présente ma mère.* ~是什么? ~ shì shénme? What's this? *Qu'est-ce que c'est (que ça)?*

~是我说过的那个地方。 ~ shì wǒ shuō guo de nàgè dìfang. This is the place I was talking about. *C'est l'endroit dont je parlais.*

这个（這個）zhègè N, G (1), **this one, this, *ce, cela, ceci, celui-(celle-)ci*** ~是我的，那个是你的。 ~ shì wǒ de, nàgè shì nǐ de. This one is mine and that one is yours. *Celui-ci est le mien, et celui-là est le tien.*

由于~原因我没来。 yóuyú ~ yuányīn wǒ méi lái. I didn't come for this reason. *Je ne suis pas venu pour cette raison.*
(2), [口] **so, such, *tellement, si, comme*** 我们玩儿得~痛快! wǒmen wár dé ~ tòngkuai! We had such a good time! *On s'est tellement bien amusé(s)!* 我~饿呀，本来能都吃掉。 wǒ ~ è ya, běnlái dōu néng chīdiào! I was so hungry I could have eaten it all. *J'avais si faim que j'aurais pu tout manger.* 我做了后~遗憾啊! wǒ zuòle hòu ~ yíhàn a! How I regret having done it! *Comme je regrette de l'avoir fait.*

这么（這麼）zhème G, S1 **so, such, this way, like that, *comment, un de ces..., le don de*** 她~叫人生气。 tā ~ jiào rén shēngqì. She makes me so angry. *Elle a le don de me mettre en colère.*

他~勇敢! tā ~ yǒnggǎn! He has such courage! *Il a un de ces courages!* 我~做。 wǒ ~ zuò. I do it this way. *Voilà comment je fais.* 别跟我~说话! bié gēn wǒ ~ shuōhuà! Don't talk to me like that! *Ne me parle pas sur ce ton!*

这些（這些）zhèxiē G, N, S1 **these, *ces, ce*** ~书是谁的? ~ shū shì shéi de? Whose are these books? *A qui sont ces livres?*

现在~日子存钱不容易。 xiànzài ~ rìzi cúnqián bù róngyi. Saving money isn't easy these days. *Faire des économies n'est pas facile de nos jours.* 你认识~人吗? nǐ rènshi ~ rén ma? Do you know these people? *Connais-tu ces gens?*

这样（這樣）zhèyàng G, S1 (1) (定语、状语) (= 这么 zhème) **such, this way, like that, *un de ces..., comment, ce*** 他~勇敢! tā ~ yǒnggǎn! He has such courage! *Il a un de ces courages!*

我~做。 wǒ ~ zuò. I do it this way. *Voilà comment je fais.* 别跟我~说话! bié gēn wǒ ~ shuōhuà! Don't talk to me like that! *Ne me parle pas sur ce ton!*
(2) (补语、谓语) **that kind of, *ce genre de*** 您如果喜欢~的东西，就没有问题。 nín rúguǒ xǐhuan ~ de dōngxi, jiù méiyǒu wèntí. It's all right, if you like that kind of thing. *C'est bien si vous aimez ce genre de chose.* 你知道他总(是)~。 nǐ zhīdào tā zòng(shì) ~. You know how he always gets his own way. *Tu sais bien comment il est.*

这种（這種）zhèzhǒng G **a sort of, this type of, one's kind, *ce modèle de, de son espèce*** ~电影很怪。 ~ diànyǐng hěn guàn. It's a strange sort of film. *C'est un drôle de film.* 你开~车吗? nǐ kāi ~ chē ma? Do you drive this type of cars? *Est-ce que tu conduis ce modèle de voiture?* 我看透了你~人! wǒ kàntòu le nǐ ~ rén! I know your kind! *Je connais les gens de ton espèce!*

着（著）zhe D, H2, S1 **[expressing a continued state or action], *[exprimer un état ou une action qui continue]*** 你听~! nǐ tīng ~! You just listen! *Ecoute bien!*

我一整天都 站~ / 是站~的。 wǒ yìzhěngtiān dōu zhàn ~ / shì zhàn ~ de. I've been standing all day. *Je suis resté debout toute la journée.* 她听~收音机做功课。 tā tīng ~ shōuyīnjī zuò gōngkè. She was listening to the radio while doing her homework. *Elle écoutait la radio tout en faisant ses devoirs.*

真 zhēn H2, S1 **true, real, genuine, *vrai, comme, intimement, réellement*** 这是~的。 zhè shì ~ de. That is true. *C'est vrai.* 这~是你说的吗? zhè ~ shì nǐ shuō de ma? Did you really say that? *As-tu vraiment dit ça?*

您 / 你 / 你们~好! nín / nǐ / nǐmen ~ hǎo! How kind of you! *Comme c'est aimable!* 我~以为他是无辜的。 wǒ ~ yǐwéi tā shì wúgū de. It is my genuine belief that he is innocent. *Je suis intimement persuadé de son innocence.* 他们~觉得能成功。 tāmen ~ juédé néng chénggōng. They truly believe they'll succeed. *Ils croient réellement qu'ils vont réussir.* 一些演员咬字不~是时髦。 yīxiē yǎnyuán jiǎozì bù~ shì shímáo. It is the fashion among certain actors to slur their speech. *C'est la mode chez certains acteurs de ne pas prononcer clairement.*

正在 zhèngzài H2, S1 **be going to, *être en train de*** 她 ~ / 在 / 正 唱歌儿。 She is singing. *Elle est en train de chanter.* 舆论~转变。 Public opinion is changing. *L'opinion publique est en train d'évoluer.*

政策 zhèngcè N, H5, S2 **policy, *politique f, mesure f***

做这个大概是一项 好的 / 坏的~。 zuò zhège dàgài shì yíxiàng hǎode / huàide ~. It would be good / bad policy to do that. *Ce serait une bonne / mauvaise politique de faire cela.*

公司这方面的~是什么? gōngsī zhè fāngmiàn de ~ shì shénme? What is the company policy on this matter? *Quelle est la ligne suivie par la compagnie à ce sujet?* 我的~向来是等着瞧。 wǒ de ~ xiànglái shì děngzhe qiáo. My policy has always been to wait and see. *J'ai toujours eu pour règle d'attendre et de voir venir.*

政府 zhèngfù N, H5, S1 **government, *gouvernement m***

他组成了新~。 tā zǔchéng le xīn ~. He has formed a new government. *Il a formé un nouveau gouvernement.*

这一规划是~投资的。 zhè yí guīhuà shì ~ tóuzī de. The project is financed by the government. *Le projet est financé par l'Etat.* 他在市~工作。 tā zài shì ~ gōngzuò. He works for the (local) council. *C'est un employé de mairie.* 社会党人参加了联合~。 shèhuì-dǎng rén cānjiā le liánhé ~. The Socialists have joined the coalition government. *Les socialistes sont entrés dans le gouvernement de coalition.* ~垮台了。 ~ kuǎtái le. The government has fallen. *Le gouvernement est tombé.*

政治 zhèngzhì N, H5, S1 **politics, political affairs, *politique f, affaires politiques***

他的~观点到底是什么? tā de ~ guāndiǎn dàodǐ shì shénme? What exactly are his politics? *Quelles sont ses opinions politiques au juste?*

她在大学学的是~学。 tā zài dàxué xué de shì ~ xué. She studied politics at university. *Elle a étudié les sciences politiques à l'université.* 他一直对~很感兴趣。 tā yìzhí duì ~ hěn gǎnxìngqu. He's always very political. *Il s'est toujours intéressé à la politique.* ~对他们从 没 / 未 有过什么吸引力。 ~ duì tāmen cóng méi / wèi yǒuguò shénme xīyǐng lì. Politics has never attracted them. *La politique ne les a jamais intéressés.*

证件 (證件) zhèngjiàn H5, S1 **credentials, papers, logbook, *papiers (d'identité), carte d'identité, carte grise***

请出示~。 qǐng chūshì ~. Please show your papers. *Présentez vos papiers, s'il vous plaît.* 警察要看他的~。 jǐngchá yào kàn tāde ~. The policeman

asked to see his credentials. *Le policier lui a demandé ses papiers (d'identité).*

之 zhī D, H4 **of, *de***

这是他们拒绝的原因~一。 zhè shì tāmen jùjué de yuányīn ~ yī. That's one of the reasons (why) they refused. *C'est une des raisons de leur refus.*

我知道为什么要我走，你要取而代~。 zhè shì tāmen jùjué de yuányīn ~ yī. I know why you want me to go -- you will replace me. *Je sais pourquoi tu veux que je parte -- tu veux me remplacer.* 我们要以我~长，攻敌~短。 wǒmen yào yǐ wǒ ~ cháng, gōng dí ~ duǎn. We must utilize our strong points to attack the enemy at his weak points. *Il faut profiter de nos points forts pour attaquer l'ennemi sur ses points faibles.*

支持 zhīchí N, H4, S1 **back, sustain, support, *(se) soutenir, subsister, appuyer***

我 ~不下去了 / ~不住了。 wǒ ~ bú xiàqù le / ~ búzhù le. I'm ready to drop. *Je ne me soutiens plus.* 你在会上~我吗? nǐ zài huì shàng ~ wǒ ma? Will you back me up in the meeting? *Tu vas me soutenir dans la réunion?*

他们靠仅有的果干和水~了下去。 tāmen kào jǐn yǒu de guǒgān hé shuǐ ~ le xiàqù. They had only dried fruit and water to sustain them. *Ils n'avaient que des fruits secs et de l'eau pour subsister.* 民主党将~这一法案。 mínzhǔ-dǎng jiāng ~ zhè yí fǎ'àn. The Democrats will support this bill. *Les Démocrates appuieront ce projet de loi.*

知道 zhīdào G, H5, S1 **know, realize, be aware of, *connaître, se rendre compte de, savoir***

你~她的电话号码吗? nǐ ~ tā de diànhuà hàomǎ ma? Do you know her phone number? *Tu connais son numéro de téléphone?*

我不~这么晚了。 wǒ bù ~ zhème wǎn le. I didn't realize how late it was. *Je ne m'étais pas rendu compte qu'il était si tard.* 那些风险他~得很清楚。 nàxiē fēngxiǎn tā ~ dé hěn qīngchu. He's well aware of the risks. *Il sait très bien quels sont les risques.*

只 zhǐ D, H3, S1 **just, only, *juste, ne...que***

你要白酒吗? --- ~要一点点。 nǐ yào báijiǔ ma? -- ~ yào yìdiǎndiǎn. Do you want some alcohol? – Just a drop. *Est-ce que tu veux de l'alcool? – Juste une goutte.*

我一个星期~剩下二十英镑过日子了。 wǒ yígè xīngqī ~ shèngxià èrshí yīngbàng guò rìzi le. I only left myself £20 a week to live on. *Je n'avais plus que 20 livres par semaine pour me nourrir.*

只有 zhǐyǒu G, S1 **only, nothing but,** *seul* ~我们知道。 ~ wǒmen shīdào. We are the only people who know it. *Nous en sommes seuls à le savoir.*

~他相信我。 ~ tā xiāngxìn wǒ. He's the only one who believes me. *Il est le seul à me croire.* ~奇迹才能救我们。 ~ qíjì cái néng jiù wǒmen. Nothing but a miracle can save us. *Seul un miracle pourrait nous sauver.*

制造 (製造) zhìzào H4, S1 **make, manufacture,** *fabriquer, produire, manufacturer* 公司~汽车零件。 gōngsī ~ qìchē língjiàn. The company manufactures spare parts for cars. *La société fabrique des pièces détachées pour automobiles.* 把东西给~商退回去。 bǎ dōngxi gěi ~shāng tuì huíqù. Send it back to the manufacturers. *Renvoyez-le au fabriquant.*

中 zhōng D, S1 **middle, centre, on, in the process of,** *mi-, centre m, en cours de* 我十月~去的。 wǒ shíyuè ~ qù de. I went in the middle of October. *J'y suis allé à la mi-octobre.* 她住在市~心。 tā zhù zài shì ~xīn. She lives in the city centre. *Elle habite dans le centre-ville.*

他心~有事(儿)。 tā xīn ~ yǒu shì(r). There's something on his mind. *Il y a quelque chose qui le tracasse.* 这正在讨论~。 zhè zhèngzài tǎolùn ~. It's in the process of being discussed. *C'est en cours de discussion.*

中餐 zhōngcān S1

(1), lunch, *déjeuner m* 她 吃~ / 吃中午饭 去了。 tā chī ~ / chī zhōngwǔ fàn qù le. She's gone out for lunch. *Elle est partie déjeuner.* 欧洲人几点吃~? ōuzhōu rén jǐdiǎn chī ~? What time do the Europeans have lunch? *A quelle heure est-ce que les Européens prennent leur déjeuner?*

(2), Chinese food, *repas chinois* 您喜欢吃~吗? nǐ xǐhuan chī ~ ma? De you like Chinese? *Vous aimez bien manger chinois?* 我今天晚上想吃~。 wǒ jīntiān wǎnshang xiǎng chī ~. I feel like Chinese food tonight. *J'ai envie de manger chinois ce soir.* 这条街上有一家很好的中(国)餐馆。 zhè tiáo jiē shàng yǒu yìjiā hěn hǎo de zhōng(guó) cānguǎn. There's a good Chinese restaurant in this street. *Il y a un bon restaurant chinois dans cette rue.*

中国 (中國) Zhōngguó G, N, H1, S1 **China,** *Chine f* ~是世界人口最多的国家吗? ~ shì shìjiè rénkǒu zuìduō de guójiā ma? Is China the most populated country in the world? *La Chine est-elle le pays le plus peuplé du monde?*

我四月去~旅行。 wǒ sìyuè qù ~ lǚxíng. I'll take a trip to China in April. *Je ferai un voyage en Chine en avril.*

中华民族 (中華民族) Zhōnghuá Mínzú S1 **Chinese nation,** *nation chinoise* ~有四千二百多年有考证的文明。 ~ yǒu sìqiān èrbǎi duō nián yǒu kàozhèng de wénmíng. Chinese nation has had an attested civilization of more than 4,200 years long. *La nation chinoise a eu une civilisation attestée de plus de 4 200 ans.*

中文 zhōngwén H4, S1 **Chinese language, Chinese,** *chinois m, langue chinoise* 您讲 / ~ 汉语 吗? nín jiǎng ~ / hànyǔ ma? Do you speak Chinese? *Parlez-vous (le) chinois?* 玛丽(说)~说得很好。 mǎlì (shuō) ~ shuō dé hěn hǎo. Mary speaks Chinese very well. *Marie parle très bien chinois.* 他~一句话 都 / 也不会说。 tā ~ yíjù huà dōu / yě búhuì shuō. He doesn't speak a word of Chinese. *Il ne parle pas un mot de chinois.* "这里讲~", "zhèlǐ jiǎng ~", "Chinese spoken", *"Ici on parle chinois";* 我学了一些基础 ~ / 汉语。 wǒ xué le yìxiē jīchǔ ~ / hànyǔ. I have learned some basic Chinese. *J'ai appris les bases du chinois.*

中午 zhōngwǔ H1, S1 **noon, midday,** *midi m* ~十二点了。 ~ shí'èr diǎn le. It's midday / twelve (noon). *Il est midi.* 我~(十二点)停下来。 wǒ ~ (shí'èr diǎn) tíng xiàlái. I stop at lunchtime. *Je m'arrête à midi.*

中学 (中學) zhōngxué S1 **middle school, high school (US),** *lycée m* 这孩子过年该上~了。 zhè háizi guònián gāi shàng ~ le. The child is going to secondary school next year. *L'enfant ira à l'école secondaire l'année prochaine.* 她在~教书。 tā zài ~ jiāoshū. She teaches at the secondary school. *Elle enseigne dans le secondaire / l'école secondaire.*

中学生 (中學生) zhōngxuéshēng S1 **middle school student / pupil, high school students,** *collégien(enne), lycéen(enne)* 他们是~。 tāmen shì ~. They're secondary school pupils (UK) / high school students (US). *Ce sont des collégiens (âgés de 12 à 14 ans) / des lycéens (âgés de 15 à 17 ans).*

中央 zhōngyāng N, H6, S1 **central, centre,** *central, centre m* 他是~委员会委员。 tā shì ~ wěiyuán-huì wěiyuán. He's a member of the central committee of the party. *Il est membre du comité central du parti.*

我们把塑像摆到了大厅~。wǒmen bǎ sùxiàng bǎidào le dàtīng ~. We put the state in the centre of the hall. *Nous avons mis la statue au centre de la grande salle.*

中医（中醫）zhōngyī S1

(traditional) Chinese medicine, doctor of ~, *médecine (traditionnelle) chinoise,* *praticien-enne de la ~* 你学的是~还是西医? nǐ xué de shì ~ háishì xīyī? Which have you studied, Chinese medicine or Western one? *Qu'est-ce que tu as étudié, la médecine chinoise ou occidentale?* 老王是一位~。lǎo wáng shì yíwèi ~. Lao Wang is a doctor of (traditional) Chinese medicine. *Lao Wang est un praticien de médecine (traditionnelle) chinoise.*

种（種）zhǒng D, H3, S1 **race, sort of,** **kind of,** *race f, type de, sorte f* 他是黄~人。tā shì huáng~ rén. He's of the yellow race. *Il est de la race jaune.* 这是另一~问题。zhè shì lìng yì ~ wèntí. It's a different sort of problem. *C'est un autre type de problème.*

我们有几百本各~各样的书。wǒmen yǒu jǐbǎi běn gè~ gèyàng de shū. We have hundreds of different kinds of books. *Nous avons des centaines de livres de toutes sortes.* (> 种 zhòng)

种（種）zhòng D, S2 **plant, cultivate,** **grow,** *planter, cultiver* 我~洋白菜。wǒ ~ yáng báicài. I plant cabbages. *Je plante des choux.*

他们~了五年地了。tāmen ~ le wǔnián dì le. They've cultivated lands for 5 years. *Ça fait cinq ans qu'ils cultivent la terre.* 这个地区的农民~小麦。zhège dìqū de nóngmín ~ xiǎomài. In this region, farmers grow wheat. *Dans cette région, les agriculteurs cultivent du blé.* (> 种 zhǒng)

重要 zhòngyào N, H3, S1 **importance,** **important, importantly,** *importer,* *important, considérable* 这不大~。zhè bú dà ~. It is of no great importance. *Cela importe peu.* 最~的是什么? zuì ~ de shì shénme? What is the most important? *Qu'est-ce qui est le plus important?*

他们之间有很~的差别。tāmen zhījiān yǒu hěn ~ de chābié. They are importantly different. *Il y a une différence considérable entre eux.* 友谊是一桩很~的事儿。yǒuyì shì yì zhuāng hěn ~ de shì. Friendship is a very important thing. *L'amitié est une chose très importante.*

主 zhǔ D **definite view, advocate,** *idée* *définitive, préconiser* 我心里没~。wǒ xīn lǐ méi ~. I don't know what to do. *Je ne sais que faire.*

预防为~。yúfáng wéi ~. Prevention is better than cure. *Mieux vaut prévenir que guérir.* 他们~战 / ~和。tāmen ~ zhàn / ~ hé. They advocate war / peace. *Ils préconisent la guerre / la paix.*

主任 zhǔrèn S1 **director, manager,** *administrateur(trice), directeur(trice)* 田先生是公司~。tián xiānsheng shì gōngsī ~. Mr Tian is the managing director. *M. Tian est l'administrateur délégué.* 他是 财政 / 地区 / 人事 ~。tā shì cáizhèng / dìqū / rénshì ~. He's a financial / regional / personnel manager. *C'est le directeur financier / régional / du personnel.*

主席 zhǔxí N, H5, S1 **chairperson,** **chairman,** *président(e)* 今天王女士是会议~。jīntiān wáng nǔshì shì huìyì ~. Ms Wang is the chairperson of the meeting today. *Mme Wang préside la réunion aujourd'hui.*

今天上午十点中国国家~会见了美国总统。jīntiān shàngwǔ shí diǎn zhōngguó guójiā ~ huìjiàn le měiguó zǒngtǒng. The Chinese chairman met with the American president this morning at 10 o'clock. *Le président chinois a rencontré son homologue américain ce matin à 10 heures.*

主要 zhǔyào N, H3, S1 **main, chief,** **principal, major,** *principal, majeure,* *principal, grand* 你平安无事，这是最~的。nǐ píng'ān wúshì, zhè shì zuì ~ de. You're safe, that's the main thing. *Tu es sain et sauf, c'est le principal.* 这是不是~的原因? zhè shì bú shì ~ de yuányīn? Is it the chief reason? *Est-ce la raison majeure?*

他是~的有关人员。tā shì ~ de yǒuguān rényuán. He's the principal person concerned. *C'est la personne principale concernée.* 我把~的时间用来搞政治。wǒ bǎ ~ de shíjiān yònglái gǎo zhèngzhì. The major portion of my time is devoted to politics. *La plus grande partie de mon temps est consacrée à la politique.*

主义（主義）zhǔyì N **doctrine, -ism,** *doctrine f, -isme* ~是一个信念的系统。~ shì yígè xìnniàn de xìtǒng. An ism is a set of beliefs. *Un isme est en ensemble de doctrines.* 他表现出了现实~。tā biǎoxiàn chū le xiànshí ~. He is realistic. *Il fait preuve de réalisme.*

别那么浪漫~了，那种完美是不存在的。bié nàme làngmàn ~ le, nàzhǒng wánměi shì bù cúnzài de. Stop romanticizing! Nothing's that perfect. *Arrête tes idées romanesques, Rien n'est tellement parfait.* 那些人是恐怖~分子。nàxiē rén shì kǒngbù ~ fènzǐ. Those people are terrorists. *Ces gens sont des terroristes.*

祝 zhù H3, S1 **express good wishes, wish, *souhaiter, vouer*** ~一切顺利! ~ yíqiè shùnlì! Let's hope everything goes all right! *Souhaitons que tout aille bien!* (~)生日快乐! (~) shēngrì kuàilè! Happy birthday! *Bon anniversaire!* ~您有好运(气)。~ nín yǒu hǎo yùn(qi). I wish you (good) luck. *Je vous souhaite bonne chance.* ~她旅途愉快 / (旅行)一路顺风。~ tā lǚtú yúkuài / (lǚxíng) yílù shùnfēng. I wished her a pleasant journey. *Je lui ai souhaité (un) bon voyage.*

住 zhù H1, S1 **live, halt, bear it in mind, withstand, *habiter, tenir, résister*** 我们 ~(在)北京 / 在北京~。wǒmen ~ (zài) běijīng / zài běijīng ~. We live in Beijing. *Nous habitons (à) Beijing.* 他们~一个套间。tāmen ~ yígè tàojiān. They live in a flat. *Ils habitent (dans) un appartement.*

站~! zhàn ~! Halt! *Halte!* 谢谢你这个建议，我牢牢记~。xièxie nǐ zhè gè jiànyì, wǒ láoláo jì~. Thanks for the suggestion, I'll bear it in mind. *Merci de ta suggestion, j'en tiendrai compte.* 你经受得~时间的考验吗? nǐ jīngshòu dé ~ shíjiān de kǎoyàn ma? Can you withstand the test of time? *Peux-tu résister à l'épreuve du temps?*

专业 (專業) zhuānyè H4, S2 **speciality, specialized, major, *spécialisé en, matière principale, connaissances spéciales en*** 汉语是她的~。hànyǔ shì tā de ~. Her speciality is Chinese. *Elle est spécialisée en chinois.* 您大学的~是什么，英文还是法文? nǐ dàxué de ~ shì shénme, yīngwén háishì fǎwén? What is your major, English or French? *Quelle est votre matière principale, l'anglais ou le français?* 他有电脑的~知识。tā yǒu diànnǎo de ~ zhīshi. He has a specialized knowledge of computing. *Il a des connaissances spéciales en informatique.*

准备 (準備) zhǔnbèi H2, S1 **be ready, prepare, intend to, *être prêt, se préparer, avoir l'intention de*** ~好了吗? ~ hǎo le ma? Are you ready? *Etes-vous / Es-tu prêt?* 他做了一切~。tā zuòle yíqiè ~. He is ready for anything. *Il est prêt à tout.*

我们~明天出发。wǒmen ~ míngtiān chūfā. We are preparing to leave tomorrow. *Nous nous préparons à partir demain.* 您~怎么做? nǐ ~ zěnme zuò? How do you intend to do it? *Comment avez-vous l'intention de vous y prendre?*

桌子 zhuōzi H1, S1 **table, desk, *table f, bureau m*** 我有一张小~。wǒ yǒu yìzhāng xiǎo ~. I have a small table. *J'ai une petite table.*

我们围着~坐了下来。wǒmen wéi zhe ~ zuò le xiàlái. We sat down to table. *Nous nous sommes mis à table.* 这张~太大，放在卧室里不合适。zhè zhāng ~ tài dà, fàng zài wòshì lǐ bù héshì. The desk is too big for this bedroom. *Le bureau est trop grand pour cette chambre.*

...子 [刀子] ...zi (dāozi) D, S1 **[nominal suffix], [suffixe nominal]** 小心，别叫刀~割着手! xiǎoxín, bié jiào dāo~ gē zhe shǒu. Be careful, don't cut yourself with that knife! *Attention, ne te coupe pas avec ce couteau!*

我们围着桌~坐了下来。wǒmen wéi zhe ~ zuò le xiàlái. We sat down to table. *Nous nous sommes mis à table.* 我播下了向日葵种~。wǒ bōxià le xiàngrìkuí zhǒng~. I sowed some sunflower seeds. *J'ai semé des graines de tournesol.*

字 zì H1, S1 **word, character, writing, handwriting, *mot m, caractère m, écriture f*** 这个~(是)什么意思? zhè gè ~ (shì) shénme yìsi? What does this word / this Chinese character mean? *Que veut dire ce mot / ce caractère chinois?*

他写得一手好~。tā xiě dé yìshǒ hǎo ~. He has good handwriting. *Il a une belle écriture.* 你的~我看不懂。nǐ de ~ wǒ kàn bùdǒng. I can't read your writing. *Je ne peux pas déchiffrer ton écriture.* 咬~清楚一点儿，我听不懂。yǎo ~ qīngchǔ yìdiǎr, wǒ tīng bùdǒng. Speak more clearly, I don't understand. *Articule, je ne comprends rien.*

自 zì D, S2 **self, oneself, from, *soi-même, depuis, de*** 这是你~找的嘛! zhè shì nǐ ~ zhǎo de ma! You asked for it! *Tu l'as cherché!* 他 ~不量力 / 不~量力。tā ~ bú liànglì / bú ~ liànglì. He overestimates his strength. *Il surestime ses propres forces.*

这项规则~即日起生效。zhè xiàng guīzé ~ jìrì qǐ shēngxiào. The rule becomes effective (as) from this date. *La règle entre en vigueur à partir de ce jour.* 一年之内我们~三个雇员增到了十二个。yìnián zhīnèi wǒmen ~ sān gè gùyuán zēngdào le shí'èr gè. We went from 3 employees to 12 in a year. *Nous sommes passés de 3 à 12 employés en un an.*

自己 zìjǐ G, N, H3, S1 **oneself,** *soi, soi-même* 我可以~拿吗? wǒ kěyǐ ~ ná ma? May I help myself? *Puis-je me servir?*

你~看看吧。 nǐ ~ kànkan ba. See for yourself. *Tu n'as qu'à voir par toi-même.* 他们只好~来了。 tāmen zhǐhǎo ~ lái le. They had to come themselves. *Ils ont dû venir eux-mêmes.*

自行车 (自行車) zìxíngchē H2, S1 **cycle, bicycle, bike,** *vélo m, bicyclette f* 你 骑车 / 骑~ 上班吗? nǐ qíchē / qí ~ shàngbān ma? Do you cycle to work? *Tu vas au travail en vélo / en bicyclette?*

他的新~真棒! tā de xīn ~ zhēn bàng! His new bike is really great! *Son nouveau vélo est vraiment génial!*

总理 (總理) zǒnglǐ H5, S1 **premier, prime minister, chancellor,** *premier ministre, chancelier m* 记者问了~一些问题。 jìzhě wèn le ~ yìxiē wèntí. The journalists asked the Prime Minister some questions. *Les journalistes ont posé des questions au Premier ministre.* 他作~期间见两次德国~。 During his prime ministership, he met the German chancellor twice. *Pendant qu'il était premier ministre, il a rencontré le chancelier allemand deux fois.*

总统 (總統) zǒngtǒng N, H5, S2 **president,** *président m* 法兰西共和国~会见了美利坚合众国~。 fǎlánxī gònghéguó ~ huìjiàn le měilìjiān hézhòngguó ~. The President of the French Republic met with the President of the United States of America. *Le président de la République française a rencontré le président des Etats-Unis d'Amérique.* John F

约翰.肯尼迪是美国最年轻的、第一个信罗马天主教的~。 Yuēhàn.kěnnídí shì měiguó zuì niánqīng de dìyī gè xìn tiānzhǔjiào de ~. John F Kennedy was the America's youngest president and the first Roman Catholic ever to be elected. *John F Kennedy a été le plus jeune président et aussi le premier président catholique aux Etats-Unis.*

走 zǒu H2, S1 **go, walk, be on the road to,** *aller, marcher, être sur le chemin de* ~吧! ~ ba! Let's go! *On y va!* 咱们去~~吧! zánmen qù ~~ ba! Let's walk a little! *Si nous marchions un peu?* 我的表不~了。 wǒ de biǎo bù ~ le. My watch has stopped. *Ma montre (s')est arrêtée.*

我们~上了成功的道路。 wǒmen ~shàng le chénggōng de dàolù. We've been on the road to success. *Nous sommes sur le chemin de réussite.*

我的决心定下来了, 决不~回头路。 wǒ de juéxīn dìng xiàlái le, jué bù ~ huítóu lù. My mind is made up, there is no turning back. *Ma décision est prise, je n'y reviendrai pas.*

组织 (組織) zǔzhī N, H4, S1 **organize, organization,** *organiser, organisation f* 老孙~我们参观了一家农场。 lǎo sūn ~ wǒmen cānhuān le yìjiā nóngchǎng. Lao Sun organized a visit to a farm for us. *Lao Sun a organisé la visite d'une ferme à notre intention.*

她参加了好几个~。 tā cānjiā le hǎo jǐgè ~. She belongs to several organizations. *Elle est membre de plusieurs organisations.*

最 zuì H2, S1 **most / the most / -est (superlative suffix),** *le / la / les plus* 班上她~聪明。 bān shàng tā ~ cōngming. She's the cleverest in the class. *Elle est la plus intelligente de la classe.*

这是我看见过的~漂亮的房子。 zhè shì wǒ kànjiàn guo de ~ piàoliàng de fángzi. It's the most beautiful house I've ever seen. *C'est la plus belle maison que j'aie jamais vue.* 他~紧急的需要是找到一份工作。 tā ~ jǐnjí de xūyào shì zhǎodào yífèn gōngzuò. His most urgent need is to find a job. *Son besoin le plus urgent est de trouver un emploi.* 这是我所听到的~愚蠢的事儿! zhè shì wǒ suǒ tīngdào de ~ yúchǔn de shìr. This is the most idiotic thing I ever heard! *C'est la chose la plus idiote que j'aie entendue!*

昨天 zuótiān H1, S1 **yesterday,** *hier* ~下了一天雨。 ~ xià le yìtiān yǔ. It rained all (day) yesterday. *Il a plu toute la journée d'hier.*

~的报纸(在哪儿)呢? ~ de bàozhǐ (zài nǎr) ne? Where's yesterday's newspaper? *Où est le journal d'hier?*

左边 (左邊) zuǒbian H2, S1 **the left, the left side,** *gauche f, côté gauche* 他们在~开车。 tāmen zài ~ kānchē. They drive on the left. *Ils roulent à gauche.*

东西在壁炉的~。 dōngxi zài bìlú de ~. It's to the left of the fireplace. *C'est à gauche de la cheminée.*

坐 zuò H1, S1 **sit, take a seat, have its back towards, sink,** *s'asseoir, prendre place, être situé, s'affaisser* 请~! qǐng ~! Please sit down! *Asseyez-vous, s'il vous plaît / Assieds-toi, s'il te plaît!* 我们将~飞机旅行。 wǒmen jiāng ~ fēijī lǚxíng. We'll travel by air. *Nous voyagerons en avion.*

这个房子~北朝南。zhè gè fángzi ~ běi cháo nán. The house faces south. *La maison est orientée au sud.* 这个房子向后~了。zhè gè fángzi xiàng hòu ~ le. This house is beginning to slope backwards. *Cette maison commence à s'affaisser vers l'arrière.*

坐在 zuòzài G **sit on / at, *s'asseoir, être assis à*** 咱们~地上吧。zánmen ~ dìshang ba. Let's sit on the floor. *Asseyons-nous par terre.* 他们围~桌子旁。tāmen ~ zhuōzi páng. They were sitting at (the) table. *Ils étaient assis à table.*

不要光~那儿，讲几句话呀! búyào guāng ~ nàr, jiǎng jǐjù huà ya! Don't just sit there, say something! *Ne restez pas bouche cousue, dites quelque chose!*

做 zuò H1, S1 **do, make, *faire*** 你~什么呢? nǐ ~ shénme ne? What are you doing? *Qu'es-tu en train de faire?*

她给自己~衣服。tā gěi zìjǐ ~ yīfu. She makes her own clothes. *Elle fait ses vêtements elle-même.* 他饭~得很好。tā fàn ~ dé hěn hǎo. He cooks well. *Il cuisine bien.* 小李经常~诗。xiǎo lǐ jīngcháng ~ shī. Xiao Li often writes poems. *Xiao Li écrit souvent des poèmes.*

作 zuò D, S2 **do, work, as, act, *faire, ouvrage m, comme*** 你现在为什么不~功课? nǐ xiànzài wèishénme bú ~ gōngkè? Why aren't you doing your homework? *Pourquoi ne fais-tu pas tes devoirs?* 她喜欢~画儿。tā xǐhuan zuò ~ huàr. She like painting pictures. *Elle aime faire des dessins.*

这是他的新~。zhè shì tāde xīn ~. It's his new work. *C'est son nouvel ouvrage.* 我们把他看~专家。wǒmen bǎ tā kàn ~ zhuānjiā. We regard him as an expert. *Nous le considérons comme un expert.* 她~口译。tā ~ kǒuyì. She acts as interpreter. *Elle sert d'interprète.*

中文索引, Chinese index, *Index chinois*

(英文索引在80 页，法文索引在88 页)

对 (對) duì (介、动) D, H2, S1
对不起 (對不起) duìbuqǐ H1, S1
多 duō (形) (1) H1, S1
多 duō (副) (2) H1, S1
p.12
多少 duōshao H1, S1

E

饿 (餓) è H3, S1
而 ér D, H4, S2
而且 érqiě G, H3, S1
儿子 (兒子) érzi G, H1, S1
二 èr H1, S1

F

p.13
发 (發) fā D, H4, S1
发生 (發生) fāshēng N, H4, S1
发音 (發音) fā yīn *
发展 (發展) fāzhǎn N, H4, A1
法 fǎ D, S2
法国 (法國) fǎguó *
法文 fǎwén *
法语 (法語) fǎyǔ *S2
翻译 (翻譯) fānyì H4, S2
p.14
饭馆 (飯館) fànguǎn H1, S2
方 fāng (形) (1) D, H5, S2
方 fāng (名) (2) G, H5, S2
方面 fāngmiàn N, H4, S1
房间 (房間) fángjiān H2, S1
非常 fēicháng H2, S1
飞机 (飛機) fēijī H1, S1
分 fēn (名、量) (1) D, H3, S1
分钟 (分鐘) fēnzhōng H1, S1
服务 (服務) fúwù N, S1
p.15
服务员 (服務員) fúwùyuán H2

G

改革 gǎigé N, H5, S2
感到 gǎndào G, S1
干部 (幹部) gànbù N
高兴 (高興) gāoxìng H1, S1
告诉 (告訴) gàosu H2, S1
哥哥 | 哥 gēge | gē H2, S1
个 (個) gè D, H1, S1
给 (給) gěi H2, S1
p.16
更 gèng T, H5, S1

公共汽车 (公共汽車) gōnggòng qìchē H2, S1
公斤 gōngjīn H2, A1
公司 gōngsī N, H2, S1
工厂 (工廠) gōngchǎng T, H5, S1
工夫 gōngfu H5, S1
工作 gōngzuò G, N, H4, S1
共 gòng T, S2
狗 gǒu T, H1, S2
古 gǔ T, S1
p.17
怪 guài (形) (1) T, S2
怪 guài (副) (2) T, S2
怪 guài (动) (3) T, S2
关系 (關係) guānxì H3, S1
官 guān T, H5, S2
观 (觀) guān T
管理 guǎnlǐ N, H4, S1
广 (廣) guǎng T, S2
归 (歸) guī T, S2
鬼 guǐ T, S2
贵 (貴) guì H2, S1
p.18
国 (國) guó D, S1
国际 (國際) guójì N, H4, S1
国家 (國家) guójiā N, H3, S1
果 guǒ T
过 (過) guò (动) D, G2, S1
过 (過) guò (助) D, G2, S1
过去 (過去) guòqù G, H3, S1

H

p.19
还 (還) hái D, H2, S1
还是 (還是) háishi G, H3, S1
还有 (還有) háiyǒu G, S1
孩子 háizi G, H2, S1
汉语 (漢語) hànyǔ H1, S1
汉字 (漢字) hànzì S1
好 hǎo (形) (1) D, H1, S1
好 hǎo (副) (2) D, H1, S1
好吃 hǎochī H2, S1
p.20
号 (號) hào H2, S1
合 hé D, S1
合作 hézuò N, H5, S1
黑 hēi H2, S1
很 hěn H1, S1
红 (紅) hóng H2, S1
后 (後) hòu D, S1
后面 (後面) hòumiàn H2, S1
护照 (護照) hùzhào
华人 (華人) huárén S1

华语 (華語) huáyǔ S1
p.21
话 (話) huà S1
欢迎 (歡迎) huānyíng H2, S1
回 huí (动) (1) H1, S1
回 huí (量) (2) H1, S1
回答 huídá H2, A1
回来 (回來) huílái G, S1
会 (會) huì (动) (1) D, H1, S1
会 (會) huì (名) (2) D, H1, S1
会议 (會議) huìyì N, H3, S1
活动 (活動) huódòng N, H4, S1
p.22
火车 (火車) huǒchē S1
火车站 (火車站) huǒchēzhàn H1

J

机场 (機場) jīchǎng H2, S1
鸡蛋 (雞蛋) jīdàn H2, S1
几 (幾) jǐ H3, S1
几个 jǐgè G
记者 (記者) jìzhě G4, S1
计划 (計劃) jìhuà N, H4, S1
技术 (技術) jìshù N, H4, S1
p.23
家 jiā (1) D, H1, S1
家里 (家裡) jiāli S1
加强 (加強) jiāqiáng N, S1
建设 (建設) jiànshè N, H5, S1
交通 jiāotōng H4, S1
交易 jiāoyì H6, S1
叫 jiào (动) (1) H1, S1
叫 jiào (介) (2) H1, S1
p.24
教室 jiàoshì H2, S1
接 jiē T, H3, S1
结 (結) jié T, S2
解决 (解決) jiějué N, H3, S1
姐姐 | 姐 jiějie | jiě H2, S1
介绍 (介紹) jièshào H2, S1
今年 jīnnián N, S1
今天 jīntiān G, N, H1, S1
尽 (盡) jǐn T
进 (進) jìn H2, S1
进行 (進行) jìnxíng N, H4, S1
近 jìn H2, S1
p.25
经 (經) jīng D, T
经济 (經濟) jīngjì N, H4, S1
京剧 (京劇) jīngjù H4, S1
京戏 (京戲) jīngxì S1
井 jǐng T, H6, S2
九 jiǔ H1, S1

就 jiù D, H2, S1
就是 jiùshì N, S1
举行 (舉行) jǔxíng H3, S1
p.26
觉得 (覺得) juéde G, H2, S2

K

咖啡 kāfēi H2, S2
开 (開) kāi D, H1, S1
开始 (開始) kāishǐ G, H2, S1
看 kàn D, H3, S1
看到 kàndào G, S1
看见 (看見) kànjiàn G, H1, S1
考试 (考試) kǎoshì H2, S1
p.27
科技 kējì N, S1
科学 (科學) kēxué N, H4, S1
可 kě D, S2
可能 kěnéng G, N, H2, S1
可是 kěshì G, H4, S1
可以 kěyǐ G, N, H2, S1
课 (課) kè H2, S1
块 (塊) kuài H1, S1
快 kuài H2, S1
p.28
快乐 (快樂) kuàilè H2, S1

L

来 (來) lái D, H1, S1
老师 (老師) lǎoshī G, H1, S1
了 le D, H1, S1
冷 lěng H1, S1
离 (離) lí H2, S1
里 (裡) lǐ G, H1, S1
理 lǐ D, S1
p.29
两 (兩) liǎng (数) (1) H2, S1
两 (兩) liǎng (量) (2) H2, S1
两个 (兩個) liǎnggè G
两国 (兩國) liǎngguó N
领导 (領導) lǐngdǎo N, H5, S1
六 liù H1, S1
陆 (陸) lù T
乱 (亂) luàn T, H4, S1
略 luè T
旅游 (旅遊) lǚyóu H2, S1

M

p.30
妈妈 | 妈 (媽媽 | 媽) māma | mā
H1, S1

麻 má T
马 (馬) mǎ T, H3, S1
骂 (罵) mà T, H5, S2
买 (買) mǎi H1, S1
卖 (賣) mài H2, S1
麦 mài T
p.31
慢 màn H2, S1
忙 máng H2, A1
猫 (貓) māo H1, S2
么 (麼) me D
没 (沒) méi D, H1, S1
没关系 (沒關係) méi guānxi H1
没有 (沒有) méi yǒu G, N, S1
每 měi (代) (1) H2, S1
每 měi (副) (2) H2, S1
美国 (美國) měiguó N
p.32
妹妹 | 妹 mèimei | mèi H2, S1
门 (門) mén H2, S1
...们 (...們) ...men D, S1
米饭 (米飯) mǐfàn H1, S1
面 miàn (名) D, S1
面 miàn (量) D, S1
明白 míngbai G, H3, S1
明天 míngtiān H1, S1
名字 míngzi H1, S1
母亲 (母親) mǔqin G, H4, S1
p.33
目前 mùqián N, H5, S1

N

哪 nǎ H1, S1
哪里 (哪裡) nǎli S1
哪儿 (哪兒) nǎr H1, S1
那 nà (代) (1) D, H1, S1
那 nà (连) (2) D, H1, S1
那个 (那個) nàge G, S2
那么 (那麼) nàme G, S1
那儿 (那兒) nàr H1, S1
p.34
那些 nàxiē G, S1
那样 (那樣) nàyàng G, S1
南方 nánfāng S1
男人 nánrén (1) H2, S1
男人 nánren (2) [口] H2, S1
能 néng D, H1, S1
你 nǐ D, H1, S1
你们 (你們) nǐmen G, S1
年 nián D, H1, S1
您 nín H2, S1
p.35
牛奶 niúnǎi H2, S1

女儿 (女兒) nǚ'ér H1, S1
女人 nǚrén (1) G, H2, S1

O, P

欧元 (歐元) ōuyuán *
旁边 (旁邊) pángbiān H2, S1
跑步 pǎo//bù H2, S2
朋友 péngyou G, H1, S1
便宜 piányi H2, S1
p.36
瓶 píng T, S1
婆 pó T
普通话 (普通話) pǔtōnghuà H3,
S1

Q

七 qī H1, S1
妻子 qīzi H2, S2
其 qí {书} D, S2
起 qǐ D, S1
p.37
起床 qǐ chuáng H2, S1
起来 (起來) qǐlái D, H5, S1
企业 (企業) qǐyè N, H5, S2
气 (氣) qì (名) (1) T, S1
气 (氣) qì (动) (2) T, S1
汽车 (汽車) qìchē S1
千 qiān T, H2, S1
签证 (簽證) qiānzhèng H4, S2
钱 (錢) qián H1, S1
前 qián D, S1
p.38
前面 qiánmiàn H1, S1
晴 qíng H2, S2
情况 (情況) qíngkuàng N, H4, S1
请 (請) qǐng H1, S1
去 qù D, H1, S1
去年 qùnián H2, S1
全国 (全國) quánguó N, S1
群众 (群眾) qúnzhòng N, H6, S1

R

p.39
然 rán D
然后 (然後) ránhòu G, H3, S1
热 (熱) rè H1, S1
人家 rénjia G, H6, S1
人民 rénmín N, S1
人民币 (人民幣) rénmínbì H4, S1
人员 (人員) rényuán H5, S1
认识 (認識) rènshi H1, S1

香港 xiānggǎng N
想 xiǎng D, H1, S1
想到 xiǎngdào G, S1
向 xiàng (名) T, H3, S1
向 (嚮) xiàng (副) T
小 xiǎo D, S1
小姐 xiǎojiě H1, S1
小时 (小時) xiǎoshí H2, S1
小学 (小學) xiǎoxué S1
小学生 (小學生) xiǎoxuéshēng S1

p.55
笑 xiào H2, S1
写 (寫) xiě H1, S1
谢谢 (謝謝) xièxie H1, S1
新 xīn H2, S1
新年 xīnnián S1
新闻 (新聞) xīnwén H3, S1
心 xīn D, S2
信 xìn (名) (2) H3, S1
信息 xìnxī H5, S1
信用卡 xìnyòngkǎ H4, S1
星期 xīngqī H1, S2

p.56
行 xíng D, H4, S1
行李 xíngli S1
姓 xìng H2, S1
熊猫 (熊貓) xióngmāo H3
休息 xiūxi H2, S1
学 (學) xué D, S1
学生 (學生) xuésheng N, H1, S1
学习 (學習) xuéxí H1, S1
学校 (學校) xuéxiào H1, S1

Y

p.57
亚洲 (亞洲) Yàzhōu H4
研究 yánjiū N, S1
研究生 yánjiūshēng H4, S2
颜色 (顏色) yánsè H2, S1
眼睛 yǎnjing H2, S2
阳 (陽) yáng *
羊肉 yángròu H2
样 (樣) yàng D, S2
p.58
邀请 (邀請) yāoqǐng H4, S1
药 (藥) yào H2, S1
要 yào (动) (1) D, H2, S1
也 yě D, H2, S1
衣服 yīfu H1, S1
医生 (醫生) yīshēng H1, S1
医院 (醫院) yīyuàn H1, S1
一 yī H1, S1
p.59

一步 yíbù N
一次 yícì G
一定 yídìng G, H3, S1
一个 (一個) yígè N, G
一路平安 yílù píng'ān H5, S1
一切 yíqiè G, H4, S1
以 yǐ D, H4
以后 (以後) G, G3, S1
以来 (以來) yǐlái H5, S1
已经 (已經) yǐjīng G, N, H2, S1
p.60
椅子 yǐzi H1, S1
亿 (億) yì H4, S1
一点儿 (一點兒) yìdiǎnr G, S1
一起 yìqǐ H2, S1
一些 yìxiē N, S1
一直 yìzhí G, H3, S1
一种 yìzhǒng G
意思 yì si H2, S1
意义 (意義) yìyì H5, S1
艺术 (藝術) yìshù H5, S1
p.61
阴 (陰) yīn H2, S2
因为 (因為) yīnwèi G, H2, S1
银行 (銀行) yínháng H3, S1
银行卡 (銀行卡) yínhángkǎ S1
应该 (應該) yīnggāi G, H3, S1
英国 (英國) yīngguó *
英文 yīngwén S1
英语 (英語) yīngyǔ S1
用 yòng D, H3, S1
邮局 (郵局) yóujú H5, S1
游泳 yóu//yǒng H2, S1
p.62
有 yǒu D, H1, S1
有点[儿] (有點[兒]) yǒudiǎr G
有关 (有關) yǒuguān N, S2
有(一)些 yǒu (yì) xiē G, S1
右边 (右邊) yòu bian H2, S1
于 (於) yú D, S2
于是 (於是) yúshì G, H4, S2
语 (語) yǔfǎ T
p.63
语法 (語法) yǔfǎ H4, S2
语音 (語音) yǔyīn S1
雨 yǔ T, S1
育 yù T
元 yuán T, H4, S1
原 yuán T, S2
园 (園) yuán T, S2
远 (遠) yuǎn T, H2, S1
院 yuàn T, S1
怨 yuàn T, S2
p.64

愿 (願) yuàn T, S2
约 (約) yuē T, S1
越 yuè T, H3, S1
月 yuè T, H1, S1
云 (雲) yún T, H3, S2
运 (運) yùn T, S2
运动 (運動) yùndòng H2, S1

Z

p.65
杂 (雜) zá T, S2
灾 (災) zāi T, S2
在 zài (动、介) D, T, H1, S1
在 zài (副) D, T, H1, S1
再 zài T, H2, S1
再见 (再見) zàijiàn H1, S1
咱 zán T, S1
p.66
暂 (暫) zàn T
早饭 (早飯) zǎofàn
早上 zǎoshang H2, S1
怎么 (怎麼) zěnme G, H1, S1
怎么样 (怎麼樣) zěnmeyàng H1, S1
站 zhàn (名) H3, S1
张 (張) zhāng (量) H2, S1
张 (張) zhāng (动) H2, S1
丈夫 zhàngfu H2, S2
找 zhǎo H2, S1
p.67
这 (這) zhè / zhèi D, H1, S1
这个 (這個) zhègè N, G (1), (2)
这么 (這麼) zhème G, S1
这些 (這些) zhèxiē G, N, S1
这样 (這樣) zhèyàng G, S1 (1)
这种 (這種) zhèzhǒng G
着 (著) zhe D, H2, S1
真 zhēn H2, S1
正在 zhèngzài H2, S1
p.68
政策 zhèngcè N, H5, S2
政府 zhèngfǔ N, H5, S1
政治 zhèngzhì N, H5, S1
证件 (證件) zhèngjiàn H5, S1
之 zhī D, H4
支持 zhīchí N, H4, S1
知道 zhīdào G, H5, S1
只 zhǐ D, H3, S1
p.69
只有 zhǐyǒu G, S1
制造 (製造) zhìzào H4, S1
中 zhōng D, S1
中餐 zhōngcān S1

78

中国 (中國) Zhōngguó G, N, H1, S1

中华民族 (中華民族) Zhōnghuá Mínzú S1

中文 zhōngwén H4, S1

中午 zhōngwǔ H1, S1

中学 (中學) zhōngxué S1

中学生 (中學生) zhōngxuéshēng S1

中央 zhōngyāng N, H6, S1

p.70

中医 (中醫) zhōngyī S1

种 (種) zhǒng D, H3, S1

种 (種) zhòng D, S2

重要 zhòngyào N, H3, S1

主 zhǔ D

主任 zhǔrèn S1

主席 zhǔxí N, H5, S1

主要 zhǔyào N, H3, S1

主义 (主義) zhǔyì N

p.71

祝 zhù H3, S1

住 zhù H1, S1

专业 (專業) zhuānyè H4, S2

准备 (準備) zhǔnbèi H2, S1

桌子 zhuōzi H1, S1

...子 [刀子] ...zi (dāozi) D, S1

字 zì H1, S1

自 zì D, S2

p.72

自己 zìjǐ G, N, H3, S1

自行车 (自行車) zìxíngchē H2

总理 (總理) zǒnglǐ H5, S1

总统 (總統) zǒngtǒng N, H5, S2

走 zǒu H2, S1

组织 (組織) zǔzhī N, H4, S1

最 zuì H2, S1

昨天 zuótiān H1, S1

左边 (左邊) zuǒbian H2, S1

坐 zuò H1, S1

p.73

坐在 zuòzài G

做 zuò H1, S1

作 zuò D, S2

英文索引, English index , *Index anglais*

(Chinese index is at page 74, and French index is at page 88)

local 9
logbook 68
long 5, 9, 26, 42
look at 17
look forward to 2
looking for 66
loud 7
love 1
luggage 56
lunar 61
lunch 51, 69

M

ma 30
mad about sb 1
Madam 46
main 70
major 70, 71
make 69
make 73
make 3
make angry 37
make up 10
man 34, 39
manage 17, 29
manager 70
Mandarin 21
Mandarin Chinese 36
manufacture 69
many 11
mark 14, 20
market 43
martial ar 51
martial arts 16
masculine 57
masses, the ~ 38
matter 43
may 27
maybe 27
ma 吗: a question word, placed at
the end of a sentence 30
me 么: particle 31
mean 55
meaning 60
meanwhile 48
medication 58
medicine 58
meet 39
meeting 21
mén 门: classifier 32
men ...们 plural suffix 32
mention it, don't ~ 4
merry 28
mess 29
message 55
method 13

miàn 面: classifier 32
midday 69
middle 69
middle school 69
middle school student / pupil 69
Midi (the South of France) 34
mike 35
minor 54
minute 14
miscellaneous 65
Miss 54
mistake 7
mister (Mr) 53
mobile 43
mobile phone 43
mode 13
moment, at the ~ 33
money 37
month 64
moon 64
more 11, 16
more...more / less... 64
more...than 4
morning 41, 66
most 72
mother 30, 32
motion 10
motor vehicle 37
move 11, 21
moving picture 10
Mr 53
Mrs 46
much 11, 66
mum 30
mummy 30
must 61
mutton 57

N

name 32
nation 18
nationwide 38
naturally 8
near 24
necessarily 59
negation 5
negotiate 46
negotiation 46
never mind 31
nevertheless 19
new 55
New Year 55
news 55
newspaper 3
newspaper, our ~ 4
next 52

next to, be ~ 2
next week 53
nice 19
night 49
nine 25
no good 7
noise 29
noodles 32
noon 69
not be able to 5
not have 31
not have done 31
not know 5
not up to 66
nothing 41
nothing but 69
nothing, for ~ 2
noun +的: demonstrative 9
nouveau 55
now 53
number 20
numerous 2

O

o'clock 10
obedience 40
observe 17
Occident, the ~ 51
occupation, a woman in a certain ~
36
odds and ends 65
of 9, 68
of course 8
of that kind 34
off [distance or period] 28
on 69
on account of 61
once 59
once more 65
one 58
one + noun 59
one another 60
one's kind 67
oneself 72
only 68, 69
open 66
opinion 60
or 19
oral comprehension 47
organization 72
organize 72
original 63
ought to 61
out 49
output 42
overcast 61

service 14
set 4
seven 36
several 19
several 22
shape 57
share 16
she 46
shelter 66
shop 40
should 61
shout 23
show 53
shutter 2
side 14, 35
side by side or presenting another
level, placing ~ 12
side of a boat 3
since 59
sing (a song) 6
sink 72
sir 53
sit 72
sit on / at 73
situation 38
six 29
skill 22
sky 47, 64
sleep 44
slight 29
slow 31
small 54
smile 55
so 19, 33, 34, 67
so as (not) to 50
society 41
solid 42
solution 24
solve 24
some 22, 60, 62
someone 41
something 41
son 12
sorry 11
sort of 70
sound 42
south 34
southern part of China 34
spare time 16
speak 44, 45
speciality 71
specialized 71
sport 64
spread 66
square 14
staff 39
stand 25, 66

stand up 37
start 26
start work 41
starting point , a ~ 62
starve 12
state 18
step 59
stiff 2
still 19
still have 19
stop 48
story 3
straight 42, 60
strange 16
stranger 49
strong point 5
student 56
study 56, 57
subject 47
such 34, 67
sudden(ly) 48
suit 20, 27
sun 40
suǒ 所: auxiliary word 45
suǒ 所: classifier 45
supply 64
support 68
surely 59
surface 32
surname 56
sustain 68
swear 30
swim 61
switch on 26

T

table 71
Taiwan 46
take 6, 59
take a rest 56
take a seat 72
take the place of 8
talk 21, 44, 45
talks 46
tasty 19, 53
taxi 6
taxicab 6
tea 5
teacher 28
technology 22
telephone 10
television 10
telly 10
temporarily 66
ten 42

terrible 7
test 26
thank you 55
thanks 55
that 33
that place 33
that's all right 31
that's why 45
the faintest 60
the most 72
the right 62
then 33, 39
there 33
therefore 45
thereupon 62
these 67
they 46
they (animals or objects) 46
they (female sex) 46
thing 11, 43
think 26, 40, 54
think of 54
this 4, 67
this one 67
this type of 67
this way 67
this year 24
those 34
though 45
thought 55
thousand 37
three 40
time 6, 42
to 15, 54
today 24, 53
together 60
toilet 52
told, be ~ 47
tomorrow 32
tongue 62
too 46, 58
too dear 17
topic 47
tour 29
tourism 29
towards 54
trade 23
traditional Chinese medicine 70
traffic 23
train 22
training 42
translate 13
translator 13
treasure 3
trivial 4
true 67
trumpet 20

法文索引, French index, *Index français*

(L'index chinois se trouve page 74 et l'index anglais se trouve page 80)

debout 66
debout, être ~ 66
débuter 26
décision, prendre la ~ 10
décliner 4
déjà 11, 25, 59
déjeuner m 51, 69
délégué(e) 8
délicieux 19
délivrer 13
demain 32
demande pardon, je vous / te ~ 11
demander 50
dépendre 65
déplacer, se ~ 21
depuis 59
dernier 41
derrière 20
dès 25
des 60
dès que 58
désastre m 65
descendre 52, 53
désirer 58
désordre m 29
deux 12, 29, 44
deux pays 29
devant 37, 38
développement m 13
développer, (se ~) 13
devenir 6
devoir 61
diable 17
difficile, être ~ 2
dire 15, 44, 45, 64
dire au revoir 45
dire la vérité 32
directeur(trice) 70
direction f 14, 54
diriger 29
divers 65
dix 42
docteur m 58
doctrine f 70
doigt, au ~ et à l'œil 40
dollar m 63
domaine m 14
don de, le ~ 67
donc 45
donner 15
donner à manger 50
donner naissance à 63
donner un résumé de 24
dormir 44
double m 44
doué pour, être ~ 5
droit 60

droite f 62
drôle 16
durer 18

E

eau f 44
école f 56
école primaire 54
écolier(ère) 54
économie f 25
économique 25
écouter 47
écrire 55
écriture f 50, 71
éduquer 63
également 58
élève du primaire 54
élève nmf 56
élever 47
éliminer 44
elle 46
elles 46
emballage 3
emploi m 16
employé(e) 44
en ce cas 33
en cours de 69
en même temps 48
en rapport avec 62
en tain de, être ~ 65, 67
en tout 16
enchanter 52
encore 19
encore avoir 19
encore une fois 65
endroit m 9
énergie f 34
enfant nmf 19
enseignant(e) 28
ensemble 60
ensuite 39, 59
entendre 47
entreprise f 37, 37
entrer 24
entretemps 48
envie f 64
envoyer 13
épingler 4
épouse f 36
épreuve f 26
erreur f 7
espèce, de son ~ 67
espèces fpl 53
espérer 52
esprit m 55
est en ouest, d' ~ 11

est et l'ouest, l'~ 11
Etat m 18
Etats-Unis [d'Amérique] 31
étranger(ère) 49
être 43, 65
être à (une école) 40
être à l'école 41
être d'accord avec 48
être d'avis que 26
être de l'avis de qn 48
être de retour 21
être humain 39
être le bienvenu / la bienvenue /
les bienvenu(e)s, être le ~ 21
étudiant(e) chercheur(e) 57
étudiant(e) de deuxième cycle 57
étudiant(e) de troisième cycle 57
étudiant(e) universitaire 8
étudient(e) 56
étudier 56, 57
EU 31
euro m 35, 63
éveiller 36
exact 42
examen m 26
excellent 19
exceptionnel 14
excusez-moi 11
exercice m 16, 21
exprimer une raison 12
extensive 17
extraordinaire 14

F

fabrique f 16
fabriquer 42, 69
face f 32
facile 19
faim f 12
fainéant(e) 17
faire 2, 3, 25
faire des recherches 57
faire savoir 15
faire tout seul 3
faire travailler 21
falloir 61
famille f 23
famille, de la ~ 23
fantôme m 17
faute f 7
femme dans certaine occupation
36
femme f 35, 36
fermer 20
feux m 20
fille f 35

参考书目
A list of reference books
La liste d'ouvrages de référence

辞海 缩印本 上海辞书出版社 1980 年 8 月 第 1 版
法汉词典 Dictionnaire français-chinois 上海译文出版社 1982 年 1 月 第 1 版
汉法词典 Dictionnaire chinois-français 商务印刷馆出版社 1990 年 11 月 第 1 版
汉英词典 A Chinese-English Dictionary 商务印刷馆 1979 年
汉英双解 新华字典 Xinhua Dictionary with English translation 商务印刷馆国际有限公司 2000 年 5 月
汉语水平词汇与汉字等级大纲 北京语言文化大学出版社 1992 年 6 月 第 1 版
汉语国际教育用 音节汉字词汇等级划分 北京语言文化大学出版社 2010 年 10 月 第 1 版
现代汉语词典 修订本 商务印刷馆 1996 年
现代汉语通用字表 国家语言文字工作委员会汉字处编 语文出版社 1989 年 9 月第 1 版
新英汉词典 A New English-Chinese Dictionary 上海人民出版社 1976 年 12 月 第 1 版
中国汉语水平考试模拟试题集 北京语言文化大学出版社 2011 年 3 月 第 1 版

French-English English-French Dictionary, Robert & Collins first published 1978
Grand Dictionnaire français-anglais anglais-français, Larousse, 2010
Harrap's Shorter French and English Dictionary, Harrap Books Limited, entirely re-set 1991
International Dictionary of English, Cambridge University Press, first published 1995
Larousse Business, Dicionnaire bilingue, Larousse 1990
Oxford Guide to British and American Culture, Oxford University Press, 1999
Word Menu, Random House, The Estate of Stephen Glazier, 1992

Printed in the United States
By Bookmasters